TEMPERANCE ESSAYS,

AND

Selections from Different Authors.

COLLECTED AND EDITED BY

EDWARD C. DELAVAN,

SOUTH BALLSTON, N. Y.

FOURTH EDITION.

PUBLISHED BY

THE NATIONAL TEMPERANCE SOCIETY AND PUBLICATION HOUSE,

172 WILLIAM STREET, NEW YORK.

1869.

Copy of Resolution adopted by the Board of Managers of the National Temperance Society and Publication House, at a meeting held January, 1866.

Resolved—That this Board recognize in the collection of Temperance Essays of E. C. Delavan a book of very great importance and value to the present state of the Temperance Cause, and we earnestly and cordially adopt it as one of the publications of this Society, and recommend measures be taken to give it a wide circulation.

JAMES B. DUNN, *Recording Secretary.*

CONTENTS.

PAGE

TRACT 1. Presidential Declarations, etc. 7
Address to the Army of the United States 11
2. The Pathology of Drunkenness, illustrated with Dr. Sewall's Plates 17
3. Comparative Temperance View of England's Commerce, Taxation, and Charities 21
Adulterations of Wine. Extract from Dr. Nott's Sixth Lecture on Temperance 28
4. Prohibition in Great Britain 29
The Light Wine Delusion 31
Responsibility of Moderate Drinkers, more especially of Christian Moderate Drinkers, whether in Church or State 32
Manifesto of the United Kingdom Alliance to its Members and Adherents throughout the Nation 33
Resolutions of a Conference of Alliance Friends in London 36
Address to Members of Parliament 37
5. The American Temperance Movement 41
6. Letter to General J. H. Cocke, of Virginia, on the Communion Question 53
General Cocke's Letter in Reply 64
Extract from a Letter by Hon. Neal Dow 66
Extracts from Father Mathew's Speeches 66
7. Letters of E. C. Delavan Relative to Communion Wine 67
Wherein Consists the Difference? 100
8. A Condensed Report of the Trial of the Cause of John Taylor *vs.* E. C. Delavan, for an alleged Libel 103
9. Letter to the President of the "Woman's National Covenant." 129
Bishop Potter, on the Drinking Usages of Society 130
Extracts from the Westminster Review 134
Dr. Nott, on the Adulteration of Liquors 135
Extract from Cowper's Essay on Charity 137
Comparison between the Dangers arising from Railroad Travel and the Liquor Trade, etc 140

PAGE
TRACT 10. Temperance of Wine Countries 141
11. A Thrilling Scene, illustrating Moderate Drinking 161
Another 163
To Truth-Seekers 164
Trial of John Burnett for Murder 166
Words of Wisdom from Great and Wise Men 167
The Little Golden-Haired Boy and his Elder Brother 169
Note by the Executive Committee of the New York State Temperance Society, relating to Dr. Sewall's Plates, etc. 171
Demoralization of the Rebel Armies 172
Franklin a Water-Drinker 174
12. Letter from Mr. Delavan to Governor King 175
13. Temperance Lecture No. XI., by Dr. Nott 187
14. Extract from President Nott's Lecture No. IX 199
15. Sketch by the Hon. Wm. H. Seward 207
The Use and Abuse of Alcoholic Liquors in Health and Disease, by Dr. Carpenter 209
Lord Byron 210
16. Chipman's Report on the Poor-Houses, Jails, and Orphan Asylums of the State of New York 211
A Short Sérmon from the Old Testament 216
" " " " " New " 217
17. Temperance, a Source of National Wealth 218
18. Reduction in Rate of Insurance on Temperance Ships 230
A Good Creature of God 235
19. The "London Star" and "London Times" on Temperance, etc 236
The Influence of Wine-Drinking, Hundreds of Centuries before the Art of Distilling was known 242
20. Schedule of Bible Texts relative to Wine 243
21. Summary of the Temperance Scripture Argument, condensed from the Works of Dr. Lees 255
Views of Richard Cobden, M. P., on Total Abstinence ... 267
22. Dr. Higgenbottom, of England, on Constitutional Difficulties 269
23. Pathology of Drunkenness; or, the Physical Effects of Alcoholic Drinks, by Dr. Sewall 273
The Expediency Doctrine Explained and Vindicated ... 307
Remarks on Dr. Sewall's Letter 308
24. Doctors and Drink 310

MOTTOES.

(From the English Edition of Dr. Nott's Work, &c.)

"Bias, by importing its own foregone conclusions into the Word of Scripture, and *by refusing to see*, or to acknowledge, what makes against its own prejudices, has proved the greatest known hindrance to all fair interpretation, and has tended, more than anything else in the world, to check the free course of Divine truth." BISHOP ELLICOTT.

"Why refuse homage to just that part of the Divine wisdom to which our own depravity cares not to consent?" DR. STEUDEL.

"Even now, after eighteen centuries of Christianity, we may be involved in some tremendous error, of which the Christianity of the future will make us ashamed." VINET.

"Each age of the Church has, as it were, turned over a new leaf in the Bible, and found a response to its own wants. We have a leaf still to turn—a leaf not the less new because it is so simple."

A. P. STANLEY, D. D.

"History leaves no doubt, that amongst the great moral and social influences that preceded the Advent of Christ, a temperance sentiment and reformation must be numbered. It is now as of old. The Church can conquer vice by becoming 'a city set on a hill'—lifted up visibly to a living *moral elevation*, which shall stand out in unmistakable contrast to the worldly, sensual conduct of existing profession—and in no other way. An abiding sense of religious duty is only possible under the reign of true temperance; since the spirit of wine is essentially incompatible with the influence of the Divine Spirit. UNTIL THE CHURCH LEARNS THIS TRUTH, ITS HISTORY WILL BE ONE OF ALTERNATE CONQUEST AND COLLAPSE—OF SPASMODIC SUCCESS INSTEAD OF CONTINUOUS ADVANCE."

DR. F. R. LEES.

"The progress of Temperance science is like that of other branches of science, speculative and practical. At whatever point science conflicts with prejudice, ignorance, interest, appetite, or superstition, it will excite the hostility of the human mind darkened by these influences. Chemistry, astronomy, geography, political economy, geology, and even such movements as those organized for the circulation of the Bible and the extinction of slavery, have all in turn had to pass through the ordeal of sharp, acrid, and continuous controversy; each in turn has been virulently opposed on biblical or on religious grounds; and each in turn has taken its place amongst the settled verities of the universe, or the moral and social necessities of the age. Some may lament all this; I do not, but accept it as the providential and necessary method for the development of truth and the enlargement of the human soul. Life is a battle, and the advent of truth as certainly brings the sword of controversy into play for the destruction of error and its baneful practices, as it ultimately brings a peaceful harvest of positive blessings. It is weakness and folly, if not cowardice, for the friends of light to decline the inevitable conflict. Sooner or later every question must be probed to the bottom—and why not this?"—IBID.

TO THE

FRIENDS OF TOTAL ABSTINENCE

AND PROHIBITION.

Permit me to inscribe to you the following pages, consisting of articles before published, now republished, and bound together, for preservation, free distribution, or sale.

I am almost daily in receipt of letters asking for temperance publications; I see in this an indication of a general movement throughout the country. My stock is exhausted; I have not a copy to one in fifty of the publications issued by the Albany Temperance Press during the thirty-five years it has been at work. I have thought a publication like this might be of some value, as a kind of text-book. In each of the articles something may be found of use to those seeking light, on one of the most important, moral and religious questions of this or any other age, being, as I believe, immediately connected with the building up of the Saviour's Kingdom on earth, and the welfare and happiness of the human race.

EDWARD C. DELAVAN

SOUTH BALLSTON, N. Y., *July* 4, 1864.

No. 1.

PRESIDENTIAL DECLARATIONS, ETC.

Being satisfied from observation and experience, as well as from medical testimony, that ARDENT SPIRIT, as a drink, is not only needless, but hurtful, and that the entire disuse of it would tend to promote the health, the virtue, and the happiness of the community, we hereby express our conviction, that should the citizens of the United States, and especially the young men, discontinue entirely the use of it, they would not only promote their own personal benefit, but the good of our country and the world.

JAMES MADISON,	JOHN TYLER,
ANDREW JACKSON,	Z. TAYLOR,
JOHN QUINCY ADAMS,	MILLARD FILLMORE,
M. VAN BUREN,	JAMES K. POLK,
FRANKLIN PIERCE,	JAMES BUCHANAN,
ABRAHAM LINCOLN,	ANDREW JOHNSON.

CORRESPONDENCE.

ALBANY, *December* 1, 1862.

To the CHAPLAIN, (if none) to the COLONEL, LIEUT. COLONEL, or any Officer in the Regiment:

The object in sending this parcel of 500 of the Appeal is, to place a copy in the hands of every Officer and Soldier in your Regiment. Parcels are made up for all Regiments. I make no suggestion as to the manner of distribution, but would respectfully recommend, that before making it, the following letters, and the certificate above, should be read to the companies or the Regiment.

The certificate of *eleven* Presidents I deem interesting as well as instructive. When I obtained the signatures of the *first three,* about thirty years since, by a personal visit to each, the movement against Alcohol, as a beverage, was confined to *distilled spirit;* then the impression was general that fermented drinks were safe, in moderation; but science has since settled the question, that Alcohol is exactly the same poison, in what are termed fermented drinks, as in distilled; indeed, that in both, it is formed by fermentation, and that there would be no impropriety in calling all kinds of intoxicating drinks *ardent spirits.* Pure brandy is distilled from wine, and should be called distilled wine.

It would be very gratifying to be informed as to the result of this effort to promote the cause of Temperance in the Army.

Respectfully, yours,
EDWARD C. DELAVAN.

NOTE.—The edition for the army having been printed, it has been suggested that this document might do good *outside the camp;* when *thus* distributed, may I not hope those receiving it, *after perusal,* will *preserve* and *circulate* it. E. C. D.

Extract of a letter from Maj. Gen. Dix.

FORT MONROE, *November* 1, 1862.

MY DEAR SIR:—I decidedly approve of your intention to publish for circulation, such an address to the army as you describe. Let it be short.

I am sincerely yours,

EDWARD C. DELAVAN, Esq. JOHN A. DIX.

Letter from Lieut. Gen. Scott.

NEW YORK, *November* 11, 1862.

MY DEAR SIR:—Much indisposed, and yet much occupied, I have read your excellent address to the army, which, I hope, may be read and re-read by every officer and man in it. It could not fail to do much good to efficiency and moral discipline; for drinking and drunkenness, among the rank and file of an army, soon become one and the same thing, and drunkenness destroys subordination, discipline and efficiency.

My sentiments on this subject cannot be too strongly stated, and consequently I do not object to your quotation of a remark of mine many years ago. With the greatest esteem, truly yours,

E. C. DELAVAN, Esq. WINFIELD SCOTT.

Archbishop Hughes writes:

"I approve highly of the purpose to which your tract is devoted, viz: the diminution, if not the abolition, of intemperance in the army and everywhere else."

NOTE.—At the last interview I had with this venerable man, now no more, he said to me: "I have read all your publications, and approve of all the principles you have advanced, except *one*, and that is not as important to the Roman Catholic church as to the Protestant." I stated to him that it had been one of the devices of my opponents, to place me, if possible, in a false position before the public, and then hold me to it, as if it was really mine. To what point do you refer? He replied, "the Communion question." This good man really had received the idea that I was opposed to the use of wine at the Lord's Supper. When I stated to him that such a thought had never entered into my head; that inasmuch as the proof was positive that at the time the Lord's Supper was instituted, various kinds of wine were recognized, good and bad; intoxicating wine, "the mocker," the unintoxicating, a blessing. I expressed a belief that the unintoxicating was more suitable for use on an occasion so sacred. The Archbishop at once replied in the most emphatic manner, "You are right." [*May* 2, 1864.]

Letter from Rev. Dr. Nott, President of Union College.

E. C. DELAVAN, Esq.—My Dear Sir:—Your "address" to the army has been received and read to me, and meets my entire approbation. My prayer is, that it may be blessed to every officer and soldier.

Very truly your friend,

UNION COLLEGE, *Nov.* 17, 1862. ELIPH'T NOTT.

Letter from Rev. Dr. Wayland, of the Baptist denomination.

PROVIDENCE, *November* 18, 1862.

MY DEAR MR. DELAVAN:—I have read your address to our army with the deepest interest. Its facts are as unanswerable as its arguments are convincing. I hope that it may be extensively read by all the army, both officers and men, and that the Spirit of God may attend it with a blessing from on high. May it thus tend to stay the ravages of intemperance, which I fear are awful among our soldiers.

I am, my dear Mr. Delavan, yours truly,

E. C. DELAVAN, Esq. F. WAYLAND.

Letter from Rt. Rev. Bishop McIlvaine, of Ohio.

CINCINNATI, *November* 21, 1862.

MY DEAR SIR:—I am thankful that anybody of influence will labor to promote temperance in the army; but especially that a gentleman of your thorough acquaintance with the subject, and experience in the *modus operandi*, is so engaged. We hear much of want of discipline in the men, and of efficiency in the officers—of surprises, and stragglers, and prisoners taken when they should not be, and of many still worse evils. What hand DRINK has in all of them—drink, with or without intoxication, who can measure? I hope, dear sir, you will carry out your plan of circulating the well prepared address of which you have sent me a copy; and may God bless it with great usefulness among those to whose devotedness to their country we are all so indebted.

Yours, very respectfully,
CHAS. P. McILVAINE.

Letter from the Rt. Rev. Bishop McCloskey, of Albany, N. Y.

ALBANY, *November* 24, 1862.

MY DEAR MR. DELAVAN:—I have read with much interest your earnest appeal addressed to the officers and soldiers of our army, in favor of temperance; and I most sincerely hope that it may be productive of beneficial results. It is not to be doubted that there is hardly any evil to which the soldier is more exposed—hardly any more dangerous and fatal, either in tent or field—than the terrible evil of intemperance. And it is equally undoubted, that its surest preventive as well as *only* effectual remedy, after God's grace, is *total abstinence* from the use of all intoxicating drinks.

With best wishes and regards, I remain, Dear Sir,
Your friend and obed't servant in Xt.,

E. C. DELAVAN, Esq. †JOHN, Bp. of Albany.

NOTE.—There appears to be but one feeling, and that of gratification, on the part of Protestants as well as Catholics, that the mantle of Archbishop Hughes is to fall upon Bishop McCloskey. It will be perceived that this Reverend Ecclesiastic takes the ground that "Total Abstinence" is the only cure for the mighty evil under which the world totters and groans. [*May* 2, 1864.]

Letter from Hon. Erastus Corning, M. C.

ALBANY, *November* 25, 1862.

EDW. C. DELAVAN, Esq.—My Dear Sir.—I have perused your appeal to the Army, and approve of it. If you carry out the plan for its circulation as suggested, I doubt not great good will follow.

Your assured friend,
ERASTUS CORNING.

Note from Hon. Ira Harris, U. S. Senator.

ALBANY, *November* 25, 1862.

I most cordially and earnestly unite in commending the effort which Mr. Delavan is about making to reduce and mitigate the evils of intemperance in the Army. IRA HARRIS.

From the Rev. Dr. E. S. Janes, Bishop of the M. E. Church.

NEW YORK, *Dec.* 1, 1862.

E. C. DELAVAN, Esq.—My Dear Sir.—I deem the circulation of your "Address to the Army of the United States" of the highest importance to the welfare of the soldiers. It furnishes to them what they much need and strongly desire—"Something to read." It also gives them a timely, judicious and friendly warning of a terrible peril to which they are all seriously exposed. I believe the army will appreciate your philanthropy in favoring them with the document. Yours, with much esteem,

E. S. JANES.

Letter from the Rt. Rev. Alonzo Potter, Episcopal Bishop of Penn.

MY DEAR MR. DELAVAN:—I have received your "Appeal to the Army." It is most seasonable. What untold and incalculable disasters, disgrace and death would have been averted, if our entire army, officers and men, had acted on the principle of TOTAL ABSTINENCE. The evil is most alarming, and threatens, in the future, consequences to the nation and to families which cannot be measured. May God bless your effort to arrest it.

Yours faithfully,

PHILADELPHIA, *Dec.* 10, 1862. ALONZO POTTER.

Letter from the Rev. Dr. Hawes, of the Congregationalists.

HARTFORD, *Dec.* 31, 1862.

MY DEAR MR. DELAVAN:—Your excellent and timely address to the army of the United States, which I have just read, has my entire approbation. Let it have the widest circulation both in and outside of the camp. The facts and reasonings which it contains, cannot fail to awaken interest and draw forth thought in the minds of all who read it; and though it may not, and will not entirely root out the "tremendous evil" against which it is directed, it will most assuredly accomplish great good in putting the officers and soldiers of our army on their guard against one of the greatest and most ruinous temptations to which they are exposed.

Affectionately, and truly yours,

J. HAWES.

From the Rev. Dr. Pohlman, President of the Evangelical Lutheran Ministerium of the State of New York..

ALBANY, *Dec.* 31, 1862.

MY DEAR SIR:—I am much obliged to you for the privilege of reading your "Appeal to the Army of the United States," on the subject of Temperance. It seems to me that it must be productive of much good WHEREVER READ, and especially among the brave men who are now so heroically battling for the Union, the Constitution and the Laws.

As ever, yours sincerely.

HENRY N. POHLMAN.

Letter from the Venerable Thomas De Witt, of the Reformed Dutch Church.

NEW YORK, *Jan.* 1, 1863.

E. C. DELAVAN, Esq.—Dear Sir.—I have received yours, with the accompanying document. The object proposed by you is an important and excellent one. You are at liberty to attach my name to any paper recommending it. I trust a blessing will attend the effort to counteract the great evil spreading through our army. Yours truly,

THOMAS DE WITT.

TO THE ARMY OF THE UNITED STATES.

Officers and Soldiers: I have been requested to prepare an appeal to the Army of the United States, officers and privates, in favor of Temperance. I have been assured the motive would be appreciated.

Permit me to express to you my astonishment and wonder at what has taken place since the first gun was fired in this terrible war. Your antagonists have been as fearless and as brave as you are; but the great and remarkable fact is, that you, to the number of about a million of men, have given up *voluntarily* your domestic pursuits, your homes, relatives and friends, to yield your lives, if need be, on the battle field, for your country's sake. . . . . Words cannot do justice to the sublimity of this wonderful fact. The historian will record it to your never ending fame.

I am well aware how delicate a point it is, for an individual to advise as to the personal habits of even his own brother. This difficulty may be surmounted by your considering me your Physician on Alcohol, as well as your brother in the bonds of our common humanity. I can assure you, I have studied for about thirty-five years the effect of Alcohol on the human system, and my experience and advice may benefit some of you.

Let me commence by assuring you, that even in pure intoxicating wine, beer, cider, as well as all kinds of distilled spirit, Alcohol is the substance for which all these various liquors are desired and drunk. Let us see what Alcohol is. We will begin by acknowledging it to be a good creature of God, for certain purposes; but never good for pouring down one's throat as a beverage, any more than burning coals are good to be taken into your hands. It is classed by medical and scientific men of the highest grade, as a poison, and if prescribed as a medicine, should be prescribed with as much care as any other poison. But it is a most dangerous remedy at any rate, and millions of drunkards have been made by the *unguarded* prescription of alcohol by their physicians.

Dr. T. Romeyn Beck, in his great work on medical jurisprudence, remarks: "that alcohol, whether found in rum, brandy or wine, *is* a poison, is conceded on all hands." European, as well as numerous American physicians and chemists, fully support Dr. Beck. Rev. Dr. Nott, President of Union College—yet living—an abstainer of half a century or more, and now about ninety years of age, says: "that pure alcohol is a poison, is an admitted fact." Shakespeare, in Othello, says: "O thou invisible spirit of wine, if thou hast no name to be known by, let us call thee Devil!" That "invisible spirit" is ALCOHOL, which the great enemy of mankind has so long employed as a decoy to ruin such vast numbers of the human race.

The ancient Greeks, instead of saying "the man is drunk," were in the habit of saying "the man is poisoned." Our word intoxication is derived from the Greek word toxicon, which signifies poison. That eminent French physician, Broussais, about fifty years since, discovered that, by the repeated use of alcoholic wine, a diseased state of the stomach was produced. The late eminent physician, Dr. Sewall of Washington, after deep study, and numerous dissections, prepared a drawing of the moderate drinker's stomach, showing conclusively that such drinking brought on an incipient disease of the stomach, and if continued, would induce diseases of various kinds, and ultimately, in many cases, death by delirium tremens. Those celebrated anatomists, Drs. Warren, Mott and Horner, of this country, at the time, sustained Dr. Sewall in his position; and now, within a year or two, and after the most labored examination and experiments, celebrated chemists and physicians in France and England, have also sustained Dr. Sewall, proving beyond question, that alcohol is a poison, and should be treated as such by every one. God, the highest of all authorities, says wine (intoxicating) "wine is a *mocker*," not much, or little, but, "*it is a* mocker." No man can drink this mocker in health without being mocked by it, in the degree he permits himself to use it. The London Times says, wine (alluding to weak French wine) is less poisonous than gin.

The polite commander of one of the forts near Washington, recently informed me, that since Government had prohibited the entrance of strong drink within the lines, drinking had diminished therein nine-tenths; still, there is some smuggling of liquors, and this, said he, "makes the men who drink it mad."

I have thus far only alluded to pure intoxicating drink; the poison, alcohol, in it, alone makes it intoxicating. I conclude the strong drink smuggled into the camps, is made and concocted (in addition to poison alcohol), of drugs of the most deadly and life-destroying character, and that none but a crazy man would drink it were he made certain of the real character of this smuggled "fire water." You may be sure, that ninety-nine hundredths of all the strong drinks now consumed, from the (so called) choice wines of the high and fashionable down to the whiskey of the soldier, are so fabricated as to cheapen the article and prevent the most conceited judge from detecting the fraud. The Rev. Dr. Nott says, in his admirable lectures: "I had a friend who had been himself a wine dealer, and having read the startling statements made public in relation to the brewing of wines and the adulterations of liquors generally, I inquired of that friend as to the verity of these statements. His reply was: '*God forgive me for what has passed in my own cellar, but the statements made are true, all true, I assure you.*' "

Dr. Lewis Beck, an eminent chemist, was engaged three months in analyzing a large private stock of wine, supposed to be of the best and purest quality. He found all adulterated, not fit to be used as a beverage or for medicine, and they were consequently destroyed.

The Government has now, in its benevolence, prohibited the spirit ration in the navy as well as in the army. Why has it done this? It is because it has come to the knowledge that intoxicating drinks, as a beverage, are intoxicating poisons.

Soldiers, ponder over the battles that have been fought during this unfortunate war. Ask yourselves how many engagements would have terminated more favorably to the honor of our beloved country, if all of you (officers and men) had been total abstainers from the use of intoxicating drinks.

It is also a remarkable fact, well worthy of your careful consideration, that, in the armies of all nations, the most distinguished generals and officers have been men of temperate habits. ***Promotion*** seldom falls to the lot of the intemperate. If you do not wish to disappoint your friends, who are anxious for your advancement, by all means avoid, as your worst enemy, the intoxicating cup.

Very many years since, Gen. Scott assured me, that he had rather march at the head of 5,000 temperance men, than at the head of two or three times that number of topers. After perusing this appeal, he writes, "I hope it will be read, and re-read, by every officer and man in the army."

Major General Dix has forwarded me General Orders No. 11, authorizing its publication.

HEAD-QUARTERS, MIDDLE DEPARTMENT,
BALTIMORE, MD., *April* 16*th*, 1862.

* * * The Commanding-General can not pass by this court without a few words of admonition to the officers under his command. Two commissioned officers have been found guilty of drunkenness by this court, and dismissed the service, and not a court-martial is held without having such cases before it; every sentence in these cases, however severe, will be carried out with the utmost rigor.

Drunkenness is the bane of the military profession; it has gained a strong foothold in the commissioned grades, and the Commanding-General is constrained to believe that it is to be traced in some instances to the bad examples which the older officers set to the younger by drinking in their presence, and inviting them to drink in their tents and quarters at all hours of the day. Moreover, the influence of these examples upon the non-commissioned officers and privates is pernicious in the extreme. Nine-tenths of all the crimes and offenses for which officers and soldiers are brought to trial are the fruits of this degrading and ungentlemanly vice; and the Commanding-General earnestly appeals to the officers under his command, in the name of the honorable profession of arms, which it is their duty to preserve from all taint, and in the name of the distracted country in whose service they are imperiling their lives, to banish from their encampments and quarters all intoxicating liquors, which add no vigor either to their mental or physical powers, and which are a certain source of demoralization, and often of indelible disgrace. * * *

By command of Major-General DIX.

D. T. VAN BUREN,
Ass't Adj't-General. [OFFICIAL.

Some people yet consider strong beer as one of the great blessings of life; but did space allow me to spread before you all the facts I have in possession as to the use of the most filthy water, as well as the most poisonous drugs in the manufacture of malt and beer, you would hesitate long before you would touch a drop of it. And here permit me to add, that physicians, in this and other countries, have testified in the most emphatic manner, that when sickness overtakes the drinker of intoxicating liquors, his chance of recovery is not near as good as if he had confined his drink to water.

Aside from the moral degradation flowing from the use of strong drink in its effects upon life, character, &c., &c., its drain upon the purse is enormous.

It has been computed by an individual, who, about thirty-five years ago, abandoned the use of all intoxicating drinks, and who, at that time, was expending at the rate of about $1,000 a year in the purchase of wines, &c., that in thirty-five years, at compound interest, it would have amounted to the sum of $147,672.69. Now, soldiers have leisure at times, so have officers; let them see if this calculation is correct.

Provided by Government with liberal compensation, food and clothing, the soldier need scarcely expend a dollar of his pay. Let him make a calculation what the saving would be by abstaining from strong drink, to the amount of five or ten cents only per day, for a year, and so on for any term of years, compounding the interest, and he will find how easy it is to keep poor and wretched by the use of this poison, and how easy to become independent, if industrious, by giving it up entirely.

And now brethren of the United States Army, officers and men, who still use intoxicating drinks as a beverage, why will you not adopt my principles and practice ?

While I was a moderate drinker, I made a mental resolution (after reading a temperance tract placed under my plate by an unknown hand,) that I would for one month try the experiment of total abstinence from all intoxicating drinks. Much to my astonishment I found it a severe trial. The poison had almost become a necessity, without my being conscious of it. This month gave me the victory over appetite, and the experiment has made me a total abstainer ever since, and may have saved me a drunkard's fate. Drinkers, moderate or immoderate drinkers, please try the like experiment, and my prayer is that it may influence you as it did me.

It is an historical fact, that after the war of the Revolution, officers and men in great numbers returned to their homes, victims to strong drink, and became a disgrace to their families and to their country, and vast numbers of them died at last, miserable drunkards. This is the great fear in regard to our present army, when disbanded after peace, with the Union restored. May this fear never be realized in a single case, but may officers and men return with minds and bodies unimpaired by the use of alcoholic drinks, that they who desire to enter upon civil pursuits, may engage in them with capital saved, and with such principles and habits, as will enable them effectually to assist in making onr beloved country one of the purest and strongest of the nations of the earth, the home and refuge of the poverty-stricken and oppressed of all lands. It is impossible in a brief document like this, to do justice to an issue involving interests so overwhelming to individuals and nations, as that of true temperance—total abstinence from all that can intoxicate. It is a question involving the morals of a nation, as well as its prosperity in a financial point of view, It is a question well worthy of the serious consideration of the rulers of all nations, of all statesmen, political economists, philanthropists and Christians. The saving of only one cent a day to each of our population of 31,000,000, in the use of intoxicating drink, would amount in a single year to $113,150,000, and pay the interest of nearly three thousand millions of dollars of public debt, at five per cent. How we all dread the public taxes, but how little we think of the enormous tax we lay upon ourselves, in the purchase of articles, the use of which tends to produce disease, poverty, crime and premature death.

I have only aimed to draw your thoughts to this great question, and with the hope that God will bless the words I send you, to your present, future and everlasting good. I am,

Very truly, your friend,

EDWARD C. DELAVAN.

ALBANY, *December* 1, 1862.

NOTE.—About 1,000,000 of this document have been circulated. It is reprinted in this form, more especially to perpetuate "the Presidential Declaration," and the endorsement of the principles contained in the address "To the Army of the United States," which contains every principle, I believe, which has been advanced by the friends of temperance during the progress of the reform.

No. 2.

THE PATHOLOGY OF DRUNKENNESS.

THE STOMACH IN VARIOUS STAGES,

From Health to Death by Delirium Tremens.

These diagrams are taken from drawings made from actual dissections in 1842, by Dr. Sewall, of Washington, D. C.

Perfect accuracy is not claimed, as no two cases would probably present exactly the same appearance ; but it is claimed that they give a truthful illustration of the ravages resulting from the introduction of the poison, alcohol, into the healthful stomach, and forever settle the question that the injury commences with the *first glass*—with the moderate (falsely termed temperate) use of this poison.

Before these representations were submitted to the public in 1842, those celebrated surgeons, Dr. Warren, of Boston, Dr. Mott, of New York, and Dr. Horner, of Philadelphia, endorsed them. In 1843, after a lengthened discussion as to the principle more especially involved in the second stomach in the series, the same distinguished anatomists re-endorsed them, and recommended universal circulation for the instruction of all classes.

Correspondence between the Executive Committee of the New York State Temperance Society, and Drs. Warren, Mott, and Horner, in relation to the republication of Dr. Sewall's Pathology of Drunkenness, for the use of Schools.

Gentlemen — The Executive Committee of the New York State Temperance Society having it in contemplation to re-publish, for the use of the Common Schools in the State of New York, Doctor Sewall's Pathology of Drunkenness, (the same to be accompanied with his Drawings of the Human Stomach, as affected by the use of intoxicating liquors, from the first inception of disease occasioned thereby, to death by

Delirium Tremens,) hereby request your consent to the republication of the original testimonials severally given by you in favor of said work; and that you will accompany such consent with an expression of your opinion in relation to the tendency of temperate drinking, as defined by Doctor Sewall, to produce such an incipient disease as Plate No. II. (labelled the Temperate Drinker's Stomach) is intended to exhibit and illustrate.

PHILIP PHELPS, IRA HARRIS,
AZOR TABER, BARENT P. STAATS,
I. N. WYCKOFF, B. T. WELCH,
ERASTUS CORNING, BRADFORD R. WOOD,
S. W. DANA,
Executive Committee.

Dr. Warren's Reply.

Understanding that "Doctor Sewall's Pathology of Drunkenness" is about to be republished, I cordially agree to the republication in this work of the testimonial I gave some years ago to its utility and faithfulness. I can also add to that testimonial the expression of my opinion, that temperate drinking, as defined by Dr. Sewall, has a tendency to alter the condition of the mucous membrane of the stomach, and give origin to that state of it which is represented in Doctor Sewall's Plate No. II. JOHN C. WARREN.

BOSTON, *December* 2, 1843.

Dr. Mott's Reply.

Finding that it is the intention of the New York State Temperance Society to republish Doctor Sewall's Pathology of Drunkenness, with the Prints of the Human Stomach, for the benefit of the Common Schools in our State, I am happy to repeat my hearty recommendation of this great and good work, and to add, that it is my full conviction that the pernicious practice of even temperate drinking, as set forth by Doctor Sewall, cannot be too severely reprobated. By whomsoever this is practiced, it will be found to be the beginning of that sad derangement of the mucous membrane represented in Plate No. II., which will sooner or later lead to the most disastrous results.

VALENTINE MOTT.

NEW YORK, *December* 5, 1843.

Dr. Horner's Reply.

The New York State Temperance Society having desired an additional expression of opinion from me on the subject of Doct. Sewall's plates, being his Pathology of Drunkenness, this is to certify that since my original communication to the learned Professor, and also my letter of March 11, 1843, to E. C. Delavan, Esq., I have seen no reason to modify or retract sentiments advanced on these occasions. On the contrary, I now renew them with a pleasure increased at the progress of the cause they are intended to support, and at the admirable improvement this cause has made in the condition of individuals and of families.

That a reformation was needed in the customs of society in regard to inebriating drinks, no one ought to doubt ; and that this reformation, limited as it yet is, has done incalculable good, must be apparent to every sincere inquirer into its present state. A wide circulation of Doctor Sewall's valuable Plates, by infusing a just dread and abhorrence of intoxication into the minds of all having their understandings now matured, will of course, by the influence of example, deter the rising generation from the dangerous practice of even temperate drinking, as thus defined and illustrated; and I shall therefore be glad to witness their greater extension.

W. E. HORNER, M. D.

PHILADELPHIA, *December* 6, 1843.

Letter from the Private Secretary of Prince Albert.

WINDSOR CASTLE, *November* 5, 1843.

Sir—I am commanded by His Royal Highness Prince Albert, to acknowledge the receipt of your letter of the 1st September, and to return you His Royal Highness' sincere thanks for the set of Dr. Sewall's Drawings of the Human Stomach as affected by drinking, which you have been so good as to send, and which His Royal Highness thinks are admirably calculated to deter persons from giving way to the abominable vice of drunkenness.

It gave His Royal Highness much pleasure to hear of the success with which they have been used in America, which makes him anxious that the same success may attend them here.

I am also to thank you for the kind expressions you have used to his Royal Highness personally, and I beg to remain,

Sir, with great respect, your obedient servant,

E. C. DELAVAN, Esq. G. E. ANSON.

Westminster Review, London, &c., &c.

This influential Review, in 1855, defended the moderate use of alcohol in health, as necessary, indeed, as food for the body. Prof. Youmans, and others, of the United States, and learned writers in Great Britain, exposed the fallacy of this position.

Now, in 1860, this same Journal magnanimously acknowledges that recent scientific French investigators of the highest rank, have exploded this doctrine, asserting that alcohol is a poison, and always pernicious as a beverage in health. By the use of alcohol, they say: "The *pathological* alterations are *very vivid inflammation of the mucous membrane of the stomach.*"

"Very lately," says Dr. James McCulloch, of Scotland, "Messrs. Lallemand, Perrin and Duroy in France, and Dr. Edward Smith, LL. B., F. R. S., in London, have published a number of carefully conducted experiments, and most important discoveries, proving that alcohol undergoes *no change in the body*, it being expelled unchanged by the lungs, skin and kidneys;" and that, in the words of Dr. Smith, "*it should be prescribed medicinally, as carefully as any other poisonous agent.*"

The *British Medical Journal*, lately in a leader, appears willing to accept the improved scientific *status quo* as touching alcohol. It says: "The subject of the use of alcohol is daily becoming one of more importance. The question of its influence on the body in health is being daily canvassed by the chemist and physiologist; and, *as far as their lights reach*, it would seem that not only is alcohol not of service to the body, but is actually injurious."

No. 3.

COMPARATIVE TEMPERANCE VIEW

OF

ENGLAND'S COMMERCE,

TAXATION AND CHARITIES.

INTRODUCTION.

ALBANY, *January 6th*, 1864.

To Members of Congress—

Gentlemen: Now, that the question is under consideration of advancing the tax on tobacco and intoxicating drink, I take the liberty of enclosing to members of Congress a brief document on British taxation, &c., &c.

Prohibition of the sale of intoxicating drink, as a beverage, as also of tobacco, would, in my opinion, not only be humane, but the true policy of governments. But such prohibition can only be sustained where a large proportion of the people are convinced that the principle is sound, and stand ready to sustain it, not only by *vote*, in the *courts*, but by the *practice* of total abstinence.

While discussing the question of excise, Lord Chesterfield, in his address before the house of Lords, 125 years ago, touched the point exactly. He said: "luxury, my lords, is to be taxed, but vice prohibited, let the difficulty of the law be what it will. Luxury, or that which is pernicious by excess, may very properly be taxed, that such excess, though not unlawful, may be made more difficult; but the use of those things which are simply hurtful in their own nature, and in every degree, are to be prohibited."

Imported liquors (as well as domestic), as a general rule, are mere vile adulterations, and poisonous. How wise it would be in Congress, to order to the public stores all imported liquors, there to be tested by reliable chemists, and if found to be fabricated, through the agency of poisonous drugs, have them destroyed. No act would be more merciful, just and popular.

There are no articles of trade which produce so great a percentage of profit, especially by retail, as tobacco and intoxicating drink. Take the wholesale price of all kinds of strong drink, and then estimate the price *by the glass*, and it will be seen the profit is an enormous per cent.; a very heavy tax could therefore be sustained on all kinds of intoxicating liquors and on tobacco. Should the tax be placed so high as to diminish income by diminished use, let it be remembered, that in proportion to such diminution, crime, pauperism, domestic taxation, and a host of other evils, would be also diminished, and a vastly increased demand for other taxable commodities, useful and beneficial, would be created.

A famine was once feared in Ireland; the Government, by way of precaution, prohibited, for one year, the destruction of grains by the distillers and brewers. A lessened revenue was anticipated, but a greater was realized by the lessened consumption of strong drink, and by an increased use of healthful and useful taxable articles.

A very recent report comes to our shores from the famished districts of Lancashire, England. I quote in brief: "One very remarkable fact presents itself with this period of destitution. It is the astounding decrease of crime; as poverty has increased, crime has diminished. It is a common thing to have a session where not a crime is brought before the magistrate."

Very respectfully your ob't servant,

EDWARD C. DELAVAN.

TEMPERANCE STATEMENTS
OF
BRITISH TAXATION, &c., &c.

The great Temperance Reform of the present century was sent to England from the United States. That nation has responded gloriously, and the friends of the reform here rejoice to know that in our Fatherland so many noble hearts are perseveringly engaged in enlightening the masses. The advance now making in England will aid us when we renew the struggle. The cause will languish here until this gigantic rebellion is put down and the Union restored. When this is achieved the friends of Temperance will renew their labors, until all that man can do will be done to arrest an evil now assuming proportions so vast, that if not checked, will in time sink us to the level with the most degraded nations of the earth.

In 1866 there is to be a convention in the State of New York to make any changes in the Constitution desired by the people. The friends of Temperance in the State look forward with the hope that the voters will send such delegates to the convention as will introduce Prohibition into the organic law of the State. Prohibition, thus established, will be beyond the reach of party or party judges ; and when established *here*, other states, not already prohibitory, will hasten to become so. Prohibition is now the basis of all laws in all countries with regard to the sale of intoxicating drinks. It prohibits the sale to the masses, and gives commission to a few—for gold—to carry on the work of poisoning their neighbors by wholesale, and filling the poor-house, the prison-house, the grave-yards with victims innumerable, and burdening the temperate and industrious with unequal and unjust taxation.

The facts, statistics and arguments which England is spreading before her people, on the great question at issue, are as instructive and as applicable to us here, as to the people of that country.

The following pages are taken from a work, put forth some years since, by J. S. Buckingham, Member of Parliament. I give them to the public at this time with the hope that good may follow them wherever they go. Could Christians be brought to see it to be their duty to abandon the use of those poisons, named in the highest obelisk, as taxing England to the amount of seventy-seven and a half millions sterling per annum—that obelisk (which represents the origin of vice of every grade) would rapidly diminish, and the charitable one, which now makes such a miserable figure, would rise in proportion as the other would sink.

ALBANY, Jan. 6, 1864. EDWARD C. DELAVAN.

MR. BUCKINGHAM'S REMARKS.

The accompanying outline engraving will tell its own startling tale, and needs no further explanation than will be found on the following pages. The several obelisks and their subdivisions will show the respective amounts expended in each of the branches designated; and when it is seen that all that can be raised for religious and benevolent societies named, falls short of a million sterling, while beer, wine, spirits and tobacco—all unnecessary in the most moderate use, and the source of immense evil when taken in excess—cost the British community nearly eighty millions sterling, or nearer one hundred millions, if illicit distillation and smuggling be added, in actual expenditure, independently of all the enormous charges involved in the maintenance of police, prisons, hulks, lunatic asylums, hospitals, workhouses, &c., mainly resulting from intemperance in their inmates—we may well doubt whether, as a people, we are entitled to the praises we so often bestow on ourselves, for our wisdom, piety and philanthropy, in which we frequently boast that we are superior to all other nations now upon the face of the earth.

Our drinking and smoking taxes are half as much again as the entire taxation of the United Kingdom; twelve times as much as our poor rates; and more than seventy times as much as we give to the twelve largest societies for promoting the cause of religion and morality, whose united annual income does not amount to one million. (Pound sterling about five dollars.)

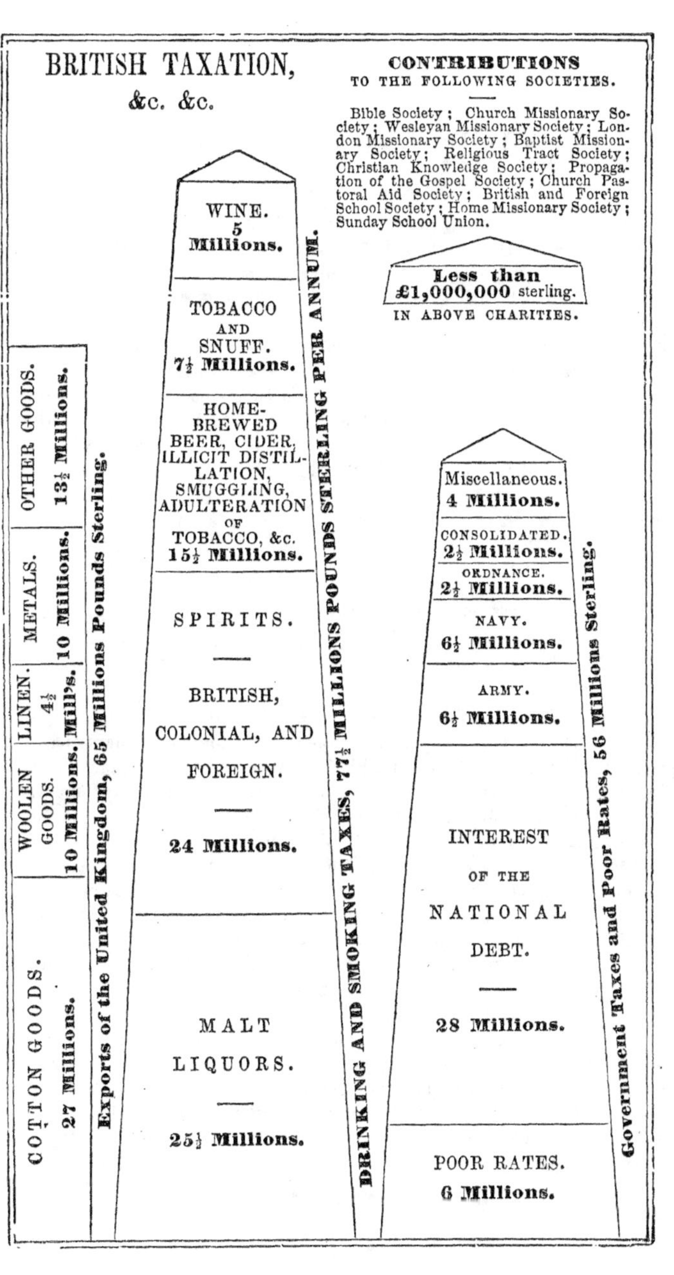

BRITISH TAXATION,
&c. &c.
CONTRIBUTIONS
TO THE FOLLOWING SOCIETIES.
Bible Society; Church Missionary Society; Wesleyan Missionary Society; London Missionary Society; Baptist Missionary Society; Religious Tract Society; Christian Knowledge Society; Propagation of the Gospel Society; Church Pastoral Aid Society; British and Foreign School Society; Home Missionary Society; Sunday School Union.
Less than
£1,000,000 sterling.
IN ABOVE CHARITIES.
OTHER GOODS. 13½ Millions.
METALS. 10 Millions.
LINEN. 4½ Mill's.
WOOLEN GOODS. 10 Millions.
COTTON GOODS. 27 Millions.
Exports of the United Kingdom, 65 Millions Pounds Sterling.
WINE. 5 Millions.
TOBACCO AND SNUFF. 7½ Millions.
HOME-BREWED BEER, CIDER, ILLICIT DISTILLATION, SMUGGLING, ADULTERATION OF TOBACCO, &c. 15½ Millions.
SPIRITS.
BRITISH, COLONIAL, AND FOREIGN.
24 Millions.
MALT LIQUORS.
25½ Millions.
DRINKING AND SMOKING TAXES, 77½ MILLIONS POUNDS STERLING PER ANNUM.
Miscellaneous. 4 Millions.
CONSOLIDATED. 2½ Millions.
ORDNANCE. 2½ Millions.
NAVY. 6½ Millions.
ARMY. 6½ Millions.
INTEREST OF THE NATIONAL DEBT.
28 Millions.
POOR RATES. 6 Millions.
Government Taxes and Poor Rates, 56 Millions Sterling.

BRITISH TAXATION, &c.

The pyramids are intended to present an idea of the various sums, in their relative proportions, expended by the British people upon different branches of the public service, and upon religious and philanthropic objects, in contrast with those expended upon intoxicating drinks and tobacco.

The statements relating to the general taxation and expenditure of the country, military and civil, are taken from the government returns, and those respecting intoxicating drinks and tobacco, from a paper read by Mr. G. R. Porter, of the Board of Trade, before the last meeting of the British Association for the Promotion of Science. It is necessary, however, to observe, that Mr. Porter in this instance only calculates the expenditure of *the working classes* upon the articles referred to, which he estimates at £57,000,000. The following is his statement :—

British and Colonial spirits	£20,810,208
Brandy	3,281,250
Total of spirits	£24,091,458
Beer of all kinds, exclusive of that brewed in private families	25,383,165
Tobacco and snuff	7,588,607
	£57,063,230

He does not include in that calculation £5,000,000 annually spent upon wine, nor does he make any calculation for the immense quantities of spirits supplied by smuggling and illicit distillation, for the quantities of cider and home-brewed beer annually consumed, nor for that which greatly exceeds in amount all these items put together—the enormous quantity added by the adulteration of every kind of intoxicating drink, as well as of tobacco. Had these items been included, the amount for the whole kingdom would have been at least one-fourth more than that which is stated by Mr. Porter ; and at that increased sum it is stated in the large pyramid. To this enormous sum expended in the purchase of alcoholic drinks and tobacco, we must add the loss sustained by the destruction of food every year, which is sufficient to maintain 6,000,000 of our population. A considerable proportion of the amount paid for poor rates, and also of the large sums annually expended in the prosecution and maintenance of our criminal population, must likewise be added. If the cost of strong drinks and tobacco, and the losses in various ways resulting from their use, be thus great, it surely becomes a duty to ascertain what benefits we derive in return. With respect to strong drink we have the following testimony, signed by about 2.000 of our most eminent medical men :—

"We, the undersigned, are of opinion,—

"I.—That a very large portion of human misery, including poverty, disease and crime, is induced by the use of alcoholic or fermented liquors, as beverages.

"II.—That the most perfect health is compatible with total abstinence from all such intoxicating beverages, whether in the form of ardent spirits, or as wine, ale, porter, cider, &c., &c.

"III.—That persons accustomed to such drinks, may, with perfect safety, discontinue them entirely, either at once, or gradually after a short time.

"IV.—That total and universal abstinence from alcoholic liquors and intoxicating beverages of all sorts, would greatly contribute to the health, the prosperity, the morality and the happiness of the human race."

These views of the utter worthlessness of such drinks as an article of diet, are confirmed by the experience of thousands of working men and others, in all parts of the united kingdom.

Of strong drink as an incentive to crime, and a powerfully demoralizing agent, our Judges have frequently spoken in the most decided terms. Amongst others we have the following :—

JUDGE COLERIDGE : "There is scarcely a crime comes before me that is not, directly or indirectly, caused by *strong drink*."

JUDGE GURNEY : "Every crime has its origin, more or less, *in drunkenness*."

JUDGE PATTESON : "If it were not for this *drinking*, you (the jury) and I would have nothing to do."

JUDGE ALDERSON : "*Drunkenness* is the *most fertile source of crime ;* and if it could be removed, the assizes of the country would be rendered mere nullities."

JUDGE WIGHTMAN : "I find in every calendar that comes before me, one unfailing source, directly or indirectly, of most of the crimes that are committed—*intemperance*."

It thus appears that we are annually expending the enormous sum of nearly £80,000,000 sterling on two articles of mere luxury, which are the chief incentives to the vice, misery and wretchedness that afflict our land.

Can a stronger case by possibility be made out for the entire abandonment of any practice ?

To the laboring classes especially, who, it is computed, annually expend half of the before-named sum, we would most earnestly appeal, and entreat them no longer to barter their means of happiness and comfort, of social and moral elevation, for a low, debasing and short-lived gratification.

Were only five millions per annum of the large sum spent in drink devoted to the purchase of land, *it would afford every year a quarter of an acre each to two hundred thousand laboring men ;* reckoning the land at £100 sterling per acre.

To the friends of religion and morality we would say : Is it wise or Christian to give your support to customs which so powerfully counteract your labors, and which absorb to so large an extent the means you greatly need for enlightening and evangelizing the world ?

Twelve of our largest and most influential religious and philanthropic Societies are unable to raise one million a-year to prosecute their praiseworthy objects, while upwards of seventy millions are annually squandered on a hurtful, crime-producing drink.

ADULTERATIONS.

From Rev. Dr. E. NOTT'S (*LL. D., President of Union College*) *Sixth Lecture on Temperance.*

"Wine indeed, 'falsely so called,' we have in abundance; but names do not alter the nature of things.

"The extract of logwood is not less the extract of logwood, nor is the sugar of lead less the sugar of lead, because combined with New England rum, Western whisky, sour beer, or even Newark cider put up in wine casks, stamped Port, Champagne or Madeira, and sold under the imposing sanction of the collector's purchased certificate, passed from hand to hand, and perhaps transmitted from father to son, to give the color of honesty to cool, calculating, heartless imposition.

"O! it was not from the vineyards of any distant grape-bearing country, that those disguised poisons, sent abroad to corrupt and curse the country, were derived. On the contrary, the ingredients of which they are composed were collected and mingled, and their color and flavor imparted, in some of those garrets above, or caverns beneath, the observation of men; caverns fitly called 'hells,' where, in our larger cities, fraud undisguised finds protection, and wholesale deeds of darkness are securely and systematically performed.

"I do not say this on my own authority. I had a friend who had been himself a wine-dealer; and having read the startling statements made in public in relation to the brewing of wines and the adulteration of liquors generally, I inquired of that friend as to the verity of those statements. His reply was: 'GOD FORGIVE *what has passed in* MY OWN *cellar, but the* STATEMENTS MADE ARE TRUE, TRUE, I assure you.'

"That friend has since gone to his last account, as have doubtless many of those whose days on earth were shortened by the poisons he dispensed. But I still remember, and shall long remember, both the terms and tone of that laconic answer.

"Another friend informed me that the executor of a wine dealer, in a city named, assured him that in the inventory of articles, for the manufacture of wine found in the cellar of that dealer, and the value of which amounted to many thousand dollars, there was not one dollar for the juice of the grape! And still another friend informed me, that in examining, as an assignee, the papers of a house in that city which dealt in wines, and which had stopped payment, he found evidence of the purchase during the preceding year, of hundreds of casks of cider, but none of wine. And yet it was not cider, but 'wine,' which had been supposed to have been dealt out by that house to its confiding customers."

No. 4.

PROHIBITION IN GREAT BRITAIN.

The friends of Prohibition in Great Britain are moving steadily onward in the noble and self-sacrificing work of relieving Her Majesty's subjects from the demoralizing influence of the License System, &c., &c. They have at last reached the National Legislature; they have now got a foothold in the right place, and as they duly estimate the beneficial results of final success, in a religious, moral, pecuniary and healthful point of view (if I do not greatly mistake the character of the men engaged in this great and good work), they will not relax their efforts until the object of their labors is accomplished.

Every position we have taken in this country, with regard to intoxicating liquors, has been fully sustained in Great Britain, after the most patient research, by large bodies of the Clergy of all denominations, Biblical Scholars, Statesmen, and Physicians, and Chemists of the highest grade. The germ of this great reform, planted in this country now about forty years since, has swelled to gigantic proportions all over the civilized world, and is yet destined, as I have faith to believe, to sweep intemperance from the face of the earth.

The following documents will serve in some slight degree to enlighten the public mind in this country as to the character of the struggle now going on in our Father Land, on the question of Prohibition. God grant that the only warfare ever to be carried on between England and America shall be, which shall do the most good in promoting the happiness of human beings.

While we of the North are straining every nerve to put down a gigantic rebellion, and restore the Union with liberty to all within our borders, it cannot be expected that the cause of Prohibition and Total Abstinence should occupy the same prominent place as before the war. The people at large now only wait the ending of the war to renew their efforts to establish Prohibition in every State of the Union. In this State there is to be a Constitutional Convention in 1866, to alter or amend the Constitution. The friends of Prohibition are looking forward to that year to secure Prohibition in the organic law of the State. It is now time that preliminary steps should be taken to secure the desired result.

Twice in years long past, the Temperance cause in the United States languished and appeared to be making no progress. A National Convention at Philadelphia was called at one time; another at Saratoga Springs, with the most happy results. The debates and resolutions of these Conventions, wide spread, had a vast influence in awaking the whole nation to a simultaneous movement.

I understand another National Convention is contemplated.

E. C. D.

SOUTH BALLSTON, *October 1st*, 1864.

THE LIGHT WINE DELUSION.

"The abundance of the harvest (in France) in 1858, diminished the poverty, and, by consequence, the crimes and offences which misery imposes; but the abundance of the VINTAGE, on the contrary, *multiplied blows and wounds*, the quarrels of cabarets, the rebellious, and outrages, and violence towards the police. These facts are again found in all analogous circumstances." [*Revue d'Economie Chretienne, Paris*, 1862, *pp*. 171–2.

Horatio Greenough, the eminent American sculptor, in a letter to a friend, from Florence, in 1838, said: "Many of the more thinking and prudent Italians abstain from the use of wine; several of the most eminent of the medical men are notoriously opposed to its use, and declare it a poison. When I assure you that one-fifth, and sometimes one-fourth of the earnings of the laborers are expended in wine, you may form some idea as to its probable influence on their health and thrift." He also said that the dealers in the weak wines did not hesitate to adulterate them in order to add a trifle to their gains.

J. Fenimore Cooper, the American novelist, said: "I came to Europe under the impression that there was more drunkenness among us than in any other country—England, perhaps, excepted. *A residence of six months in Paris changed my views entirely.*"

"Light wines," says Sir Edward Bulwer Lytton, "nothing so treacherous! They inflame the brain like fire, while melting on the palate like ice. All inhabitants of light-wine countries are quarrelsome."

"Oh, thou invisible spirit of wine! if thou hast no name to be known by, let us call thee DEVIL."—*Shakespeare.*

Cardinal Acton stated, in a letter, in 1839, the Government of Rome had more to fear from the wine shops than from any other source. The Emperor of the French has more to fear from the wine shops than all other sources united. They furnish the material for riot and revolution, and the wine drank in them is the stimulant to every vice. Americans and others visiting the fashionable walks of Paris and other continental cities, seeing but few staggering men, suppose, and honestly suppose, that wine countries are, in a great measure, free from the vice of intemperance; but it is a great mistake.

RESPONSIBILITY OF MODERATE DRINKERS,

More Especially of Christian Moderate Drinkers,

WHETHER IN CHURCH OR STATE

The ragged, squalid, brutal drunkard, who raves in the bar-room, consorts with swine in the gutter, or fills with clamour and dismay the cold and comfortless abode, to which, in the spirit of a demon, he returns at night, much as he injures himself, deeply wretched as he renders his family, *exerts but little influence in beguiling others into an imitation of his revolting conduct.* On the contrary, so far as his EXAMPLE goes, it tends to *deter* from, rather than *allure* to, criminal indulgence. From his degradation and his woes, the note of warning is sounded both loud and long, that whoever will may hear it, and hearing, understand.

But reputable [careful] Christian wine-drinkers, are the men who send forth, from the high places of society, and sometimes even from the portals of the sanctuary,* an unsuspected, unrebuked, but powerful influence, which is secretly and silently doing on every side, among the young, among the aged, among even females, its work of death. It is this reputable drinking of these disguised poisons, under the cover of an orthodox Christian name, which encourages youth in their occasional excesses, reconciles the public mind to holiday revelries, shelters from deserved reproach the bar-room tippler, and furnishes a salvo even for the occasional inquietude of the drunkard's conscience.

Regard this conduct as *we* may, there can be no question how GOD regards it. He has not left himself without a witness of his displeasure, in any city, town or hamlet, throughout the land.

PRESIDENT E. NOTT, D. D. LL. D.

* The experience of near forty years has furnished me materials for a volume, and a large one too, of most remarkable and heart-rending incidents, where the examples of moderate drinking Christian men, clergymen, have been the ruin of youth, struggling against a habit which the social drinking usages of society had fastened upon them.

UNITED KINGDOM ALLIANCE.

Offices: 41 JOHN DALTON STREET,
MANCHESTER, *June* 16*th*, 1864.

Manifesto of the Executive of the United Kingdom Alliance to its Members and Adherents throughout the Nation.

FRIENDS AND FELLOW HELPERS:

For the first time, the House of Commons has seriously discussed the principle of a Permissive Prohibitory Liquor Law. A stage of progress which it had been predicted would never be reached, has been attained. A second reading has been formally proposed and respectfully debated. The result is known, and a consideration of the facts will show what reason we have for thanking God and taking courage. When we entered upon the Parliamentary struggle, we were prepared to find an adverse House of Commons. Hostility has been usually manifested to the initiation of the greatest reforms of recent times, and we could not in the first stages expect other treatment for ours. At the last General Election, our most sanguine and earnest adherents generally contented themselves with a pledge, where it could be obtained, to support the first reading of a Bill, in order that an explanation of its nature might not be denied. This pledge has, in most cases, been creditably redeemed; but promises in favor of a second reading had then hardly any existence. In the interval since 1859, vacancies in the Representation have frequently occurred, and much commendable diligence has been shown to press our views and wishes upon the candidates who have come forward. The instances have, however, been few in which an organized and concentrated manifestation of strength has backed these efforts.

On the 10th of March, Mr. Lawson brought "The Intoxi

cating Liquors Bill," embodying our principle, into the House of Commons, and it was read a first time. Leave to bring it in was granted, by 72 votes against 38. It is probable that this division excited in the breasts of some of our friends, not well acquainted with the usages of Parliament, an exaggerated estimate of the good-will of the House towards the measure. All that was signified by this vote was a courteous inclination to have the Bill printed and discussed — this, and nothing more. We therefore could not build any hopes upon the defeat of a sudden and ungraceful opposition on that occasion. The number who would support the Bill at the next and critical stage, when its principle would be brought under review, was still uncertain. We did our duty. We called upon you to petition the House, and to supplement petitions, by electoral memorials and private communications to your respective members. This counsel was widely accepted, and too much approval cannot be expressed of the activity and enthusiasm which, in many places, you exhibited. The effect produced upon members of Parliament could not, however, be foreseen. We knew that we had to contend with much ignorance, both of our principles and of the hold they possessed upon public sympathy; and we were confident that the interests of some, and the fears of many, would prevent their co-operation with Mr. Lawson. It was possible, but not probable, that from twenty to thirty members would follow Mr. Lawson into the lobby.

The event has exceeded this calculation, and we can sincerely avow our gratification that as many as 37 members, including tellers — some of them representing influential constituencies — voted in favor of the Bill. If to these we add the three who paired in favor, we have no fewer than forty members who have recorded their approval of the vital principle of the measure — the right of the people when so disposed, to prohibit the sale of intoxicating liquors within their districts. That such success should have attended this first parliamentary effort, is remarkable, and is a proper cause of profound thankfulness to Almighty God. The fact ought not to escape notice that 324 members did not vote at all. Nearly half the House of Commons remained neutral, thus indicating an unwillingness to commit themselves against the Bill. Taking those who neither voted nor paired adversely, we have out of the 656 members, 359 who are not committed against the Bill. The debate has widely diffused more correct information of our principles and views to the country; and has imparted a prodigious impetus to the agitation, regarded as such. It has shown the argumentative weakness of the opposition. It has registered the admission of the popularity of the measure. It has extorted the confession that the present system is bad, and that something must be done. It has even originated from Mr. Bright a proposal kindred to itself in principle.

From the whole of these circumstances we gather clear and strong encouragement. The first blow has been struck in Parliament, and it must be repeated. We are bound to support Mr. Lawson, who has honorably and ably done his part, and to see that the flag once raised is carried higher and higher. This we can only effect by a closer union among ourselves, by greater liberality in behalf of the movement, and by such an electoral organization in our counties and boroughs, as shall divest the liquor traffic of its existing political influence, and induce political parties to avoid our opposition, and desire our friendship. We must endeavor to secure the adhesion of the members before they take their seats in the next Parliament. A General Election cannot be long delayed. To prepare for it is your immediate, your most urgent and imperative business. We, the Executive, and our agents throughout the country, will render all possible advice and assistance. Let us hear from you at the earliest opportunity, for on us in concert will devolve the labors and honors of the work to be done among the electors and at the hustings. It is now, in the pause that follows the first trial of our strength, that we hear afresh the voice of patriotism and humanity, demanding, in the words of the Declaration of the General Council — "That rising above class, sectarian, or party considerations, all good citizens should combine to procure an enactment, prohibiting the sale of intoxicating liquors, as affording most efficient aid in removing the appalling evil of intemperance."

Resolutions of a Conference of Alliance Friends in London.

Immediately after the division on Mr. Lawson's "Intoxicating Liquors Bill," on Wednesday afternoon, June 8th, a large number of the leading and active friends of the Alliance, who had been in attendance in the lobby of the House, and aiding in the deputation to Lord Palmerston, met at the Alliance offices, 335 Strand, to confer upon the result of the discussion that had taken place, and the future operations of the supporters of the movement. Mr. Pope presided, and very ably stated the position of the question, and the bearings of the division that had just taken place. Many very excellent practical suggestions were made by the various speakers, and the following resolutions were unanimously adopted:

Moved by Charles Jupe, Esq., seconded by Thomas Clegg, Esq.: — "That the friends of the Alliance who are present at this Conference, from various parts of the country, feel very much encouraged with the result of the first division in the House of Commons on the principle of the Permissive Prohibitory Liquor Bill, introduced by Messrs. Lawson and Bazley; and they rejoice that the agitation in its behalf has at length been recognized by Parliament as involving a question for its earnest consideration. The Conference regard the circumstances of so large a number of members being in the House at the division, as in itself a recognition of the importance of the question; and they rejoice that so many members at the very first introduction of the measure were prepared to support its principle by their votes. They earnestly recommend all friends of the movement to increase their efforts in enlightening public opinion, and informing members of the Legislature of the real nature of the Permissive Bill."

Moved by Edward Whitwell, Esq., Kendal, seconded by Rev. Canon Jenkins, M. A.: — "That the most cordial thanks of the friends of the movement are due and are hereby tendered to Wilfrid Lawson, Esq , M. P., for the able manner in which he has introduced the Permissive Bill into the House of Commons."

Moved by Thomas Richardson, Esq., Bagshott, seconded by J. R. Taylor, Esq., London: — "That the best thanks of the Conference be presented to Mr. Bazley and those members of Parliament who supported Mr. Lawson by their speeches and votes on the second reading of the Intoxicating Liquors Bill."

Address to Members of Parliament.

On the morning of the debate in the House of Commons on Mr. Lawson's bill, a copy of the following document was delivered at the residence of each member:

"*Intoxicating Liquors Bill*," *Second Reading*, *Wednesday*, *June 8th*, 1864.

"Honorable gentlemen are respectfully requested to support the second reading of the Intoxicating Liquors Bill.

"1. The numerous acts regulating the sale of drink recognize that the traffic needs treatment of an exceptional character. In fact, all persons are prohibited from selling intoxicating liquors, excepting those who are permitted by license.

"2. Licenses are now granted on the production of certificates from the magistrates, who are constituted the judges, not only of the character of the applicants, but of the wants of the neighborhood.

"3. Whilst this serious responsibility rests upon the gentlemen holding the commission of the peace, they are without any means of ascertaining the wishes of the community amongst whom the licensed houses are established.

"4. The Intoxicating Liquors Bill provides the machinery by which the public, upon the widest suffrage in existence, may indicate, by their votes, whether they desire the sale of intoxicating liquors in their midst.

"5. It provides that when a large majority—two to one—wish to be without the sale amongst them, then, and only then, shall their veto become operative.

"6. The bill does not propose to close public houses as places of public entertainment, but simply to stop the sale of intoxicating drinks when the people desire the privilege of sale to be withdrawn.

"7. Public houses, without the sale of those dangerous articles, will become more available for all classes. They will be victualling houses rather than drinking houses.

"8. The principle of the bill has been acted upon by many landowners, and the inhabitants of the district affected by this policy express the greatest satisfaction with the arrangement and its results. What is done by landed proprietors, with such beneficial effects, cannot be objectionable when accomplished by the people themselves.

"9. The bill is not coercive in any sense not applicable to all legislation, and is not a measure capable of abuse by any party or class. It enables drinkers and drinksellers to vote equally with other sections of the community. Under these circumstances, to pass the Intoxicating Liquors Bill would clearly be an extension of liberty to the people to protect themselves from the evils and taxation invariably produced or augmented by the liquor shops of a district.

"10. All classes would ultimately be benefited by the bill, and as it has the support of large numbers of the working classes, it is hoped that honorable members will be in their places to support the second reading on Wednesday, June 8th, at 12 o'clock."

UNITED KINGDOM ALLIANCE,

Offices—41 John Dalton Street, Manchester; and 335 Strand, London.
June 7th, 1864.

TO THE RIGHT HON. LORD PALMERSTON, HER MAJESTY'S FIRST MINISTER OF STATE.

The Humble Memorial of the Executive of the United Kingdom Alliance, for the Total Legislative Suppression of the Liquor Traffic,

RESPECTFULLY SHEWETH —

That your Memorialists, from a wide observation of the condition and sentiments of the people of the United Kingdom, and especially of the middle and working classes, are convinced that there is a strong opinion and a growing feeling against the present system of Licensing places for the Sale of Intoxicating Liquors.

That the efforts and teachings of Temperance and Social Reformers have resulted in a prevalent and deep conviction, that strong drink is an exceptional article of commerce, and that it is neither right nor politic for the State to sanction and uphold a system that produces poverty, vice, crime, insanity, and premature death.

That your Memorialists have observed that many leading Landowners, of late years, have recognized the pernicious and demoralizing character of places Licensed for the Sale of Intoxicating Liquors; and have exercised their influence to remove these pestilent places from their estates. And in no instance have the people of the district, from whence the liquor traffic has been thus excluded, expressed any grievances or complaints; but on the contrary, in all cases, your Memorialists believe that public sentiment has ratified and rejoiced in the beneficial change.

That your Memorialists have fo. a series of years tested the opinion of the masses of the people on this question of the Liquor Traffic, by holding public meetings, gathering petitions, and by a systematic house to house visitation and canvass. The result of these inquiries has been such as to fully convince your Memorialists that the present public house system, if submitted to the action of an effective popular control, would soon be swept away, as a public nuisance and social curse.

That, as these drinking houses are ostensibly Licensed for the convenience and advantage of the public, your Memorialists conceive that it is only just and right that the people of any district should have the power to declare by vote, that they either do or do not desire to have these places in their midst.

That your Memorialists therefore respectfully and most earnestly implore your Lordship and the Government to sanction and aid the effort now being made to pass the "Intoxicating Liquors Bill," which would enable the owners and occupiers of property, being Ratepayers, to veto the issue of Licenses for the sale of Intoxicating Liquors, whenever and wherever a majority of two-thirds shall so determine.

And your Memorialists will ever pray.

Signed on behalf of the Executive Council,

WALTER C. TREVELYAN, *Bart., President.*
WILLIAM HARVEY, J. P., *Chairman.*
SAMUEL POPE, *Barrister-at-Law, Hon. Sec.*
THOMAS H. BARKER, *Secretary.*

MANCHESTER, *June 6th,* 1864.

No. 5.

THE

AMERICAN TEMPERANCE MOVEMENT,

PREPARED BY REQUEST OF THE GREAT TEMPERANCE ALLIANCE OF GREAT BRITAIN, AND READ AT THE

International Temperance and Prohibition Convention

HANOVER SQUARE ROOMS, LONDON,

ON SEPTEMBER 3d, 1862.

BY EDWARD C. DELAVAN,

ALBANY, N. Y.

CORRESPONDENCE.

FROM E. C. DELAVAN, ESQ., UNITED STATES.

South Ballston, Saratoga County,
New York, U. S. A., Aug. 12th, 1862.

Sir—I have been notified by my friend, T. H. Barker, Esq., Secretary of the "Grand Alliance," that the committee of arrangements for the International Temperance and Prohibition Convention, to be held in London on the 2d, 3d, and 4th of September, has done me the honor of naming me the first Vice-President of the Convention, an honor which I greatly appreciate.

I was a delegate to the World's Convention, held at London in 1838. On my recent visit to England, I was much delighted and greatly encouraged with the marked advance the cause of Temperance had made during this long interval. The fact that you, sir, act as President of the Alliance, as well as the presiding officer of the Convention, with the Earl of Harrington and Lord Brougham as Vice-Presidents, makes, in my opinion, an era in the great Temperance cause.

I am older than I was in 1838, and yet, if it is possible and compatible with other duties, I shall endeavor so to manage my affairs as to sail in the Africa, the 20th instant, from Boston, with the expectation of reaching London in time to take the highly honorable place assigned me on the platform. Should I be prevented, the disappointment to me would be very great.

Permit me, sir, to express the opinion, that the Permissive Bill appears to me simple in its structure and just in its aim; and I have no doubt it is destined in due time to prevail, and cause a rich flow of blessings to the British nation. The press in this country has been the great instrument to enlighten the public mind, and bring that mind up, step by step, to the full blaze of the truth with regard to the nature and effects of alcohol.

In 1837 I hardly knew of a dozen individuals who had even thought of Prohibition. Now, I believe there are millions of true converts to the principle, who only wait the ending of the present unholy, causeless rebellion, to renew their labors until the law is fully enacted in every State in the Union.

Of a single document on the immorality of the traffic, two millions two hundred thousand were printed—a copy for every family in the nation that by any possibility could be reached. Copies of important Temperance papers have often been furnished for every family in the State. It appears to me the Permissive Bill should follow, not precede the general enlightenment of the masses, as to its value and justice.

I look upon the Alliance, and all kindred organizations, in their influence, as mutual insurance associations to preserve health, life, and property; to lessen pauperism, crime and taxation; and to promote piety, virtue, and add to national health and prosperity.

If these benevolent institutions in Great Britain can, by their efforts, diminish the consumption of alcoholic poison as a beverage a single penny a day to each of 35,000,000 of the inhabitants of the British Isles, it would amount (if my calculation is correct) to £53,229,166 sterling a year. As the pulpit, press, and the lecturer are the principal instruments of enlightenment, I trust the public bounty will flow into the treasury of the Alliance in proportion to the magnitude of the labor thrown upon it. I am, sir, yours very truly,

Sir W. C. Trevelyan. E. C. DELAVAN.

South Ballston, New York, United States,
August 16th, 1862.

MY DEAR FRIEND—I have this moment received your kind note of the 29th ult. I regret most deeply and painfully the necessity of informing you that my health will not allow me at this time to cross the Atlantic. I have never recovered from the severe accident which befel me last year. I have delayed writing till the last moment, hoping I might (as I intimated to your worthy President) take the steamer of the 20th inst. But such is my state of health that my family object, and I dare not go.

You very much overrate the importance of my presence at the Convention. To me the loss will be great; and it is also a disappointment which I feel very deeply. I spent seven years of my life in England, and have experienced so much kindness from English friends that I cannot cast them from my heart because some of them, through the agency of a depraved press, have been misled as to the cause of the great rebellion. You may rely upon it, my friend, this rebellion has been long hatching—about as long as the Temperance Reformation has had being. The war originated in the South to break up the Union, with the hope of fastening slavery on this Continent. The war was commenced in the South. The South fired the first gun. The North is fighting for its existence as a nation, for the Union, and for the final downfall of slavery, which is as important to the South as to the North. The North will continue to fight for these objects while a man or a dollar is left. To be consistent, England must sympathize with us. We want no help; we have the means and power of doing up this work. We may have reverses, but they will only stimulate to greater effort. The North have a pride in labor. It is according to God's law that man should eat bread "by the sweat of his brow." The South would set aside this law, and gain their bread by the sweat of other men's brows, and under the lash too often. Will God permit this? I think not.

It appears to me that if ever there was a time, now is that

time, when statesmen should study the Temperance cause in view of its political economy. Your laboring classes are on the verge of starvation for the want of bread, consequent upon the want of cotton. Are not the brewers and distillers, by destroying the grain of the earth, increasing the evil tenfold?

The Temperance Reformation has not yet done its perfect work in this country by any means; it has still to encounter and subdue many opposing forces. Much, however, has been done of permanent value. When the reform was inaugurated in 1826, the population was about half that it now is. The darkness was all but universal as to the true character of alcohol. Then, not one farm in a hundred was cultivated without the poison, "alcohol," in the hay and harvest field. Then, a great proportion of the farms were mortgaged to the rum seller. Now, not one in a hundred use the poison on their farms, and mortgages for liquor bills are now rare. The farmers of the nation are the strength of it, and can be relied on in any necessity involving right principles.

But I must not take up your time. I know full well, by experience, how much labor and anxiety it must cost to prepare for such a Convention as is to meet in London on the 2d, 3d and 4th of September. Do present my kindest regards to all your associates, and believe me as ever,

Your friend,

T. H. Barker, Esq., Sec'y EDWARD C. DELAVAN.

United Kingdom Alliance,

To procure the total immediate Legislative suppression of the traffic in Intoxicating Liquors,

Manchester, England.

AMERICAN TEMPERANCE MOVEMENT.

About a third of a century since, a small Band of Temperance men in the United States of America ventured to put forth their belief that distilled spirit was always injurious as a beverage. This opinion was at first assailed as ridiculous and fanatical, an outrage on public opinion and common sense.

But this small band, believing their position to be true, employed the press and other instrumentalities to bring home to every fireside in the nation, which could possibly be reached, those facts and arguments by which they had themselves been convinced.

Truth is mighty, and it *did* prevail. These efforts were eminently blessed, and after a few years of intense labor the results were truly astonishing.

Four hundred thousand persons in the State of New York, gave in their adhesion to the principle, and signed the pledge of Abstinence from the use of ardent spirits. Over ten thousand dealers abandoned the traffic, in obedience to public opinion, or from the bidding of an enlightened conscience.

Although the truth was thus blessed, in regard to distilled liquors, yet only a part of the truth had been proclaimed. Science came in, and settled the fact, that alcohol in fermented drinks was exactly the same poisonous fluid as in distilled liquors.

Before the full establishment of this fact, spirits became so universally condemned, and the trade so reduced, that the dealers resorted to skillful adulterations, by which they adroitly converted a great deal of their stock of ardent spirits into a drink bearing the name of wine, and, under this disguise, decoyed tens of thousands into drinking ardent spirits, who supposed they were living up to their pledge! This art has now become a business, so established that a pure article of liquor, even when intoxicating, is almost out of the question, whether for medicinal or sacramental purposes.

When the truth became known that it was alcohol, no matter under what name disguised, which was the "mocker," ruining the world, the friends of true Temperance had but two alternatives; either to give up the reform altogether, or fight the battle against alcohol in fermented as well as distilled liquor. They had the moral courage given them, in the face of the general opinion of the civilized, but more especially of the Christian world, to fight this battle. The opposition was all but universal; the thousands of societies formed under the ardent spirit pledge fell away, and the whole labour had to be gone over again to establish the Total Abstinence doctrine.

The political and generally the religious press uttered the cry of denunciation against this step in advance, condemning it as opposed to the teachings of the Saviour. "Did he not," said they, "make intoxicating wine at the marriage of Cana? Did not He dispense it at the institution of the Last Supper?"

It was thought to be sufficient answer to these inquiries that the Bible had denounced intoxicating wine as "a mocker," not much or little, but wine itself; had characterized intoxicating wine as "biting like a serpent, and stinging like an adder." How could the Saviour, without stultifying this teaching, make and dispense intoxicating wine? He who came into the world to save, not to destroy it! That our Saviour made wine, out of water, is true, but must it follow that He made the kind which is "a mocker."

The doctrine that the Bible sanctions the use of intoxicating liquors, as a beverage, has been the bane of the Church. It has already caused the downfall of millions within its pale, and is still leading on millions more to the same impending judgment.

The delusive doctrine that the moderate use is safe, and that it is *excess* only that is to be avoided, has occasioned most of the drunkenness of the world; and, unless this delusion is expelled, intemperance will continue to the end of time. The use of alcohol as a beverage in health, is at all times, and in all cases, a violation of the laws of life, which are the laws of God; and so long as such use is sanctioned by the Church, drunkenness will, however unwittingly, be perpetuated by the Church.

Temperance organizations have furnished the world with facts and arguments, to show that there can be no cure for the evil, save total abstinence. The early labourers in the States are passing away. The Rev. Justin Edwards, D. D., Governor Briggs, Dr. Warren, Honorable Theodore Frelinghuysen, and others of the like character, who were faithful to the last, have died; the Revs. Drs. Beecher, Nott, and Wayland; Chief Justice Savage, John Tappan, Horace Greeley, Dr. Hewitt, Dr. Mussey, Chancellor Walworth, Hon. G. Smith, Rev. Dr. Marsh, Professor Youmans, General J. H. Cocke, Bishop Potter, Professor C. A. Lee, and a host of others, who assisted to raise the Temperance standard, yet live, and have never for a moment deserted their colours. As with you, so with us, the most devoted friends of the reform have at times honestly differed as to the best mode of urging it forward; but as a rule, by friendly intercourse and public discussion, great oneness of sentiment and action has been attained. Total Abstinence men all over this nation are so numerous, and have practiced the abstinence they have preached so long, that they have become venerable landmarks, illustrating in their persons the inestimable value of the principle. These veterans cannot hereafter labour as in times past; but it is most refreshing and heart-cheering to them to know that converts to their principles are to be found by millions, including men and women of all ranks in Church and State. Our great leader in Prohibition, General Neal Dow, now engaged in fighting the battles of his country, will, we hope, when peace is restored, again lead on the prohibitory host to victory.

The latest steps adopted by our rulers are encouraging. The English public are acquainted with the well-bruited fact that spirit rations, with quinine, were issued to the army on the Potomac to ward off fever. A week's trial was sufficient evidence of its futility for good, and its power for evil, and the Commander-in-Chief at once expelled this most dangerous foe At the same time Congress ordered alcohol to be ejected from the navy, where it has nestled for fifty years ; and now both army and navy stand out before the world, in all their regulations, examples of Temperance principles. May England soon follow in the same safe and sanitary path !

Prohibition has not been a failure in this country. A very great majority of the people, outside the corrupting influence of large towns and cities, are decidedly in favor of it, and in time will have it. After the war ends and things settle down, the movement will again revive, and what you are now doing will be valuable aid to us, though the struggle will be long and arduous. We, indeed, have special difficulties, if special advantages. Our political demagogues, who appear willing to sacrifice the best interests of their country to carry out party ends, look to the grog-shop and the miserable drunkard, as their most valuable supporters. These influences will be arraigned against universal Prohibition, and it will require many Dows and Careys to conquer. That they *will* conquer, I as fully believe as that there is a God in Heaven.

I repeat, Prohibition has been no failure in America, all things considered. It has hardly had a fair trial generally; but where it has, the beneficial results in such localities have quite exceeded the expectations of its friends. With us, as with you, the opponents have been most ingenious in their arguments to prejudice the masses against the measure. One standing plea has been, that it is "a tyrannical attempt to take away the liberties of the people." "Is it right," they ask, "that any citizen should be prohibited from selling, or be embarrassed in the means of procuring, what he is accustomed to use without apparent injury to himself or the public, because others abuse it to their own detriment?" In replying, it is necessary first of all to inquire what are the invariable and inevitable social effects of the liquor-traffic? for it is on these grounds, if at all, that the State has a right to interfere. Now, it is safe to assert, that whenever human beings have been exposed to the temptation of intoxicating drinks, many have partaken of them habitually, and a considerable number have become drunkards. So long as this ensnaring temptation is publicly offered, it is certain that many will drink, and numbers will become abandoned drunkards. These propositions are confirmed by all experience, from the days of the flood until this very hour. It is equally undeniable that these drunkards are withdrawn from every duty they owe to society, and finally hurried down, through sufferings none but themselves can conceive, to dishonored and untimely graves; that in the meantime some of them become maniacs; that some, under the moral blindness and frenzy of intoxication, are guilty of murders and other crimes; that many of them inflict upon their helpless wives and children miseries, compared with which speedy death were a blessing; and that the immediate costs and terrible consequences of these misdeeds fall on citizens in no degree accountable for them. Can a law, designed to relieve these citizens from such mischiefs, by directly and absolutely interdicting their known cause, really be tyrannical and unjust? or is it not usual and proper legislation? Light may be thrown on the question by a simple definition of municipal law and of liberty:—

"Civil, or municipal law, is a rule of conduct prescribed to all the citizens by the supreme power in the State, in conformity to the constitution, on a matter of common interest. It is the solemn declaration of the legislative power, by which it commands, under certain penalties or certain rewards, what each citizen should do, not do, or suffer, for the common good of the State."

Liberty is defined as "The power of doing whatever is not injurious to others; the exercise of our natural rights, bounded only by the rights which assure to others the enjoyment of their rights. Civil liberty is the power to do whatever is permitted by the laws of the land. It is no other than natural liberty so far restrained by human laws and no further, as is necessary and expedient for the general advantage of the public."

Now, in view of the admitted wrongs to individuals, and burdens and taxes upon the public, through the sale of intoxicating drinks, compare a law simply prohibiting that sale with the above, or the narrowest definitions, of municipal law, and we shall find that the law proposed comes strictly within its terms; or compare this law with the above, or the broadest definition of human liberty, and we shall find that it is not infringed a hair's breadth by the Maine Law. If this be so; if the law merely prescribes what "each citizen should do, not do, or suffer, for the common good of the State"—if, in effect, it simply interdicts some from doing what is "injurious to others," then we may safely assume that it is neither tyrannical nor improper, but within the ordinary sphere of legislation.

A license law, in fact, involves the entire right in question, for such a law primarily prohibits all, and then excepts those licensed; and if it had not the right to prohibit them also, the license would be an idle ceremony. In this view of the case, the question of right has been practically settled foı ages.

But to some minds the application of the principle of Pro hibition, in a parallel case, may be more convincing. Thirty years since, the several cities of New York State were almost as plentifully studded with shops for the sale of lottery tickets, as with those for vending intoxicating drinks — both licensed by the State, under the notion of regulating the business. The purchaser of lottery tickets could take the same grounds as the purchaser of intoxicating drinks; he paid for what he purchased with his own money; he had too much prudence to do himself any harm; he was willing and able to dedicate all he expended for tickets to the benign objects of the lottery, thereby purchasing the possibility of drawing a prize. The vendor of tickets could, in like manner, insist on the pecuniary losses to which he would be exposed, by the destruction of a business, to which he had devoted himself under the sanction of law, and on which his family depended for support; that the business ought not to be suppressed, because a few only of those who purchased tickets were ruined by its allurements — still less should it be suppressed without ample compensation.

In principle, this lottery and the liquor trade were the same. but in two or three particulars there was a difference. Lotteries were for the promotion of science and literature, an object undeniably useful, while the liquor traffic is of worse than doubtful utility. The allurements of the lottery were considerable, but those of the inebriating cup are many times greater; while the mischief and ruin which attended the former, was as a drop to the ocean in comparison with the latter. On the ground of facts, therefore, the liquor business should have been forbidden, and the lotteries, if either, ought to have been cherished and perpetuated by State licenses. On the contrary, however, the Legislature of 1827 prohibited, under severe penalties of fine and imprisonment, the opening of any lottery scheme, or the sale of any lottery tickets, authorized or unauthorized; and the people emphatically sanctioned the enactment by vigorously enforcing it, and by causing to be inserted in the constitution, approved by their own votes, a clause forbidding any future Legislature to repeal it.

An attentive examination of our numerous prohibitory and penal laws, will show that the supreme selfishness which seeks the gratification of its own appetites, or the acquisition of gain, by means dangerous to others, is as promptly and sternly rebuked by municipal law as by Christian morality. It is the impunity in public and private mischief, hitherto enjoyed by the liquor traffic, and not the law demanded for its suppression, which really constitutes a marked and mischievous exception to the ordinary course of protective legislation.

The philanthropists of England and America are engaged in a mighty work, in spreading the Gospel throughout the world. They send their bishops and missionaries everywhere; but, as a general rule, along with the Bible they introduce intoxicating liquor, and even at the very table of the Lord the convert is expected to partake of the cup of intoxication. I pray that this great error may ere long be corrected in the churches, and when corrected by them, the world at large will follow, and one of the greatest hindrances to conversion will be removed.

No. 6.

LETTER

TO

GENERAL JOHN H. COCKE OF VIRGINIA,

(Late President of the American Temperance Union,)

ON THE COMMUNION QUESTION.

FROM

EDWARD C. DELAVAN.

SOUTH BALLSTON, *October* 1, 1856.

TO GENERAL JOHN H. COCKE,
Late President Am. Temperance Union,
7 Island Post Office, Virginia.

MY DEAR SIR:—While on your recent visit to me, you remarked that it was due to the cause of Temperance, to myself, as well as my family, that I should give to the public a brief history of the rise of the Communion question, and my true position with regard to it. That while you fully understood the whole matter, yet you had not unfrequently, even in Virginia and elsewhere, to defend me from unfounded charges with regard to this important question. Your recent letter, alluding to the same subject, has induced me to comply with your request, which I now do as briefly as possible, that the reproach and charge of my "*daring attempt to banish from the communion table the element the Son of God consecrated,*" may be removed.

In the early years of the Temperance Reform in the State of New York, the agitation of the Communion question was thought by many as most unfortunate, and calculated to retard the movement, if not threaten the overthrow of the Temperance cause entirely.

At this time, I cannot but think, that on a review of the whole question, it will be looked upon in a truer light and with a more impartial eye. And when it is considered that whatever explanation I have to make must be made soon, if made at all, I shall, I trust, be pardoned for making that explanation now.

Besides the opposition met with from dealers and drinkers, which was to be expected, great embarrassment was experienced in consequence of the position assumed even by educated men, that alcohol was the result of distillation; and that fermented liquors were, therefore not injurious but healthful as a common beverage. So little understood was the nature of the poison we arrayed ourselves against, as connected with fermentation, that our noble, intelligent and mutual friend, the Hon. Gerrit Smith, at the first meeting of the New York State Temperance Society, recommended the cultivation of the vine and the manufacture of wine. He said "it would be a useful Temperance measure to substitute wine for ardent spirits." Now this same noble and disinterested supporter of the cause, feels that he has not only the same moral but the same legal right to enter the tenement where intoxicating liquors are sold as a beverage, whether the product of the wine vat or the still, and with his own hand break the bottles, and stave in the head of the casks, and destroy the contents thereof as a *public nuisance*, as he would have to shoot a mad dog in chase of his child or neighbor. Nor was it till discussions were held, and repeated experiments made by men of science, in different countries, that the public mind was disabused of error, and the friends of Temperance vindicated for including intoxicating drinks of all kinds, whether distilled or fermented, among the articles to be avoided as always injurious as beverages. These changes in our own views from time to time, should ever remind us to judge with charity those who do not immediately change with us.

The Communion question, as it was called, the discussion of which greatly agitated the public mind, and threatened for a season to destroy the harmony, if not the very existence of the Temperance organization, was not introduced by the organization, or any branch of it, but was forced on the State Society by the opposers of entire abstinence, on the plea that while intoxicating wine was used, and commanded to be used at the Lord's Table, we had no right to condemn its use in moderation at other tables. The discussion of this question was constantly urged by opposers of total abstinence, and for a long time avoided by the Society, till at length it was boldly asserted, and publicly proclaimed in the newspapers, *that I was myself "opposed to wine at the Lord's Table."*

About this period, and before the report had been extensively circulated, a Temperance convention was held at Buffalo, in 1835, to decide whether the Society should adopt the pledge of *total abstinence from all that can intoxicate*. I took with me to that convention a resolution adopted by the Executive Committee of the State Society, of which I was chairman, disavowing all intention to interfere with this question in relation to the use of wine at the communion. But the Business Committee of the convention thought it unwise to bring such a resolution forward to arrest the progress of an unfounded rumor, put in circulation in a single locality. When I returned to Albany from the convention, which decided by only a single negative that it was the duty of the State Society to advocate total abstinence from all that can intoxicate, I found the imputation of my opposition to the use of wine at the communion had been so extended, and so generally believed, that Temperance men and Anti-Temperance men seemed to be combined against me; and the press, both political and religious, uttered only the language of denunciation. And although I published a disclaimer in the Evening Journal* immediately (October, 1835), yet falsehood traveled so fast, that truth has even yet hardly overtaken it. I saw there was no avoiding the discussion—that the *real* question at issue must be distinctly stated, and the charge implied, fully and fairly met. And although dragged before the public without provocation, I did meet it; and to show how unfounded the report was which was put in circulation, and the disadvantage under which it placed me before the public, I will give a letter from an individual who was the innocent cause of giving rise to a charge against me, which at the time bore on me with such injurious effect, and such a crushing weight. Had this letter, which follows, been published at the time, and the origin of the unfounded accusations been immediately made known, I should at once have been placed on the vantage ground before the public, but it was not so made known; on the contrary, nearly two years elapsed before its publication, which took place 10th June, 1837, in the New York American, then edited by Charles King, the present honored President of Columbia College, who while editor of that exemplary political paper, always gave me an impartial hearing; and I wish here, after a lapse of twenty and more years, to render him my public thanks for his kindness. The letter is as follows, and probably did not meet the eye of one in ten thousand who had been made to believe that I was little short of an Infidel, "BEING OPPOSED TO WINE AT THE LORD'S TABLE."

FARMINGTON, CT., *May* 17, 1837.

DEAR SIR:—It has recently come to my knowledge, that a distinguished clergyman, whilst delivering a sermon to a large congregation in the city of New York, in which he spoke of the ultraism of the times, expressed himself in substance as follows, viz: "That so extravagant and reckless were some of the advocates of the Temperance cause, *that they had* STOLEN *into the church of God, and desecrated the wine provided for the holy communion.*" Not long since, a gentleman visiting in the family of a highly respected citizen, residing in the western part of the State of New York, was told that "*Mr. Delavan had secretly entered the Second Presbyterian Church, in Albany, and mixed water with the wine, intended for the communion.*" Other misrepresentations of the same character, in which Mr. Delavan's and my

*DISCLAIMER OF THE NEW YORK STATE TEMPERANCE SOCIETY.

The Executive Committee of the New York State Temperance Society, being aware that a report has been industriously circulated, that it was their design to dispense with the use of wine at the Lord's Supper, deem it to be their duty to disclaim utterly any such intention. They believe that the "Fruit of the Vine" is one of the essential elements of that sacred ordinance. The Committee have never, for a moment, entertained a wish or thought that the "Fruit of the Vine," as used by our Lord, should be withdrawn from the sacramental table.

By order of the Executive Committee,
E. C. DELAVAN, *Chairman.*

ALBANY, *Oct.* 1, 1835

name were distinctly mentioned, have also come to my knowledge, which it is unnecessary to repeat. So long as the censure connected with the transaction that gave rise to these misrepresentations was confined to myself, and was limited in extent, I did not deem it of consequence enough to require any particular notice. But since the misrepresentation is circulated and endorsed in various sections of the country, by individuals whose standing and influence will give it currency, to the injury of the Temperance cause, and to the detriment of a friend, who had nothing to do with the transaction in question, I feel called upon to make a simple statement of the facts.

About two years since, being then a resident of Albany, and a member of the Second Presbyterian (Dr. Sprague's) Church in that city, two elders of that church called at my house, at a late hour of a Saturday evening, previous to a communion, and stated, that they had just left a meeting of the session of the church, and that Dr. Sprague had stated to the session, that he had understood that I was in possession of some pure wine, and as they had difficulty in procuring such as was pure, suggested that a committee be appointed to ask if I would furnish enough for the use of the table the next day. I replied to the elders, that I had Maderia wine, that I had no doubt came directly from that island; but notwithstanding this, I did not consider it pure, as all Maderia wines had a considerable admixture of brandy; that Dr. Beck had analyzed some of the same kind, and found it contained alcohol equal to 42 per cent. of brandy. I did not, therefore, consider it proper to be used in the communion, inasmuch as the wines of Palestine, and pure wines generally, did not contain more alcohol than was equal to about 15 or 20 per cent. of brandy; and moreover, there was good reason to suppose that even those wines were in ancient times reduced by adding two or three parts of water, when drunk by respectable people and when used in the communion.* I added that I was unwilling to furnish such wine as mine to be used in the communion; but if they chose to take it with such an addition of water as would reduce it to about the strength of the wines of Palestine, they were welcome to as much as they might want. They made no objection to my proposition, informed me how much they should want, and the next morning the sexton of the church was sent to my house, and I furnished the quantity desired, reduced in the manner proposed. The whole transaction was unsought on my part, and unexpected to me, nor did I consult or advise with any one on the subject. I was present at the communion, and left town the following morning, not dreaming that any dissatisfaction existed. On

*It is yet an open question whether water was used for diluting wine for the communion in the early history of the church, on account of its containing alcohol, or on account of the thick ropy state of the unintoxicating wine as it was usually preserved, and as abundantly proved by ancient writers. In one case water would only dilute an intoxicating drink—"the mocker," in the other to dilute a pure, healthful and nutritious wine. In a note attached to the 11th verse of the xl chapter of Genesis, in Baxter's Comprehensive Bible, will be found the following account of wine making and wine drinking in the primitive ages of the world: "FROM THIS WE FIND THAT WINE ANCIENTLY WAS THE MERE EXPRESSED JUICE OF THE GRAPE, WITHOUT FERMENTATION THE SAKA OR CUP BEARER TOOK THE BUNCH, PRESSED THE JUICE INTO THE CUP, AND INSTANTLY DELIVERED IT TO HIS MASTER."

"Thus saith the Lord, as the new wine is found in the cluster, and one saith, destroy it not, for a blessing is in it." Isaiah lxv, 3.

Pliny, who lived about the time of our Saviour, says good wine was that which was destitute of spirit. Book 4, chap. 12 Plutarch calls that the best wine which is harmless; that the most useful which has the least strength; and that the most wholesome in which nothing was added to the juice of the grape. Evidence of the above character, as to the existence and healthfulness of unintoxicating wine, could be greatly multiplied.

my return in a few weeks, I found that the church had been much excited on the subject, and that there was a general impression that I had practiced a deception, by *offering* to furnish some *pure wine* for the communion, and instead of *pure wine*, had furnished *weak wine and water*. I took no further notice of the matter than to send a written statement to the pastor, similar to what I have now written, nor should I now do so, but for the reasons already stated. I am yours very sincerely,

JOHN T. NORTON.

To give you some faint idea of the character and *spirit* of the controversy, especially *on one side of it*, and the public feeling at the time by the false charge brought against me, I quote, as specimens, and merely specimens, which might be greatly extended, of epithets applied to me by a single opponent, and a Reverend Doctor of Divinity, in his communications in favor of the wine that intoxicates for the Lord's Supper, in place of wine the fruit of the vine, advocated by me, in a state which would not intoxicate:—

"Presumptuous and impious statements—foul aspersions—assault on the most solemn ordinances of our religion—all the wise and holy men of the land are opposed to his views, and contemplate them with indignation and horror—blasphemous presumption—this is a monstrous, daring attempt to banish from the communion table the element the Son of God consecrated—presumptuous attack upon an ordinance, and through it upon the character of Christ—antidote to the poison—prevarications and perversions of Scripture—flood of error—he has impeached the benevolence, and by consequence the divinity of the Son of God—another such instance of vanity and presumption—shocking impiety, aiming, as in fact it does, a blow at the divinity of the Son of God—involves the inspiration of the Scriptures, and equally the wisdom and benevolence, and consequently the divinity of Christ—alarmed at the indignation, &c.—after all the fog in which Mr. D. has endeavored to involve his views—his pretensions to candor are pretensions and nothing more—he has practiced abundantly on the credulity of the public—I have reason to believe that there is more of poetry than truth in this excuse—shocking language—it is a deliberate attempt to deceive—a tissue of falsehoods—absurdities and blasphemies—he has the hardihood to affirm—this amazing perversion of truth—his own gross prevarication—after all his quibbling."

And after applying to me these epithets, and after a full review of them, and his labors, he remarked:—

"*I have not penned a sentence, nor a word, which with my present views I should desire to erase.*" It is only just, however, to remark, that after applying to me the epithets above quoted, and re-indorsing them as above quoted, he very charitably ascribed my views on the communion question (those views only extending to the kind of wine proper for that sacred ordinance), to an "*aberration of intellect.*" How far such epithets should have been applied by a Christian minister to a Christian brother of the same church, under an "*aberration of intellect*," is a question I will not take upon myself to decide.

The same Rev. gentleman compared me to Judas Iscariot. "*I prefer*," said he, "*the character of the impetuous Peter who drew his sword to the insinuating Judas, who betrayed his Master.*" But here, let it be remembered, that the rashness of Peter, as well as the treachery of Judas, was rebuked by Jesus Christ; and that when rebuked, Peter, whom this Reverend gentleman wished to imitate, obedient to his Lord's command, "*put up his sword;*" and in another case, "*went out and wept bitterly.*"

Happy would it be if all Christians, and especially all Christian ministers, who have heretofore offended, or are now offending, by imitating the impetuous Peter, were to cancel the offence by imitating his repentance and reformation.

As a matter of history alone, do I refer to the spirit in which this controversy was conducted. And while in some cases that spirit cannot be defended, yet I can and do fully estimate the motives of those learned divines, who wrote in opposition to my views. They undoubtedly felt that in my zeal to promote the cause of Temperance, I was laying sacrilegious hands upon one of the most holy ordinances of our Religion; and as watchmen, set to guard Truth, and arrest the spread of Error, they felt impelled, by a sense of duty to the church, to expose what they, in the commencement of the discussion, considered a great fallacy.

In 1842, this same report was revived, and circulated in the newspapers, in a modified form, to wit: "*that I was in favor of water at the Lord's Supper.*" This (understanding that I was to be crushed), I repelled, by requesting letters from leading individuals with whom I was most intimate and confidential, and with whom I had been in free correspondence on the subject. In response to that request, the following gentlemen stated, "*that in all my correspondence and conversations during this period, they never heard me express a desire to substitute anything for wine at the Lord's Table; that my only object appeared to be to ascertain the* KIND *of wine used by the Saviour, and to substitute that at the communion table, in place of the vile intoxicating and adulterated compounds known to be in use, and the use of which at the Lord's Table was plead in their own defence by the rumsellers and the rum and wine drinkers, and the profligate of all classes.*" The names of the individuals alluded to are the following:—

Rev. Dr. E. Nott, Pres. Union College; Rt. Rev. Alonzo Potter, Bishop of Penn.; Hon. Ira Harris, Supreme Judge, Albany; Gen. John H. Cocke, late President American Temperance Union, Va.; Hon. Gerrit Smith, Petersboro; Hon. Erastus Corning, Albany; John T. Norton, Farmington, Conn.; Rev. John Marsh, D. D., Secretary American Temperance Union; Archibald Campbell, Deputy Secretary of State of New York; Rev. Dr. I. N. Wyckoff, Albany; Hon. A. Tabor, Albany; Israel Smith, Esq., Albany; O. Scovill, Esq., Albany; Prof. C. R. Lee, M. D., New York; Hon. R. H. Walworth, late Chancellor of the State, Saratoga; Hon. Bradford R. Wood, Albany; Rev. Dr. Justin Edwards, Andover, Mass.

You will understand that the above gentlemen are here cited only as witnesses to a matter of fact; and not that they are from this to be held committed to the views which make up the body of this communication.

And now my dear friend, after the excitement of the discussion growing out of the controversy has passed away, a controversy in which I caused to be circulated near seven millions of documents, I wish to ask of you, in all sincerity, whether, if this controversy had not taken place, and the facts established as to the nature and effects of intoxicating drinks, the Temperance host now would with such unanimity and zeal be urging forward the cause of prohibition of the sale of all that can intoxicate as a beverage?

As my sole object was the development of truth, it was my practice in all these controversies on these great questions, to publish and scatter broadcast, and at great cost and labor, the facts which had been ascertained, and the arguments which had been employed on both sides—taking it for granted, that those openly and under their own signatures, opposing my views, did so from an equal desire to arrive at truth with myself.

You are aware that I have published five numbers of the "Enquirer" principally devoted to this question. I may, if my life is spared, and the cause of Truth demands it, continue the "Enquirer," on my own responsibility, and publish all communications on both sides, which are written in a Christian spirit, Even this communication, you of course understand, is on my own personal responsibility, and commits no Temperance Society or Committee with which I may be connected.

I do not make these statements for the purpose of renewing the question by Temperance organizations. That question has been already, as will be perceived, extensively discussed, and it is now for the churches to decide as to the *kind* of wine proper for the Lord's Table Still, as an individual opinion, speaking on my own responsibility, and for myself only, I cannot refrain from saying, that it crosses my sense of propriety, to find in laws inhibiting the sale of intoxicating drink as a beverage, an exception in favor of their sale FOR SACRAMENTAL PURPOSES.

Not that I have ever been opposed to the use of wine at the communion, but merely to the use of spurious, enforced and intoxicating wine, a kind of wine I believe never made, used or sanctioned by our blessed Lord. "The fruit of the vine," is the only term used in the sacred volume connected with the Lord's Supper.* It is now gener-

*We know that our Lord and his disciples had met to celebrate the feast of the Passover; and we know that the Jews were scrupulous in using at this ceremony none but unleavened bread and unfermented wine. And it is certain that we have no account that any other kind of wine was introduced when our Saviour merged the Passover into the Lord's Supper. Indeed, the only words used to define the contents of the "cup," are "the fruit of the vine." Here is the language of the three evangelists who record the occasion:

Matt. xxvi, 27-9.—And he took the cup, and gave thanks, and gave it to them, saying: Drink ye all of it; for this is my blood of the new testament, which is shed for many for the remission of sins. But I say unto you, I will not drink henceforth of

ally admitted, by those who have examined the subject, that the "fruit of the vine," is wine, whether intoxicating or not.* This being the case, I would ask, and with becoming deference, and in view of the mighty reform in progress, of all professing Christians of every sect, whether it would not be becoming in them at once to look deeply and prayerfully into the bearings of this question; and if it is found that the presence of the intoxicating cup, as now generally administered at the table of the Lord, is a stumbling block, and that stumbling block can legitimately be removed, by the substitution of the "fruit of the vine" in an unadulterated and unintoxicating state, whether it is not their bounden duty to substitute the same as soon as practicable ?†

Here is a great, important and vital question, lying, as I think at the *very root* of the Temperance Reform, which belongs to the church to consider and settle. As a member thereof, I speak as I have a right to speak, and I trust every other member who feels as I do will speak in the same manner. It has long been my belief, and still is my belief, that the purchase by the churches, for the communion, of intoxicating liquors, generally, if not always, of the most impure and disgusting character, and the "*except for sacramental purposes*" in Prohibitory

the fruit of the vine, until that day when I drink it new with you in my father's kingdom.

Mark xiv, 23-5.—And he took the cup, and when he had given thanks, he gave it to them, and they all drank of it. And he said unto them: This is my blood of the new testament, which is shed for many. Verily I say unto you, I will drink no more of the fruit of the vine, until that day that I drink it new in the kingdom of God.

Luke xxii, 19, 10.—This do in remembrance of me. Likewise also the cup after supper, saying : This cup is the new testament in my blood, which is shed for you.

The only words used by our Saviour defining the ingredients of the "cup," it will be seen, are "the fruit of the vine;" now the "fruit of the vine" when "new" is not intoxicating. When it has become intoxicating, it is no longer new, but *old.* Besides, it can be abundantly proved that the wines of commerce are made up of other ingredients besides "the fruit of the vine." Nay, most of it has none of "the fruit of the vine" in it. "The fruit of the vine"—in its fresh and newest state—is unintoxicating. The wines which we substitute are not only intoxicating and adulterated, but absolutely forged and counterfeit—the product not of the "vine," but of the Still, the Brew-house and the Drug-shop ; and the common use of which tends to debase and destroy mankind. Is it possible that an inquiry into so solemn a departure from the original institution can injure either Religion or Temperance ? In this connection, the learned and pious Dr. Clarke, has left on record the following emphatic language :—"This is a most wicked and awful perversion of the Lord's ordinance The matters made use of by Jesus Christ on this solemn occasion, were unleavened bread and the produce of the vine, *i. e.*, pure wine. To depart in the least from his institution, when it is in our power to follow it literally, would be extremely culpable."

* "The fruit of the vine" may be legitimately fermented or unfermented.—*Rev William B. Sprague, D. D.*

† Christians, is it not part of almost every prayer you offer, that God will soon open upon the world the millennial day? Are you acting in consistency with your prayers, by lending your influence to help forward this glorious cause of moral improvement, which *must* prevail ere the millennium shall fully come? Are you exerting any influence, directly or remotely, to retard this cause? Do you make the poison, or do you USE it, or do you sell it? Never open your lips then to pray for the millennium.—*Rev William B. Sprague, D. D.*

The alcohol, whether found in rum, brandy or wine, *is* "poison," is conceded on all hands. It is classed among poisons, because, says a learned writer, it is one of "those substances which are known by physicians as capable of altering or destroy-

Laws, are among the greatest hindrances to the final triumph of Prohibition and the Temperance Reformation.*

The clergyman who preached the sermon referred to in the letter already given, before a congregation of over 2,000 persons in the city of New York, was direct from Albany. One of his hearers, a personal friend of mine, took steamboat the next day to ask of me an explanation, "for" said he, "no man present supposed for a moment but you were the person alluded to." I wrote to this clergyman explaining the whole transaction, asking him in common fairness and Christian obligation to do me justice, and correct the unfounded report to which he had given so wide a circulation; *but I got no reply*—and even at this day, individuals, friends, have told me that they were under an impression that I had in some way been led into acts of great impropriety on this question—*and no wonder*. In all this severe trial and controversy, I suffered greatly in feeling and estrangement of valued friends; my locks whitened rapidly; of about one hundred and fifty families in Albany, who were in the habit of visiting mine, over one hundred immediately drew off—for said some of them, "if Mr. Delavan will by his folly disregard the usages of society, try to banish wine from the Lord's table, and render himself ridiculous, he must take the consequences." A few noble friends however stood by me, but they were very few. Had it not been for them and an abiding conviction that God was with me and near me, I should, I do believe, have sunk under the pressure, for the odds against me were fearful—learned men—scholars, were against me; as I trust honestly against me. While I, on my part had but little to sustain me but faith and a deep conviction that the truth and God was on my side. But this is now all past—I yet live, thank God; and without a single unkind feeling towards any one of my old opposers yet living. I feel it to be my duty to devote whatever is left of me to the furtherance of this great cause, which you love so well, either to aid in purifying the communion cup, or in any proper shape it may present itself, so far as that shall be compatible with those other duties which in the providence of God I may be required elsewhere to perform.

In conclusion, let me here reply to the practical question which is almost invariably asked when the communion question is discussed, viz:—"How can we procure wine, the fruit of the vine, in an unintoxicating state for the sacrament, so as to avoid resorting to the vendors

ing, in a majority of cases, some of the functions necessary to life."—*Dr. Romeyn Beck's Medical Jurisprudence.*

"The testimony of physicians is uniform and unequivocal. They pronounce alcohol a poison. They tell us that it is so considered and classed by all writers on Materia Medica; and they will even point out the precise place which it occupies among the 'vegetable narcotic poisons.'"—*Rt. Rev. Horatio Potter, Episcopal Bishop of New York.*

"That pure alcohol is poison, is an admitted fact."—*Rev. Dr. E. Nott, President Union College.*

*"You are right; it is preposterous to fight against alcohol in other places and welcome it at the Lord's Table."—*Hon. Gerrit Smith.*

of intoxicating liquors, and using their fabricated compounds, and thus avoid the inserting in laws against the sale of intoxicating liquors as a beverage the clause of "*except for sacramental purposes?*"

In reply to this inquiry, I remark that in my opinion there is hardly a church, whose officers could not secure grapes in their season, in quantities sufficient to prepare wine for sacramental purposes. All they would have to do would be to press out the wine from the grapes, put it into bottles—cork the same, then plunge the mouth of the bottles thus corked into some melted substance, beeswax and rosin, or other substances used to secure preserves from fermentation, and then keep the bottles in the same position, upside down, and deposit them in a cool place in the cellar for use when required. Thus the pure blood of the grape—the fruit of the vine—wine—unintoxicating wine, could always be secured. Or the same fruit of the vine could be boiled down to one-third, then bottled in the same way as above stated, and when wanted for use diluted with water; this would also be wine—inspissated wine. When I was in Italy, I had one hundred gallons of the pure fruit of the vine-wine, thus boiled down, and after keeping some of it for years here in my cellar, I sent a bottle of it to Professor Silliman, of New Haven, who after subjecting it to chemical test, informed me he could not find a particle of alcohol in it.

Gerrit Smith writes me: "It must be more than twenty-five years since the little church with which I am connected, refused to use intoxicating liquors at the Lord's Table. During all this time we have used unintoxicating and pure wine. It is obtained from the dried grape or raisin."

Thus you perceive, my friend, there need not be an insurmountable barrier in the way of introducing even in this country the fruit of the vine—WINE—at the communion table, in an unintoxicating state—all that is wanting is the WILL, and, in my opinion, an enlightened conscience in regard to the question.

Having been called upon by an elder of the church to which I belonged in Ballston, late on Saturday, for some of my pure unintoxicating wine for the communion next day (the same as tested by Professor Silliman), I declined, fearing another commotion like the one I had passed through in Albany. But being assured that the communion would have to be omitted unless I complied, I reluctantly furnished the wine, but on the condition that it must not be used without the consent of the pastor and officers of the church; and although thus used, a great commotion followed, and a grave charge brought against me for lending myself to such an *innovation, if not desecration, of the holy communion*. The whole matter was brought before an ecclesiastical court, before which I appeared, and although I was cleared from all blame in the premises, yet had I not so appeared (having been sent for by express), I should doubtless have been censured. The church went back to the use of the liquor of commerce, called wine, two samples of which were furnished me, which J. W. Draper, M. D., Professor of Chemistry and Natural History, New York, examined, one sample contained (to say nothing of drugs) forty-four and two-thirds per cent., the other forty-two per cent. PROOF SPIRIT.

To my mind it is as clear as the noonday's sun, that the Bible recognizes various kinds of wine, good and bad; that ancient writers who lived before, at the time, and since our Saviour, recognized intoxicating and unintoxicating wines, pronouncing the former bad, and the latter good as a beverage; but learned men heretofore have treated the idea of the two kinds of wine, intoxicating and unintoxicating, with contempt, branding those having that idea as "*conceited innovators*," insisting that nothing could be truly called wine except intoxicating, consequently nothing fit for the communion but such wine, and this too in the face of numerous texts in scripture, clearly defining the distinction. "AND THE PRESSES SHALL BURST OUT WITH NEW WINE." Prov. iii, 10. Could the wine here referred to have been intoxicating, bursting out immediately from the press? If the views of these learned men are sound they should be sustained; if not sound, and it is found that the church has *departed from the original pure symbol*, and adopted a corrupting one, the sooner the church makes the correction the better—and it does appear to me that the word wine is of small amount in the controversy, the "fruit of the vine," is the *thing*. That when the Bible recommends the use of wine, and without qualification, it is good wine; when it condemns the use of wine and without qualification, it is bad, deleterious and crime producing wine; for such wine no moderate use as a beverage or for communion, can, in my opinion, be defended. And it appears to me also, by making this distinction, the word of God is cleared from the charge of inconsistency, which the infidel has attempted to bring against it, by making it call the same thing "*good*" without qualification in one place, and "*bad*" without qualification in another. Because pure water is pronounced one of the greatest blessings as a drink, in the Bible, does it follow that the filthy water of the gutter and the fen is a blessing also for the like purpose? I found even the use of my unintoxicating wine exposed me to the charge of wine drinking, indeed, to intemperance on wine, so that on the ground of expediency I abandoned its use, for I conclude the doctrine of expediency with regard to the use of wine applies to *good* wine, not *bad* wine.

I am, as ever,

Your devoted friend,

EDWARD C. DELAVAN.

NOTE.—It is now about eight years since I was called upon by General Cocke of Virginia to make some explanation as to my course with regard to the Communion question—the letter to him now republished in this volume, was prepared in compliance with his wishes; the eight years which have elapsed since the letter was written, have not in any degree served to lessen in my mind the importance of the question to which the letter refers

The general use of intoxicating and fabricated liquor, called wine (but as a rule undeserving the name), on the Lord's Table, is of vast import, and as I believe stands most formidably in the way, not only within, but without the pale of the Church of Christ, to the advance of true temperance, total abstinence from all that can intoxicate as a beverage. So long as "the mocker" holds possession of the Communion cup, the great enemy of the human race will not in my opinion be much disturbed by the Temperance Reformation. And may not the timidity with which even temperance advocates approach this question, be one of the causes why the reformation is now in an inactive state?

In a letter received within a few days from a valued friend, he remarks: "The great fault I have to find with you and Dr. Nott's temperance writings, is the undue use you make of the Bible." Perhaps we are chargeable with this fault, if fault it is, still, as we are bid to "search the Scriptures," why not search them relative to the wine, as well as other questions, seeing that it is a question largely introduced in the Bible--and seeing also it is appealed to by a large body of Christians as sanctioning the use of intoxicating wine as a beverage, as well as a proper element for the Lord's Table; and in addition thereto, they assert that the Savior of the world made and dispensed wine, intoxicating wine, the kind denounced in the Bible as "a mocker" On the other hand, a rapidly increasing host in Great Britain and in this country, after labored and devout examination, have come to the conclusion that the Bible, rightly understood, does not sanction any kind of intoxicating liquor as a beverage in health or for Communion purposes. How important then, that discussion should go on, until the question is finally settled The real friends of temperance do not favor "fallacies," but truth—and nothing but the truth will satisfy them; they labor to destroy those "fallacies" which have held the world in bondage to strong drink, ever since the fall of Noah and Lot. E. C. D.

SOUTH BALLSTON, August 15, 1864.

GENERAL COCKE'S LETTER IN REPLY.

BREMO, VIRGINIA, *Nov*. 20, 1856.

Edward C. Delavan, Esq.,

MY DEAR FRIEND:—My late absence from home, must be my apology for not acknowledging the receipt of your late letter sooner.

Had my mind reverted fully to all the reminiscences which your comprehensive letter has so clearly brought back to my recollection, I know not that I should have been able to command the moral courage to urge you to recapitulate the history of the communion question as connected with the great Temperance reform; but, when I reflect, that great principles cannot be waived for personal consideration, I am brought fully to the conclusion—it is due to yourself, as well as the cause with which your name is identified, that a subject so connected with the success of the greatest moral revolution of the age, should be clearly set forth to the world. It appears to me hard to conceive a case to which the maxim more manifestly applies—*Fiat justitia, ruat cœlum.**

In answer to your letter of the first October, I cannot hesitate to say, that but for indefatigable efforts in collecting and circulating the facts established as to the nature and effects of intoxicating drinks, in the course of this controversy especially, the Temperance host would have been greatly retarded, in attaining the high position it now triumphantly occupies in the cause of Prohibition.

It is manifest, at first glance, at every contested point in the discussion, that disinterestedness and self-denial, on the one hand, stand in array against sordid interest and self-indulgence, on the other. Christianity is essentially a religion requiring sacrifices. Witness Christ himself, the great

* Let justice be done, though the heavens fall.

example of this truth; and the whole tenor of his gospel; all at open warfare with the opposing host, under the self-indulgent banners of the world and the flesh.

How this simple view of the matter does not bring over all the Christian world to the right side of the question, can only be accounted for by the fact that the insidious evil of intoxication has so long had dominion over the human mind, as to have become established--a legalized strong delusion; let it be exposed.

It would seem hardly necessary to do more for the ultimate success of the cause than to keep the above view before the public mind; but for the daring and outrageous pretensions of our adversaries, while ignoring the following undeniable facts, which require a passing notice, viz:—

1st. That there was unintoxicating wine in common use when Christ was upon earth; and that the terms he used in the institution of the eucharist, unequivocally mean this unintoxicating beverage.

2dly. That the art of distillation, the principal instrument of giving to wine of commerce its intoxicating character, was not discovered until centuries after the canon of Scripture was closed.

3dly. That since the discovery, it has become the means, together with the other discoveries of modern chemistry, of changing the character of all the wines of commerce, and that to a degree of making a deleterious compound called wine, without a particle of the fruit of the vine in it.

Yet, nevertheless, this anti-Christian doctrine is still maintained and acquiesced in, that the now universally adulterated and enforced wine of commerce, unavoidably including the base and often poisonous counterpart already alluded to, is as suitable an element of the Lord's Supper as the consecrated fruit of the vine.

But the most adroit stroke of policy yet devised by our adversaries is the exemption clause in the Prohibitory Laws—virtually changing the consecrated element with which Christ instituted the sacrament, viz: "the fruit of the vine," and substituting therefor the injurious distilment of man's invention—ardent spirit. And while the church of Christ do not protest against this desecration, and by their mighty power and only delegated authority on earth put it down, the consummation of their mission to evangelize the world, must be awfully postponed.

How can the conclusion be avoided, that He who knew all things from the end to the beginning, "and is of purer eyes than to behold iniquity," intended to exclude from the holy sacrament this wicked alcoholic invention of man—the most prolific source of evil on earth.

But why, it may be asked, did He not expressly forbid it—forestalling the evil growing out of the invention. The answer presents itself—to try the faithfulness of his professing followers. That it might be made manifest to the world who are willing to be led by the spirit of the Gospel at the expense of self-denial, and who are willing to shelter their self-indulgence and protect their cupidity under the absence of literal prohibition in Holy Writ.

Here the question may still be urged upon every fair-minded Christian is it possible to conceive, consistently with what we know and believe of the immaculate and omniscient character of Christ—who instituted the eucharist with the fruit of the vine, unintoxicating wine—that to celebrate it as a matter of choice and not of necessity, with the wine of commerce, now known to be universally enforced by the intoxicating principle, and at the risk of using a foul compound without a particle of the juice of the grape in it—must be an offence, a crying offence against the Master of the feast.

In conclusion, it may be remarked that in the providence of God there are constantly occurring new developments in connection with the Temperance reformation, proving that this wonderful movement in the moral history of man has been brought forth to "try men's souls."

Yours, &c.,
JOHN H. COCKE.

EXTRACT FROM A LETTER BY HON. NEAL DOW.

PORTLAND, MAINE, *Nov.* 20, 1856.

Edward C. Delavan, Esq.,

MY DEAR FRIEND:— * * * * * * * * * .

As to the "*communion question*," I have no fear but the truth will finally prevail. One great aid to this, undoubtedly, will be the fact that in all the nation there is not to be purchased a gallon or *bottle* even, of the pure fruit of the vine, unless it may possibly be some relict of an old importation. *All* the wines of commerce are fabrications—the base being the neutral spirit of the shops—made from new rum or whiskey, flavored and colored to imitate *exactly* the various brandies, wines and other liquors, and reduced with water to the proper standard, and very often mixed with poisons more active and concentrated than alcohol is.

In the wine countries, this same neutral spirit is also employed; and in France the beet root spirit is employed by all the "wine houses" in the fabrication of brandies, wines and other liquors; the whole "*brew*" being utterly innocent of grape. All this I had recently from a Frenchman, an agent of a great wine house in France; who admitted to me that this fabrication was universal, the grape crop having been cut off for years. But he maintained, that if no deleterious drugs were introduced—and his house never used them—the article thus produced was in every respect equal to the genuine, because the imitation in every particular is so exact. that the most skillful and experienced judges cannot tell the difference. All this must in time convince the most obstinate, that by employing the wines of commerce in the communion, they do not obey the injunction or follow the example of Christ—but in fact do violence to the whole tone and spirit of the Gospel.

Truly yours,
NEAL DOW.

EXTRACTS FROM FATHER MATHEW'S SPEECHES.

"I have no hesitation in saying that strong drink was ANTI-CHRIST; *it was opposed to the principles of Christ—to His example—to his design and to his reign.*"

"All are bound by the Gospel precept to practice Temperance, and that the same Gospel advises to aspire to perfection, *and that total abstinence is the perfection of Temperance.*"

"Total abstinence is not a novelty or an innovation, strong drink is the innovation, and it had no sooner been introduced than men were led astray by it."

"Total abstinence is evidently the lever by which great good could be effected. It therefore becomes the *duty of all to assist in working that 'lever.'*"

No. 7.

LETTERS RELATIVE TO COMMUNION WINE.

INTRODUCTION.

By the written request of several valued friends, I republish in this work a series of letters which originally appeared in the first number of "The Enquirer," December, 1841, with regard to "the *kind of wine most suitable for Communion purposes.*" To these Letters was attached an extended appendix, containing numerous communications from learned and distinguished clergymen, chemists, physicians, and laymen, sustaining every position set forth in the Letters; these evidences are of great value, but space will not allow of their introduction here. These Letters occupy in this fourth edition of this work the space occupied in the former editions by a valuable essay on tobacco; that article can be issued in a separate tract, if desired, as the National Society holds the stereotype plates of that essay as well as this work. I will add, that this volume has been in the printer's hands for several years, added to from time to time. It was originally intended to be limited to 100 pages, *not* for sale, but to answer calls on me for Temperance Publications, my stock having become exhausted. With these explanations I send the Letters, as requested, to the printer, feeling assured that the reader will make all due allowance for imperfections, considering the *period* in which they were penned, and the little light (at the time) which had been shed on the question; as also for the want of system in the arrangement of this volume, made up as it has been at long intervals of time. E. C. D.

New York, 1866.

LETTER I.

South Ballston, Saratoga Co., *Dec.* 1, 1841.

Dear Christian Brethren.—The great principle of the Temperance Reformation, that intoxicating drinks are never beneficial, but always injurious, to persons in health, seems now to be firmly established; not that the practice of all, or even of the majority, conforms to this principle, but few or none now publicly advocate the use of such drinks as a means of keeping in good order either the physical or moral nature of man.

The effect of Total Abstinence on communities and individuals is n longer doubtful, and examples are now so numerous, that the most skeptical must be convinced that the world would be the better and not the worse were the principles universally practiced.

The fears of some good men, that somewhere or somehow in this new scheme for the improvement of human beings, infidelity would be found concealed and nourished, seem also to have passed away; and all agree that men are not only as good citizens, but as good Christians, though they never taste the intoxicating cup.

The reformation having, by the blessing of the Almighty, been thus far so wonderfully sustained and established, it has seemed to me in the last degree important that some one should strive to awaken professing Christians to the propriety and expediency of banishing the intoxicating cup from the table of the Lord, and substituting in its place the "Fruit of the Vine," free from fermentation or adulteration of any kind. While I regret that a more able writer than myself has not appeared to address you, I trust you will bear with me, and not think it presuming in an unlearned layman to beg your kind attention to a subject which seems peculiarly the province of ministers of the Gospel, or learned men whose researches and studies have qualified them to instruct you. My apology for trespassing on your time is, that my mind has for several years been deeply interested, and I have been led to consider with great care whatever has been written in Great Britain or our country in reference to this question; moreover, the use of intoxicating wine at the Sacrament has appeared to me one of the greatest hindrances in the way of those who are laboring to induce all to abstain from strong drink as a beverage.

I fear many sincere Christians will be alarmed at what they think the boldness, if not the actual impiety, of this suggestion. There are around the sacred ordinances of the Supper so many sanctified associations, so many solemn interests, that the pious mind shrinks from this discussion, lest the hallowed institution should suffer, or the Saviour they love be dishonored; and I am far from being insensible to the value of this principle; it ought to be cherished; the pious mind should never be disturbed without good reasons, and to answer some great end. I hope to be able to convince you that there are reasons of sufficient magnitude, and of great practical importance, now in operation, to demand an immediate investigation as to the *kind* of wine proper to be used at the Communion table. The cause of Total Abstinence, as a beverage, is no longer in danger from an unpopular, or even a wrong movement by an individual member, and I desire to be expressly understood that it is as a Christian, and not as an officer of any association, that I make this appeal; and that no Temperance Association is at all responsible for errors, if such be found in the letters I am about to address you. Affectionately yours, etc.,

E. C. D.

LETTER II.

Dear Brethren—In order to understand what is called the "Communion Question," it is well to go back to the period in our country when there was no thought or discussion as to the kind of wine proper to be used, because none, or very few, understood the nature of the substance they drank. They called everything the Fruit of the Vine that was sold *under the name of wine*, and thus the wine dealer, or the wine fabricator, became the judge of what was proper for the Sacrament, and the Gospel, which distinctly specified *not wine*, but "the Fruit of the Vine," was overlooked as authority, and whisky distilled from corn, rye, or potatoes, cider pressed from apples, the juice of the currant preserved with alcohol, and all frequently mixed with drugs of the most poisonous character, were drank as wine, though they contained not a drop of the juice of the grape. I know that many churches did endeavor to procure the purest fermented wine, which was generally Madeira, well enforced with distilled spirits, and this was only obtained by the more wealthy societies. An extensive dealer informed me that he had for many years served a large district of country with Communion wine; that he not only kept imported wine, but manufactured large quantities himself from whisky and drugs, and that in nine cases out of ten, officers of churches would take the whisky wine because it was the cheapest, although frequently informed that it did not contain a drop of the Fruit of the Vine. It will, I think, readily be conceded, that if it is certainly ascertained that liquors not containing the "Fruit of the Vine" are constantly sold and drank under the name of wine, that to use such for the Gospel symbol will in no manner promote holiness or sanctification in a church—and it may be said no symbol can do this; but there will generally be found an aptness in the symbol to the thing signified. God insisted on cleansing in the ancient ritual, and thus pure water is used in baptism. Let us illustrate the Sacrament of the Supper by the water used in baptism. What Christian parent would be willing to have the water with which his infant child is baptized in the name of the Father, the Son, and Holy Ghost, mingled with such substances as compose the liquor generally used at the Supper? Pure water is the only proper symbol of baptism. The pure blood of the grape for the Supper. May not the Church of Christ have greatly suffered from this ignorant use of this impure substance? And will she not certainly suffer in purity, if, when the means of knowledge are in the hands of all her members, she still continue its use?

Yours, etc., E. C. D.

LETTER III.

Dear Brethren—I will now endeavor to state how of necessity the Communion Question arose out of the change of the pledge of abstinence from ardent spirit to that of total abstinence from all that can intoxicate. Not that the most strenuous advocates of that change *then* saw this effect. They plead for the abandonment from all alcoholic drinks, because they felt that drunkenness would still prevail, though not a soul drank rum, brandy, whisky, or gin under their appropriate names; and though the moderate drinker had the right to drink fermented liquors, yet that it was expedient and Christian to yield that right to effect a great and benevolent object. But a very few then understood that the principle of intoxication, which was the great enemy the Temperance Cause aimed to overthrow, was created entirely by fermentation, and not the product of distillation. My own conviction of this truth was established by the analysis of my own stock of wines by Prof. Lewis C. Beck; they consisted of the most celebrated, and were all or nearly all imported; he found them to contain alcohol (the Port and Madeira) equal to 42½ to 48½ per cent. of the strength of brandy, or more than double the alcohol resulting from natural fermentation. With this general ignorance of fermented wines, or the liquors sold and used as wine, it is not wonderful that few were found willing to place it in the same class with what was termed ardent spirit, which had come very generally to be considered as a poison when used as a beverage in health, therefore immoral to drink it. It is not surprising that good and learned ministers of the Gospel, and Christian laymen, who had been good old pledged Temperance men, who had raised their voices and opened their purses freely to advance the cause on that ground, should, when the new pledge was introduced or advocated, throw their influence against it, and that they should declare publicly that the triumph of Total Abstinence would be the triumph of infidelity. In the first Temperance convention ever held in this country for discussing the Total Abstinence question, which took place in Albany, Feb. 25th, 1834, I introduced the following preamble and resolution:

Whereas, There is so much evidence of the almost universal adulteration of fermented liquors, and of wines particularly, by the use of alcohol, and of the great extent to which the manufacture of factitious wines is carried, as to render it almost, if not quite, certain that the pure juice of the grape is seldom procured in this country; and

Whereas, It is now understood and generally believed that the reformation of the drunkard is utterly hopeless so long as he continues to use the smallest quantity of any intoxicating drinks, and

Whereas, It is important to remove all objections against uniting with

Temperance societies, now urged by a numerous and efficient portion of our citizens; therefore

Resolved, That those members of Temperance societies who wholly abstain from intoxicating liquors as an ordinary drink, present to the world a consistent and efficacious example, which this meeting would warmly commend to the imitation of every friend of Temperance.

The passage of this preamble and resolution was powerfully, and I doubt not conscientiously, opposed, not only by a doctor of divinity, but by a doctor of law. Says one, "The Scriptures permitted and sanctioned the use of (intoxicating) wine. Jesus Christ used it, and consecrated it by making it one of the elements in a religious ordinance, instituted by himself; and more than this, *he manufactured it*, and would gentlemen condemn the example of the Lord of Glory?" Says another, "We are looking to the Great Head of the Church for success in this cause; shall we proceed contrary to his example? If the whole world should go for the preamble and resolution, the speaker should stand by the Bible and the example of the Saviour." Of the document containing these remarks, and others of a kindred character, the New York State Temperance Society circulated 100,000.

What were the friends of Total Abstinence to do in these circumstances? They were fully convinced that the Temperance Reformation must either be given up, or that all means of intoxication must be abandoned, distressed as they were to hear themselves condemned in public assemblies, from the pulpit, and by the press, as inculcating doctrines contrary to the Word of God and the example of Christ, denounced on all sides as fanatics and ultraists, and an almost universal cry that they had ruined the noblest of causes; yet they felt strong in the *truth* of their position, and persevered in efforts to sustain it. Here and there one and another began to ask, "Was it really fermented intoxicating wine that our Saviour made at Cana, and that he used as the symbol of his blood at the institution of the Supper?" Thus they were led to the Bible and to history to ascertain whether in fact they did sanction the use of such wine.

Many thanks are due to those who in the face of persecution and obloquy first discussed this question. Among these were Prof. Stewart, Edwin James, M.D., L. M. Sargent, Esq., Mr. Wm. Goodell, Rev. Mr. Duffield, Rev. Dr. Chapin, and others. These gentlemen appreciated at that early day the leading facts and principles which have established the reputation of the valuable Essays known by the titles of Bacchus and Anti-Bacchus, and indeed there is no doubt that the early discussion of these gentlemen, and others in this country, first induced the author of these Essays to think and write on the subject. A very general excitement was produced by this slight agitation of the question; many good men were for a time distressed and offended, and walked no more with those so universally denounced as fanatics, but the greatest concern and distress were evinced by makers and venders of factitious drinks. They saw clearly that if they could no longer plead the example of the Saviour and its use at the Sacrament, good men would soon cease purchasing and drinking their importations and mixtures. We are sorry to declare, but truth demands it, that the clamors for a while prevailed; the opposition appeared to triumph, and "Temperance down" was echoed from tavern to grog-shop—from one extremity of the nation to the other. Still the friends of Total Abstinence held on; though truth compels me to say—and I say it with deep mortification—they were for a time obliged to suppress the public discussion of the Communion Question.

Yours, etc., E. C. D.

LETTER IV.

Dear Brethren—There were several reasons why even some of the warmest friends of the *new pledge* felt obliged to discontinue the discussion of the Communion Question in their publications. A powerful one was found in the very imperfect understanding of the principles of *Total* Abstinence; it was a new thing, and required much discussion before it could be made clear, even to many of the best friends of the old pledge, that it was wrong, or even inexpedient, to drink intoxicating wine in moderation. The nature of fermentation was to be developed, the effects of fermented wine pressed on the attention and conscience, and the adulterations exposed; and driven as the friends of Total Abstinence were by their opposers to the table of the Lord, before they had even begun to purify common usages, it is not wonderful that they for a time were almost overwhelmed. Another, and by far the most powerful reason, was the reports so industriously circulated, that some of the leading friends of the new pledge *were determined not to rest until they had driven wine from the table of the Lord.* I have never known a person connected with a Temperance association who wished this; I have never heard an individual express such a desire; but while conducting the Temperance press at Albany, one correspondent, a clergyman, proposed the substitution of water, in consequence of the impossibility, as he supposed, to procure the Fruit of the Vine free from alcohol or adulterations; all they desired was to substitute the unfermented for the fermented. Had the case been fairly stated, or had not the opponents been themselves under a misapprehension, or been deceived by the common belief that nothing could be the "Fruit of the Vine" but that substance which contained the principle of intoxication, I verily believe there would have been little or no trouble on this point. What conscience, however tender, what Christian, however timid, would have feared to use what alone is mentioned in Scripture as the Gospel symbol, the "Fruit of the Vine?" Was it not the "Fruit of the Vine" the friends of this measure were contending for? Do we hesitate to call the juice of the apple, cider, before it is fermented? As a proof, if any is needed, that they wanted wine, and no other substance, for the Sacrament, four persons in Albany subscribed $5,000, twelve hundred and fifty dollars each, in 1835, to send a competent person to Palestine, to examine into the history of ancient wines, their manufacture and use—giving him orders to make a large shipment of the "Fruit of the Vine," free from alcohol. Just as this plan was completed, and the individual ready to embark, we were informed that Messrs. Pomeroy & Bull had recently received a large importation of the article; this, of course, rendered another experiment unnecessary. In consequence of the stopping of the discussion, all demand for the article ceased; the discussion having again revived, that old importation, which had been lying in the cellar for five years, meets with a ready sale, and vast orders have been sent for more.

Another reason for not continuing the public discussion of this question will be found in the want of firmness of those that sincerely believed in the vast practical importance of the question. If they had stood firm a little longer in the position where they had been placed by their opponents, and permitted the inquiry to go on in their publications, God alone knows what would have been the result. We can not doubt that the truth would have earlier been found. But they felt obliged to put forth a disclaimer, in which they denied any intention to interfere with wine at the Communion, and abandoned the discussion.

It was doubtless needful for the friends of Total Abstinence to pass through these times; it tried their temper, their character, and their faith, and doubtless there was much to be purified and corrected; it is not common to human nature, even while striving for the truth, to bear with becoming meekness the lash of opponents, sometimes applied in sly satire or cold irony—under the mark of sanctity, or in the filth of drunkenness—in the eloquence of the pulpit and the ribaldry of the bar-room; and I doubt not that the friends of Total Abstinence were too often provoked to feel and retort railing for railing, and they were tried and mortified by being forced, for a time, to yield to their opposers. From this trial let them learn *their* weakness; *it is not in their cause*—there they are on a rock—let them but be faithful to it *in all its bearings* and to themselves, be patient in adversity, and meek and humble in prosperity, and seek diligently for that wisdom which is first pure and then peaceable, and truth in due time will prevail.

Yours, etc., E. C. D.

LETTER V.

DEAR BRETHREN—Having given some account of the rise of the Communion Question, and of its suppression in the Temperance publications in this State, in 1835, we arrive at its present position; and I wish briefly to ask your attention to some of the advantages which the present period presents for its candid discussion, which were not enjoyed at that time. As one of its greatest obstacles, on its first introduction, was want of knowledge and experience of the principles of Total Abstinence from intoxicating drinks as a beverage—so the understanding and settlement of that principle leaves the Communion Question free to be discussed *on its own merits.* We are no longer in the dark as to the practical results of Total Abstinence from all that can intoxicate. It is acknowledged by all to be the only method of reforming the inebriate; and in no instance have we a record of evil resulting either to the drunkard or temperate drinker from abstaining entirely from all intoxicating liquors. Another encouragement which the present period presents for pressing this subject is the vast army of total abstainers. We have now friends in all professions and stations in society, instead of here and there one, when this question was first introduced. The ministers of our holy religion are now almost universally advocating Temperance on the principle of entire abstinence. There exists a vast many churches where all the members are pledged to entire abstinence. In our own State it is ascertained that already about eight hundred churches have substituted the unfermented Fruit of the Vine for alcoholic liquor at the Lord's table. A great number of the old established churches of New England, who are not likely to be blown about by every wind of doctrine, are beginning to examine and *feel* on this subject, and some of their associations have entirely abolished the fermented or intoxicating wine at the Communion.

Other advantages exist in the theological and medical knowledge that has been elicited. There is also much encouragement to believe that the religious and political press, now so universally advocating the Total Abstinence principle as a beverage, will, in a good degree, lend their powerful assistance in publishing facts which may be collected in the course of this discussion.

With these and many other sources of encouragement, may not the friends of the Communion Question take courage and go on in efforts, at least to persuade the professing Christians of their country to faithfully and prayerfully examine the subject, and if they find nothing unscriptural in the use of unfermented wine at the Lord's Supper, to labor, each in his own church, in a proper and Christian way, to bring about so desirable a change? Yours, etc., E. C. D

LETTER VI.

Dear Brethren—With these and many other important advantages which the present period possesses over 1835 for the impartial discussion of this question, we can not fail to see that many imposing obstacles yet remain in the way of substituting the unfermented "Fruit of the Vine" for the intoxicating liquor which has heretofore been used at the table of the Lord, and even to free and candid discussion of the benefits to be derived from such a change. The most powerful of these consists in the fact that the misunderstanding which formerly occasioned so much mischief still pervades many minds. I mean the idea that the change desired is to do away with wine altogether, and the ignorance of the distinction between fermented and unfermented wine. Even among professing Christians, if you ask them *what word* is used to express the substance to be used at the Lord's table, they will answer with the utmost confidence, "wine, to be sure;" and when they thus answer, they only think of the liquid sold under the name of wine, without connecting with it the pure "Fruit of the Vine." Now the fact that in the four different places where the Supper is mentioned in the New Testament, the word wine never once occurs, does not enter their minds, because they have so entirely accustomed themselves to the idea that fermented wine is the only proper symbol, that they think the introduction of the real substance mentioned in Scripture *an innovation.*

This remaining ignorance of the true point at issue, or the precise change desired, is the source of another obstacle yet to be overcome, viz., a sort of indefinite *fear;* with some it is the fear of disturbing the church with with they are connected; they feel that it is better even to suffer evil rather than to create agitation and perhaps discussion by introducing the question, forgetting that God has made the path of duty the path of safety, and finally the path of peace With another person it is the fear, to which we have before alluded, of disturbing the pious mind; but let this question be freely and kindly stated and truly understood, and I do not believe it will disturb any such.

Another mortifying, but yet a positive obstacle in the way of this discussion, is that custom and appetite which I fear still in too many cases influence the church of the living God. The Christian, living as he does in this sinful world, is apt to be overcome in part. It is yet the custom with many such to drink alcoholic wine as a beverage, and it is to be feared that many yet love it—and many more continue its use as a tribute to the long-established usages of what is called good society. If such consent to remove it from the table of the Lord, where will they find refuge when pressed by their Total Abstinence brethren to drink no more wine for their brother's sake? What will become of their excuse, that what Christ made must be good for common use?

Another obstacle is one which the Temperance reform has met in its every effort, viz., opposition to voluntary associations and an idea that it is a work belonging exclusively to the Church. No one more readily grants than myself, that to raise the fallen, to support the weak, to heal the broken-hearted, *to remove temptation to sin*, are surely the office of the follower of Him who while on earth went about doing good.

And whatever may be said of Temperance organizations to cure and prevent intemperance, surely nothing can be said against professing Christians, whether belonging to Temperance societies or not, who wish to inquire into what is alleged to be an evil in the Church, and who determine, if they find it so, to labor each in his own sphere to do away with that evil. Are they not members of the Church? and is not the Communion Question a legitimate one for their discussion? Therefore I do not address you as members of the Temperance associations, but as members of the Church of God. Yours, etc., E. C. D.

LETTER VII.

Dear Brethren—After speaking of the present as a favorable period for the discussion of the Communion Question, and noticing some of the obstacles that still require to be overcome before the change from fermented to unfermented wine can be effected, we will just review a few of the reasons why such a change is desirable.

The first reason is derived from what *we believe* to have been the example of Christ, and our reason for thus believing is found in the fact that the Supper was instituted after Christ and his disciples had been eating the Passover, and most probably the symbols were taken from materials already on the table. Now it is well known that nothing of a fermented nature was allowed at that feast, or even to be found in the house of any Jew for seven days. In Europe, as well as in this country, the Jews of the present day use no other than unfermented wine on the Passover night. It may be possible that in the corrupt state of the Jews at certain periods, or at the time our Saviour was on earth, many of them might have evaded the command, and permitted that in their *drink* which the law did not allow in their houses nor in their vessels. But we are sure that Christ, in whom was no guile, and who expressly declared that "He came not to destroy, but to fulfill the law," would not do this. The only instance on record where wine was ever offered to our Lord he refused it. "They gave him to drink wine mingled with myrrh, but he received it not." Learned men have settled for us the fact, that in the time of our Saviour there were two kinds of wine in use at Palestine—the one unfermented and pure, the other fermented and often drugged; thus teaching us what might otherwise appear contradictory in the Scriptures, which in one place declares, and without any qualification, "wine is a mocker;" and in another speaks of it as a blessing "to cheer the heart of God and man." The one like milk, generally nutritious and good, the other stealing away the senses, and is indeed, as the Word of God declares, "a mocker." Now it seems to me that the innocent, unmixed, unfermented juice of the grape comes much nearer the Gospel symbol, which is "the Fruit of the Vine," than the fermented and drugged liquor now in general use, and which in ninety-nine cases in the hundred is the runnings from the still, either in whole or in part, and without any certainty of containing a single drop of the "Fruit of the Vine."

Let us suppose, for argument sake, that milk had been used originally as the symbol, instead of the Fruit of the Vine, and it should be found that cows grazing in one particular field produced a milk which was poisonous, but in an adjoining field free from every injurious quality, who can doubt which should be used? Now it is a well-known fact that in Indiana *the milk sickness* is the occasion of the loss of a vast many lives yearly. Dr. Leland has lately taken a tour through the region where it prevails, for the purpose of observing the symptoms of the disease and investigating the causes. He attributes it to arsenic, which he finds scattered in great abundance, in the form of arsenical iron pyrites, throughout every section where the milk sickness prevails. While it would be entirely innocent to use the milk when free from the poison arsenic, who can doubt that it would be a sin to use it *after ascertaining* its poisonous qualities? Let us divest our minds of all preconceived opinions and all prejudice, my dear brethren, and see if we can find any substantial argument that will not apply as powerfully against the use of fermented, intoxicating wine, when the Fruit of the Vine can be had free from that principle, as against the milk found to be incorporated with the deadly poison arsenic.

I know the example of the Corinthian Church is introduced as opposed to our views. As to that point I find very little agreement, even among the learned, and I leave that inquiry only with them.

Many refer to the marriage of Cana as authority in the moderate use of intoxicating wine. The governor of the feast makes allusion to wine, and says, "*but* thou hast kept the *good* wine till now." There is no question that there are various qualities of unfermented wine, some much better than others, and that the term good and bad was applied in ancient times as well to the product of the vine in an unfermented state as in the fermented state. I have several specimens of wine, all differing, all unfermented, but one decidedly superior to the others, so that while this specimen has always been commended as very good, the others have been spoken of with qualified praise. A worthy and conscientious Christian said to me not long since, "You almost persuade me to adopt your extreme views; but how can you get along with the wine called "good" at the marriage? was that not intoxicating?" Being now a total abstainer of some eight or ten years' standing, I stated that to my mind it was very easy, much easier than when I was in the daily use of intoxicating wine, and when I judged of its quality by its strength. Then perhaps I should have called, and indeed did call my old doubly fortified Madeira which I drank, good, but I have since found that my opinion was then formed on a vitiated taste; but now my taste having become as that of a child with regard to such drinks, I am a better judge of what is good or bad than I was then. Now I should pronounce the delicious, nutritious, unfermented "*fruit of the vine*" the "good," and the other, that wine "which is a mocker," *bad.* Let any one place before a child, whose appetite was unimpaired, of a year old, the two kinds, and while it would receive the Fruit of the Vine as it is supposed Pharaoh drank it, with pleasure, and if it could speak would pronounce it good, it would struggle and resist the other, no matter how highly estimated, as against a dose of nauseous medicine. The taste for alcohol is artificial, but once acquired, no one can tell to what it will lead. It is hard to convince an old alcoholic wine-drinker that anything in the form of the juice of the grape can be "*good*" unless it will produce intoxication in a greater or less degree. All such for a time will ridicule the pure unfermented Fruit of the Vine when they taste it, for the reason that the first thing they notice is the absence of the alcohol, for which alone the fermented wine is drank, and many will go on drinking and increasing their dose of "*good*" wine, when, had they commenced their first potation with a quantity equal to the last, it would have landed them in the gutter.

Another reason why the change should take place is, that the Church of Christ should no longer countenance the use or traffic in intoxicating drink. At present, the dealer and the drinker have a formidable answer to all who censure their trade. May we not drink what Christians take at the table of the Lord? May we not sell what the Church buys to celebrate the death of Christ? Now, if the Bible had said, or Christ had said, "As oft as ye drink this fermented or intoxicating cup, do it in remembrance of me," our mouths would be stopped, even should reformed, converted drunkards hasten from the Communion table to the grog-shop. But, as the "Fruit of the Vine" is what we are directed to use, may we not choose to use it in its most innocent form, and thus take a formidable excuse away from those who drink and sell what experience has found to be evil, and evil continually?

Another reason for this change is, that many consciences are greatly troubled, and their numbers are rapidly increasing by the present usage. In our country it is supposed that there are about two millions who adopt the principle of Total Abstinence from all that can intoxicate; a vast number of these are members of Christian churches, and it is not a large calculation to suppose that two hundred thousand are dissatisfied with alcoholic wine as the symbol of salvation. It may be said they are troubled without cause; and they may be called weak brethren. Grant this, and the Bible rule is, that the strong should give way for the sake of the weak. "It is good neither to eat flesh nor drink wine, nor anything whereby thy brother stumbleth, or is offended. or is made weak." Since it is the article mentioned by Christ we plead for, "the Fruit of the Vine," do not cast us all out from the Church because our consciences refuse to take it in a form which may satisfy others. We do not wish for innovation, but to return to what we believe to be the original symbol.

Yours, etc., E. C. D.

LETTER VIII.

Dear Brethren—God in his wonderful providence has raised up a powerful argument, which, until within a few years, hardly occupied the mind of the Christian even in a remote degree—an argument to which it appears to me every follower of the Lamb must now give heed. It comes to us as a voice from the Almighty, and will any one of us answer to this voice, "Am I my brother's keeper?" This comparatively new argument is found in the reformation of thousands and tens of thousands of drunkards in this and other lands. The devout mind, accustomed to watch the current of events, can not but say, Truly this is the finger of God. Whatever may be said of the Temperance enterprise, as having its foundation in human wisdom, it will not be denied that this wonderful revelation has on it the stamp of divinity. It appears to me the words applied to the rise and progress of Christianity are not less applicable to this: "But God hath chosen the foolish things of the world to confound the wise; and God hath chosen the weak things of the world to confound the things which are mighty; and base things of the world, and things which are despised, hath God chosen, and things which are not, to bring to nought things that are."

The argument here is—the reformed converted drunkard is in imminent danger of having his disease of intemperance forced back upon him by the alcoholic cup presented to him through the hands of God's ministers. And let it be borne in mind, as one of the remarkable features in the great work now in rapid progress, that the reçlaimed inebriate never thinks himself safe till he finds refuge in the Church of God. Let all who have heard them speak, either privately or publicly, bear me witness to this. As a general rule, religious speech becomes their natural language. The cause of this appears plain to me. I regard the Temperance enterprise in all its bearings eminently the work of God; hence revivals of religion have almost invariably followed in the train of revivals in Temperance. Who can doubt, therefore, that vast numbers of the reformed will become Christians, and every church in our widely-extended country be blessed with a sprinkling from this class. It is estimated that we have 14,000 churches in the United States, and 500,000 drunkards; this gives about 35 drunkards to each church. Now, can there be a question that should each of those churches put forth proper effort, more or less of these lost ones might, with God's assistance, be brought within the fold? And if brought there, should their safety be endangered by presenting to them, within the holy sanctuary, the very substance which had all but destroyed them in the grog-shop?

It is a fact, founded on undoubted experience, that the *sight* of liquor, known to contain alcohol, has been followed by the most disastrous consequences to those who have been considered long reformed. Sight, in this case, acts with great power, producing a desire almost irresistible. Solomon, I suppose, grounds his warning against intoxicating wine upon this very principle: "Look not thou upon the wine when it giveth its color in the cup." I knew a man who had been a drunkard of long standing, but through the influence of kind neighbors and friends, had broken away from his fetters, and had abstained for a year or more; he had even been made an officer of a Temperance society on the old pledge; but one day having occasion to enter a grocery on some errand for his family, he found the keeper of it at the moment tapping a newly received barrel of strong beer; the sight of the foaming liquor, as it flowed out, revived his long dormant desires, which he found uncontrollable; like a bird charmed by the eye of the snake, he fell powerless in the embrace of the destroyer; one glass followed another, until he became a raging maniac, and in that state followed me with a club, from which I only escaped by a miracle; but my excellent friend Chancellor Walworth, on whom he next fixed his gaze, did not escape so well, and on whom he inflicted a blow. The next day the miserable man called upon me and made an apology. But his self-respect was gone; confidence in himself was lost; he resorted again to the waters of death; in a week he had another fit of the delirium, and in another he filled a drunkard's grave.

There is great danger from the smell, still more than from the sight. The fumes passing through the olfactory nerves, revive in the brain all the old feeling, and his desires come upon him like a strong man armed. The enemy of the reformed man, aware of this, has been known to sprinkle the deceitful liquor in his way, and then watch him with the eye of a fiend, hoping again to have him within his toils, and rob him of his daily earnings, by which his family should have been fed. Will the Church of God continue to offer the same substance to the smell of the reformed converted man by placing it on the Lord's table?

Still more certain is the danger arising from *the taste of the alcoholic cup.* Perhaps this can not be better illustrated than by comparing the body of the reformed to a cask of gunpowder that is entirely safe so long as fire is kept from it—but the smallest spark will explode the whole as fully as if a shower of sparks had fallen upon it.

The duty of Christians to sustain their weak brethren need not be urged; all admit it. In the case of the reformed brother, he is "willing, but his flesh is weak;" and when he comes into our company we are bound to hold him up; we are bound also to remove from his sight, smell, or taste that substance which may be his ruin, not only in time, but in eternity.

Let each one of us, my dear brethren, bring the case home to himself; suppose each one of you had a near and dear relative who had become reformed and converted to the religion of our blessed Lord and Master, would you not tremble for him, with the light now shining upon the question, while the alcoholic cup was presented to him at the table of the Lord, would you not fear the influence the sight, the smell, the taste might have upon him? would you not feel safer if the cup contained the fruit of the vine free from the principle of intoxication?

In former years the reformation of the drunkard was a rare occurrence, consequently there were few from them as a class to make a profession of religion, and it was still more rare that an attempt at reformation was successful; what watching and warning was needed to sustain them —one of the secrets of the failure has at last been discovered. *The Church herself in ignorance has helped to send them back.* The reformed convert, on the communion morning, prayed, "Lead me not into temptation," and on that very day the strongest temptation meets him in the smell, the sight, and the taste of the alcoholic cup, blessed and handed to him to drink to commemorate the dying love of his Saviour!!

It may be said by some, if these men be Christians, they will not fall before so slight a temptation. If I understand this objection, it is the same that might be urged against all exhortation. Paul, I think, viewed the question in a different light: "Through thy knowledge shall the weak brother perish for whom Christ died?" This objection assumes another and more general form. When it is said a man who has not resolution to stand such a temptation is not to be relied upon, let us ask what kind of resolution the reformed inebriate is expected to have?

Moral of course; but is this sufficient to meet the cruel and insatiate antagonist he has to contend against? His enemy is a physical evil, which has produced a moral debility, so that on the supposition that his moral resolution is as firm as any man's who sits down at that table with him, his physical nature is not equal to the same encounter, and until this defect in his bodily frame is removed, neither his spiritual or moral nature have strength to resist. His case is exactly like those who are predisposed to certain diseases. Moral resolution is not sufficient to prevent them. It may avail before going within the region of infection, but once there, he must yield to the influence. The drunkard's disease slumbers within him; the moment he comes within the influence of the cause which originated it his longings begin, and in too many cases his moral resolution fails. Drunkenness is therefore not like some other moral evils, which have the seed in the thoughts; it exists immediately in the *flesh*, and through its influence holds the mind in subjection; therefore to discipline the sensual nature by entire abstinence from all that would in the least degree provoke the return of the disease, is not only consistent with true religion, but sound philosophy.

Some think that this reformation is but temporary—that it is a new thing, and that any violent change to meet their case is not desirable or important. We acknowledge that until within a year or two the reformation of drunkards has been rare; but recent events have astonished us all, and set all ordinary rules at defiance. Who could have predicted two years ago what has taken place since that time in this marvelous work? Instead of waiting to see if the good will pass away, and leave no trace of it behind, would it not be wiser to do all in our power to *establish it*, and "to work while it is day, for the night cometh when no man can work?"

My attention was forcibly called to this important subject while I had charge of the Temperance press at Albany on the old ardent spirit pledge. A single year brought in reports of 5,000 drunkards reformed on that pledge in the State of New York alone; the next year full half of them were reported from the same sources as having gone back to their old habits of intemperance without breaking their pledge, on fermented drinks; so that on that pledge we ceased to report the reformation of drunkards. Many had joined churches, and went immediately from the alcoholic cup, received from the hands of the minister, to the grog-shop, and abandoned themselves to drunkenness, and became lost to their families, to themselves, and I fear to Heaven.

Though the reformation on the wide scale we now see it be new, the change for which we plead, and for the same reason, has been urged for a long time; but then it was to meet a single case here and there scattered over the country, but now their numbers can be counted by thousands.

The Church did not see any necessity for preparation to receive accession to her ranks from this class; but they have come, *and she is not ready to receive them.* They have come without her aid, and certainly with but slight invitation, if any. They have come by thousands, and may come by tens of thousands. They have left the temples of Satan, the grog-shops—have fled from alcohol as from the face of the serpent; and many of them are running to the Church of the living God for refuge; and some of them are so much in earnest that they are clinging to the horns of the altar; but let not the infidel hear it—they meet even there, *on the sacred altar of God, their terrible foe.*

Instead of thousands, should there be only hundreds of the reformed seeking the sanctuary, the smallness of their numbers does not impair the argument. The benevolent man will rejoice over even one sinner that repenteth, and should watch over that one as the Almighty Father does over every individual penitent. What Christian would willingly put a stumbling-block in the way of his brother? and surely the Church of God should be filled with the same love in this case.

In examining both sides of this question, so pregnant with consequences to the reformed converted drunkard, who can question what stand the Church should take? Now that reformed drunkards are knocking at our church doors for admission, shall they be refused, unless they partake within its sacred precincts the very substance that all their experience tells them will send them again back to drunkenness? No, I can not believe it. The Church will without delay inquire into this question, and will, I have no doubt, offer not only to communicants generally, but to the converted drunkard, the Fruit of the Vine, in which there is nothing to *mock.*

Some suppose the agitation of this question will react disastrously upon the general cause of Temperance; to my mind the reverse will be the result. Now the religious mind of the country is beginning to understand the question, and can not again be deceived as to the real point at issue. This great and last principle, yet to be settled in the Temperance reform, belongs legitimately to the Church, not to Temperance societies, to settle; and should they unitedly resolve to use the "Fruit of the Vine," free from alcohol, they will set the key-stone in the arch of Temperance, and by this simple act do more for this great cause of benevolence than all other efforts yet made. Let her expand her doors, and proclaim to the world that the drink of the drunkard is no longer tolerated within her walls; and the reformation will, in my judgment, then rush on to final triumph with a rapidity that will astonish the world.

Your affectionate brother, E. C. D.

LETTER IX.

DEAR BRETHREN—As the reformed and converted drunkard, if he will speak, can bring the most convincing testimony, so the physician is authority to which we can appeal with the utmost confidence to help us to a just conclusion in the matter at issue. The testimony of this class of men goes the whole length of our views ; they all to a man testify that the reformed drunkard must, to be safe, declare against all that can intoxicate, in every form and in every place. What shall then be done? Shall we advise the reformed converted drunkard not to unite in our communions? or shall we at once and without delay meet the exigencies of his case? The testimony of physicians was sought and obtained generally, without, as they probably supposed, any direct reference to this important question, but which, nevertheless, tells powerfully in favor of the change. I conclude, under no circumstance would any sensible man say that a reformed drunkard could safely taste that in a church which he could not safely elsewhere taste?

The influence the physician has had in every stage of the Temperance enterprise has been vast ; he has in all cases spoken out decidedly. When this question was first agitated in 1835, I consulted some of the most learned physicians in the country, and their invariable reply to my inquiry was, "The reformed drunkard is only safe while he abstains entirely from all intoxicating drinks, and he must abstain as well at the Communion table as at any other table."

No one can doubt but that the physician is qualified to give evidence in this matter. He knows what that state of the system is, physically and mentally, which renders the reformed man liable to become an easy victim to the destructive agent which has once had the ascendancy over him. He knows the state of not only the temperate drinker, but the drunkard's stomach, for he has dissected them in all stages. He knows the state and condition of the drunkard's brain and of the whole nervous system, for he has deeply studied this also, and who is able so well to tell us the effect that alcohol will have when it comes under any form, or in any place, in contact with either stomach or brain? The late President and Professor of Theory and Practice in the Vermont Academy of Medicine, in closing his highly interesting letter, states :

"ALCOHOL, THEN, IN ALL ITS FORMS, SHOULD BE REGARDED BY THAT CLASS OF MEN WHO HAVE ESCAPED FROM ITS INFLUENCE IN THE SAME LIGHT AS THE MOST *VIRULENT POISON.* EVERY VESSEL CONTAINING IT SHOULD, IN THEIR EYE, BE STAMPED WITH THE 'DEATH'S HEAD AND CROSS BONE LABEL;' AND MUST BE AS SEDULOUSLY AVOIDED, IF

THEY WOULD REMAIN ENTIRELY SAFE, AS THAT DEADLY POISON, A FEW DROPS OF WHICH WOULD PROVE CERTAINLY FATAL."

When the minister of Christ and professing Christians can come to the same conclusion with the physician, and in imagination see labeled on the alcoholic Communion cup "*death's head and cross bones*," it can not be long before the Fruit of the Vine, free from the poor drunkard's poison, will be universally demanded for the Communion.

Yours, etc., E. C. D.

LETTER X.

Dear Brethren—The testimony of learned and influential clergymen and laymen, for and against the change now proposed, should be fairly considered, and when they are willing to send their opinions out to the world, with the sanction of their names, it is a sufficient proof of the sincerity of their motives. Perhaps there have been no writers in this country who have written more learnedly or more powerfully heretofore against the change now aimed at than the Rev. Dr. Sprague of Albany and the Rev. Prof. McLean of Princeton, and I trust neither of those gentlemen will deem it uncourteous or unkind if I endeavor to draw from their published works admissions which will seem to strengthen my position. It appears to me that the admission of Dr. Sprague would allow of the change without the least departure from Bible sanction. In one of his sermons published at the period when this question was before up for discussion, he remarks with his usual eloquence: "I say, brethren, you have no occasion for Hebrew learning, or Arabic learning, or any other learning than the plain English, to settle the question; the Master himself has settled it for the obscurest peasant as for the most eminent biblical critic, and no man, no body of men, has a right to call in question the Master's decision. I have heard the practice of the Church in the second century appealed to in justification of this usage. But if the authority of the second century is good, surely that of the first is better; and why not go a little further back and take advantage of that. And if the testimony of uninspired men is good, the testimony of those who are inspired is better; why not, then, be satisfied by simply opening the Word of God and ascertaining what is there written on this subject? Ah! it is because God says not a word about any other element to be used as a drink in this ordinance but the Fruit of the Vine." (See sermon on the Danger of being Over-wise.) Here is the true conclusion of the whole matter. The Fruit of the Vine is the proper and only substance; the Doctor's views and mine are in perfect agreement here. I have never for a moment questioned, nor have I ever heard any one else question, the duty of using the Fruit of the Vine at the Communion. Again; the Doctor in his letter to the Rev. Professor Stewart states: "It is readily admitted that there is nothing in the language which our Saviour used in the original institution of the Lord's Supper from which it can be determined whether it was fermented wine or the unfermented juice of the vine which was used on that occasion, as the Fruit of the Vine may legitimately mean either." Now, it does begin to be questioned whether alcohol is the Fruit of the Vine any more than miasma, which is the result of decomposed vegetable matter, is the fruit of the earth; yet not to pursue this, to my mind a most important thought of my valued friend and fellow-laborer in this great work, the Rev. Doctor Edwards, I think the most unreasonable must have the candor to allow, that even admitting, for argument sake, that the Fruit of the Vine may legitimately mean either fermented or unfermented wine, *there can be no wrong, no departure from the Master's command, if the unfermented is used.*

The Rev. Professor McLean has often been before the public on the general subject connected with the use of intoxicating drinks, and to do him justice, no man has been a more constant and thorough advocate in sustaining the usages of society in the moderate use of intoxicating drinks as derived from Scriptures. He has recently published a large pamphlet, which is only, as we are informed, the precursor of others that will appear in due time. To understand the object of the essay, it may be well to state to those who have not perused it, that the author labors throughout to prove that the word οινος in Greek, and *vinum* in Latin, were synonymous with that of wine in English.

In his review of the English works, Bacchus and Anti-Bacchus, he says, page 36, "that in treating of wines, these writers have mentioned modes of preserving the juice of the grape other than by fermentation; this we without the least hesitation admit, and that this unfermented juice of the grape, whether inspissated or not, was sometimes used as a drink, we do not question; but we do maintain that the *common* or almost universal acceptation of *vinum*—the Latin term for wine—is the fermented juice of the grape; and that when the term is applied to any other preparation of the grape juice, it is connected with some word qualifying the import of the word *vinum*."

"The same remark may be made of the Greek word οἶνος, corresponding to the Latin *vinum* and English *wine*."

Here is acknowledged in substance all that we contend for, that the juice of the grape was used at the time of our Saviour in its fermented and unfermented state; and the only difference between Professor McLean and the authors he reviews, is as to proportions which was the most generally used. To my mind this is a very small matter; it is admitted that both were used, and it appears to me the argument would have been more profitable, if to show which was the safest to use. I conclude that by a little closer investigation, not only Professor McLean, but the authors which he reviews may be found correct *when applied to different ages of the world.* What was common in one age might be the reverse in the next. Sixteen years since, the custom of using ardent spirit was almost universal; now, the habit, except with the degraded, has almost disappeared. So it will be with fermented drinks when their character is as fully developed. It will be seen that the existence and use of unfermented wine remain established. To be sure, the Professor says, "that when the term is applied to any other preparation of grape-juice it is connected with some word qualifying the import of *vinum.*" Very likely, just as we speak of cider in its different preparations, we use the qualifying word *hard, sweet, boiled.* He however admits that *sometimes* the word *vinum,* without any addition or qualification, was employed to designate the unfermented juice of the grape. How important these admissions when applied to the question before us! The Professor admits, also, that the same remark may be made of the Greek word οἶνος. Professor McLean calls upon the Rev. Eli Smith to sustain him, and Mr. Smith has referred to a letter of mine on the subject.

Mr. Smith says, "I am happy to find that any apparent discrepancy between the testimony here given and that of Mr. Delavan, in his letter to the editor of the New York *Observer* of August 24, *as far as facts are concerned,* is chiefly, if not entirely verbal. He certifies that the unfermented juice of the grape *can* be preserved from fermentation by boiling. My testimony goes farther, and proves that it can be, but *is in fact* thus *preserved to a great extent.* The difference is, he calls the sirup wine; I have not found it bearing the name nor used in the place of wine. Of his opinion that it was anciently regarded and used as wine, and is the wine approved in the Bible, but has gone into disuse in consequence of increased taste for alcoholic drinks, a person who has never been in Palestine is perhaps as capable of judging as myself." Observe here, Mr. Smith agrees with me in the facts that the fruit of the vine can be preserved in an unfermented state—second, that it is preserved to a *great extent* at the present time in the East; and third, he does not profess to judge what was the custom of the East in the days of our Saviour.

Professor McLean makes great use of the "verbal distinction," and when applied to the signification of a word he considers it everything. His great anxiety is to prove that the unfermented fruit of the vine can not be called wine. I think he has admitted that the Latin and Greek words signifying wine settles that question.

With regard to the great question now before us, we think we can turn this verbal criticism to good account, for whatever may befall the question of Total Abstinence from all that can intoxicate as a beverage, in consequence of a signification of a word, *the Communion Question is safe, as the word wine does not once occur with regard to the ordinance.*

Upon the whole, Prof. McLean has certainly labored hard, and has been most ingenious in his arguments to sustain his views on this subject. Still, he has had to admit that there were two kinds of wine in use in ancient times—one intoxicating, the other free from that destructive principle. Is it not incumbent on him, therefore, to prove that our Lord and Saviour made and drank that which has occasioned all the intemperance in the world, and left the innocent to others?

Toward Prof. McLean I have no feeling but that of affection. He has sometimes been a severe critic, and in his last publication classes me with the heretic, but I love him as a Christian brother, and a great and good man. In several interviews I have had with him, and by correspondence, he has ever been affectionate and kind, and he has always held up his testimony against the attempt that for a time succeeded too well to suppress the discussion. He thought all subjects in which good men might honestly differ should be fully investigated.

Yours, etc., E. C. D.

LETTER XI.

Dear Brethren—While I am opposed to fermented wine of the purest quality because it contains alcohol, and because I look upon it as a poison entirely unfit to be received into the system, except as other poisons are sometimes administered as a medicine, I propose to show to those who still consider such wine a blessing as a beverage, or a proper substance for the Lord's table, that in this country it is next to impossible to obtain it, while there is not the least difficulty in procuring the Fruit of the Vine free from fermentation or adulteration of any kind.

During the many years my attention has been called to this subject, a great variety of facts has come to my knowledge from authentic sources, only a few of which space will allow me to state, while I could fill a volume with them. I have been often astonished at the indifference evinced by many individuals to the subject of adulterations in their daily drink

It has appeared to me that they did not wish to be enlightened, fearing that they would be constrained to abandon that which habit had, in a measure, rendered necessary. I have often thought that should the bakers be detected in adulterating bread to one tenth the extent that wine fabricators adulterate wine, Lynch law world be at once administered to them.

The adulterations are of three kinds; that which is made on the spot in wine regions, and when fermented wine, is both strengthened by the addition of ardent spirit and adulterated by foreign admixtures. This kind of adulteration has a close connection with the Communion Question, for in fact the wine considered the purest, and purchased as the purest, is indebted to ardent spirit, run from the distillery, for its principal strength. As evidence of this, I will state a fact received from the lips of a large dealer and importer of wine. His conscience was aroused on the subject of Communion wine; knowing the general imposition practiced upon the churches, he resolved to import the pure fermented wine, free from any admixture whatever. He accordingly wrote to his agent at Madeira, giving strict orders that not a drop of ardent spirit should be added. The wine came, but to all appearances *undiminished in strength.* Surprised at this, he determined to ascertain the cause, and wrote to his agent for a positive answer to the question, "Was my order strictly complied with?" The reply was, "We complied with the letter but not with the spirit of your order. We put *no* brandy into the wine, but we put the wine into the brandy; and the reason was, had we not have made this addition, it would have spoiled before reaching you." Every gallon of imported alcohol wine, of the more expensive kinds, probably contains at least a quart of distilled spirit; as brandy is cheapest, it is added to as great an extent as the public taste will bear. Is such wine proper for the Lord's table? This is the purest state that alcoholic wine generally reaches this country.

There is another kind of adulteration far more extensive than the last. It is the pure fermented wine, rendered more intoxicating by poisonous drugs, because the drugs used are cheaper than alcohol. Even when wine is only worth a penny a bottle, such is the cupidity of the dealer, that he will practice this imposition to increase his gains.

Is this kind of wine proper for the Lord's table?

But by far the most extensive and alarming adulterations are the liquors sold as wine *in which there is not a drop of the fruit of the vine.* This trade is one of the secrets which the Day of Judgment can alone unfold. Some few of them have, however, come to light. The National Convention, recently held at Saratoga, offered $500 for the best essay on the adulterations of intoxicating drinks. Had it done nothing else but this, it would have been worthy of their assembling themselves together.

When this department of wickedness is thoroughly examined and laid before the public, the beer exposures will be entirely thrown in the shade. An aged divine related to me what actually took place under his own knowledge. He was called to the death-bed of a manufacturer and dealer in liquor *called wine.* In the course of his conversation with the dying man he put the question, "Are the statements made in the Temperance papers respecting the adulteration of wine true?" "Yes," said he, "they are all true, and I am now suffering the deepest pangs of remorse for what I have done in this matter." In connection with this fact, the druggist of a town admitted publicly, that while this trade was in its greatest state of prosperity, the sale of *sugar of lead* was in the greatest demand. I wonder what this dying man would have said if he had been asked, "Is the wine you have been making and selling a proper substance to commemorate the dying love of that Saviour before whom you are shortly to appear?"

I have myself received many confessions from wine fabricators and others, all going to show that the greatest iniquities are practiced, and that the health and life of the community have been held in small consideration. A gentleman of New York, of high standing, informed me not long since that he purchased a bottle of champagne, said to be pure as imported, and had it analyzed, and found it to contain one quarter of *an ounce of sugar of lead;* and this is the wine that the higher classes are now drinking in great quantities, especially the young.

A grocer, now no longer engaged in making or selling these poisons, confessed to me that he had often purchased of the country merchant whisky one day, and the next sold him his whisky back again in part under the name of wine, at a profit from two to four hundred per cent. Another large dealer that I knew full well, having purchased a receipt for turning ardent spirit into wine, and New England rum into brandy and gin, went to work on an extensive scale, and prepared a large quantity of his adulterations. He one day exhibited his receipt to his physician, and told him how rapidly he was making his fortune. His physician informed him that the ingredients he was using were rank poisons, and to sell what he had made would be *murder.* All at once his golden visions departed; still he could not be reconciled to the loss of his present stock; he concluded, therefore, to give a gallon of his liquor to a poor miserable drunkard of his acquaintance, and *if it did not kill him,* he would sell it. The drunkard being a tough subject, was not killed immediately, so he sold his stock of poisonous liquors, and continued to make and vend them for years. He grew *rich,* and DIED RICH, AND HAS GONE TO JUDGMENT.

I frequently meet with persons of intelligence who are quite incredulous as to the truth of these statements. While traveling recently, I fell in with a gentleman of great influence, whose aid I was anxious to secure to the Temperance cause. He was in favor of temperance, but thought moderate drinking temperance. Failing in my arguments to convince him, as I thought of his wrong position, I resorted to the one of adulterations, and stated to him that in order to be sure that he was drinking pure wine, and not a mixture of poisons, he would require a chemist with his laboratory constantly in attendance. After giving him a great variety of facts, to which he listened attentively, he replied, "I can not credit what you say; you must be deceived; such things could not exist without exposure so long; if true, or even half true, these wine forgers deserve the State Prison ten times more than he who writes another man's name on the back of his note. Here is Mr. B. sitting beside us; he has been listening to our conversation; he is an extensive importer of wine; let us appeal to him: is what Mr. Delavan relates true?" "Yes," replied our fellow-passenger, "all that he says is true;" and then he went to describe the iniquitous practices of the wine fabricators.

A gentleman of undoubted veracity gave me the following fact in a letter from the city of Troy:

"A spirit dealer in this city acknowledged to me that a gentleman called on him who loves *good wine*, and will drink no other. He showed him some for which he charged him twelve shillings per gallon; it cost him *two shillings and sixpence a gallon.* If he had charged it at a low price the purchaser would not have supposed it good; he was therefore constrained to ask an extravagant price, or lose the sale. A few days since the same dealer informed me that that he had made *fifteen dollars* on the sale of ten gallons of wine; that the tavern-keeper who purchased it intended to bottle it, and would make fifteen dollars more!"

The practices of wine fabricators several years since underwent a thorough examination in the British Parliament; a great mass of important testimony was adduced, and great numbers were convicted. One man was found to have more than 2,000 pounds of divers drugs and compounds intended to be used in the business; this man was convicted and punished.

There were individuals engaged in this nefarious traffic who confined their operations simply to the manufacture of the ingredients, omitting the alcohol. This substance made up with the necessary drugs to produce the flavor required, is furnished at a very small cost to the dealers, who themselves added the necessary quantity of whisky. A large shipment of this horrible stuff was made to Boston during the winter, left on the quay one cold night, and in the morning was found frozen solid, as the fire-water had not yet been added—had it been, it would have been sold as good wine, and some of it probably found its way to the table of the Lord, and there drank as representing the blood of Christ! Do I do wrong, dear Brethren, in stating these things, and in urging you to purify the table of the Lord from such abominations?

Other evidence could be adduced to strengthen what I have said, but it is unnecessary. The Temperance press has been teeming with such facts for the last five or six years, *and yet up to this day, let it be remembered, there has not appeared a man to contradict them.* In the face of open day have these practices been exposed, and in broad day are these abominations yet practiced, yet how few, especially in our cities, except the Temperance men, really give credit to these facts, but keep on drinking their liquors daily, and our churches using them at the Communion with hardly a thought that they, by purchasing and using, are in point of fact not only partakers, but co-partners in sustaining this traffic of death.

Let me with all kindness and earnestness inquire of those of my brethren who oppose the introduction of the Fruit of the Vine free from all that can intoxicate or pollute, for what is it you contend? Is it for the alcohol, the drugs, or the coloring matter?

Setting aside all higher considerations, it appears to me for the purpose of discountenancing such a trade we would be justified even in straining a point; but this is not required. The real unobjectionable and pure symbol is at hand, and will you refuse it and continue to use such compounds as I have described? May not the souls of many now be crying from under the altar, "How long, O Lord, holy and true, dost thou not judge and avenge our blood on them that dwell on the earth?"

Yours, etc., E. C. D.

LETTER XII.

Dear Brethren—No class of men possesses more influence over the public mind than ministers of religion. No class has done more to promote the cause of Temperance, and no class has derived greater benefits from it. It is hardly necessary here to refer to the custom of society and of the clergy fifteen years since, and state what their habits were then, and how many of them, especially in our cities, fell before the destroyer. But now all this has passed away, and I doubt whether there is a clergyman who has commenced his labors since the reform that is even in danger of becoming intemperate. That, with very few exceptions, the whole body of the clergy in the State of New York and in all the New England States now practically adopt the principles of Total Abstinence, tells powerfully in favor of that principle and on the agency they must have had in producing the results which are now rejoicing the hearts of the benevolent everywhere.

The question now before us, and as I think the most important in the Temperance reform, can be greatly retarded or almost immediately settled, as they incline. What little I may say to my brethren of this class shall be said with great deference, disclaiming any intention but to express my views in simplicity, without entertaining the least desire to dictate to them on this important question.

It does appear to me that the time has now fully arrived when every minister of Christ should devote his mind to the examination of this question. It will have to be met and examined on its own merits, without regard to denominations or schools in religion. All who love the Saviour will have to settle this question each for himself. The question is now fairly and openly before the Church. "Is the unfermented fruit of the vine the proper symbol of the Redeemer's blood?" I do hope and pray that no minister of Christ will decide hastily in favor of continuing the use of alcoholic wine. As I have said before, the influence of the clergy is great, and it should be great on all subjects connected with our salvation. This has been forcibly exhibited as the Temperance cause has advanced. When the minister has been forward, the people have rapidly followed; when the minister has been cold and lukewarm, or opposed, the people have been so likewise, until he was either removed or converted. Some yet from the pulpit declare that the use of intoxicating wine in moderation is according to the Word of God. Those that preach thus are doubtless sincere. Not long since a clergyman, in delivering a Temperance address, preached this *doctrine*—an aged man arose after the clergyman had finished his address, and begged the privilege of saying a few words. It being granted, he remarked that he had a son, the staff of his declining years, who had heard from the pulpit such sentiments advanced as he had listened to, and in consequence had become a moderate drinker, and then a drunkard, and then filled a drunkard's grave—and, said the aged man, the clergyman from whom he received these lessons has just addressed you.

I had a dear friend whose son had reformed for eighteen months, and all considered him safe, but happening to be at a public house, he there saw a clergyman call for a glass of beer; at once the example affected him; he said if the clergyman can take a glass of beer, why can not I? He took one and another; became again a beastly sot, and died a drunkard. I had a man in my own employ whom I had persuaded to abandon strong drink, but hearing a clergyman in a Temperance lecture allude to the ultraism of the times in condemning fermented wine, he went immediately from the church to the tavern and called for a glass of rum and drank the minister's health, and said, "He is the man for me." I could multiply such facts to any extent, but it is unnecessary. No one doubts the overwhelming influence of the clergy for good or for evil, if by chance they take a wrong view of an important question. I wish to see every minister of Christ occupying such a position *in all its bearings* that no one can point to him and say, "It was through your example and influence I have been made a drunkard, or kept from being reclaimed," but rather that the minister of the Lord should everywhere be pointed at as leading the way, and setting the temperate a proper and constant example, and in sustaining the poor drunkard in his efforts to break the chains of the monster appetite under which he has been in bondage; and should the poor drunkard be led back to sobriety through the Total Abstinence doctrine of his pastor or others, and be converted, can that pastor administer to him without fear and trembling the cup of intoxication at the Communion table? Yours, etc., E. C. D.

LETTER XIII.

Dear Brethren—The influence the missionary has had upon the Christian Church, and upon the world at large, is acknowledged by all. That influence is rapidly extending, and the idea is spreading, that should the Church be faithful to its duty, a comparatively short period may see the whole world evangelized.

I have for years thought that an argument might be drawn from our duty to the heathen in favor of the change I advocate, even more powerful than that from the reformed converted drunkard.

In Christian lands we have had to work our way in a manner backward; we have had to labor to undo, in a great measure, what in ignorance Christian men and the Church have been doing for generations. We have had to commence far down among the lowest grade in society, and by degrees come up to the domestic hearth of the middling classes, and again to the higher walks, and intercede with them to forego the alcoholic cup as a beverage, that the world may be freed from the curse of intemperance. How all these various classes have responded, it is not now my object to recapitulate. Now we approach with hope, confidence, and faith to the altar of the living God. Will the Church listen? Will she not give a favorable response? My faith is strong that she will.

Such were the customs and fashions of past times in our country that the drinking usages had eaten into the very core of the social system, and it had become almost a part of the religion of men to drink. Said an aged divine in Edinburgh, Scotland, while I was there, "If your principle of Total Abstinence prevail, the clergy will lose their influence over their people; for now, when they come to see us, we give them something to drink; should it be known that we offer nothing, they would not come, and then we should lose the opportunity of admonishing them as to their eternal welfare.''

With regard to the benighted heathen world, all this may be reversed if we begin right now. The Church will not, centuries hence, have to undo the wrong practice in this branch of duty. The missionary goes abroad that he may exhibit the contrast between heathenism and Christianity, even to the minutest thing, and, if possible, to avoid "even the appearance of evil."

All interested in the cause of missions understand that one of the greatest hindrances to the progress of the Gospel is the awful extent of drunkenness among the heathen; and we blush to say it, the habit has been taught and sanctioned by men bearing the Christian name! To redeem this name from reproach is one of the first objects the missionary has to undertake. This he can do in one important branch of morals, and I believe he universally does abandon, himself, the use of all that can intoxicate, and endeavor to induce others to follow his example. But should a different course be adopted, I should expect that Christianity would be as little promoted hereafter by the introduction of the drink of the drunkard among the heathen, in the form of wine by the missionary, as civilization has been heretofore by the introduction of the same drink in the form of fire-water by the Indian trader.

It appears to me that the missionary should not only teach abstinence from all that intoxicates, while speaking from the pulpit, but also while ministering at the Communion table; and how can this be done so effectually as by substituting in place of intoxicating wine the mere fruit of the vine, free from poison, whether generated by fermentation or superadded by drugging?

It appears to me that the missionary should not only teach abstinence from all that can intoxicate as a beverage, but should also be permitted to teach the same principle while officiating at the Communion table; and how could this be done so effectually as by substituting the Fruit of the Vine, free from alcohol, for the intoxicating wine? The feeble disciple, then but just converted from idolatry, will see that the minister of the Lord discourages the use of alcohol *on all occasions*, and will by degrees be brought to view its common use as sinful. The appearance of it will put him in mind of his idolatry, and he will flee from it as from the face of a serpent. To taste the intoxicating cup would be like returning to kiss his false God.

We can easily conceive the danger which surrounds the new convert but just drawn by the grace of God from his idol worship, and perhaps from habits of intemperance, at his first communion season, should the intoxicating cup be presented to him. The minister of Christ holds out to him the Bible as the groundwork of his hopes, and a cup of alcohol which he must drink in obedience to the requirements of that holy Word —the Bible in one hand, and the cup of intoxication in the other! while on common occasions he has been taught to love and reverence the one and detest the other. His simple mind, unable to make distinctions, which even the most refined and intelligent begin to find it difficult to make as to time, place, or quantity, will at once associate a sacredness with the cup of intoxication; his longing desires, originating in previous habits, might blind his mind to any reasoning which fails to succeed oftentimes with more enlightened minds, and he would very soon lose his abhorrence for that as a daily drink which has been presented to him with so much solemnity at the Lord's table.

Perhaps he only takes the same liquor at the feast of his Saviour which he heretofore took at the feast of his idol, and it produces the same longings, and why may we not suppose the same consequences will follow?

There is surely no need of running such risks; the Fruit of the Vine, free from alcohol, can be had in all pagan countries as readily as the fruit of fermentation. Why, then, should not our missionaries be at once directed to make the change for which I plead?

There are also hundreds of millions of our race that yet know not God, but still abhor intoxicating wine, and by their present religion are prohibited its use. Why should we, then, by its introduction at the Lord's table, seek to introduce this deleterious drink into these regions, where it is now viewed with abhorrence? Why should we teach the converts of these countries to love this substance at the Lord's table, which, to drink on common occasions, leads to every species of wickedness and misery?

There is no part of the world where missionaries have gone where this change is not to be desired. In the region of Syria, we have the authority of the Rev. Eli Smith of the deadly influence of even the purest wine. "Of the inebriating effects," says he, "of the wines of the Mediterranean, we have often powerful evidence. On first going to Malta, at the beginning of the Temperance reformation, with the impression I had received here, that there was no danger from the pure wines of those countries, I fell in with what I found to be the prevailing custom, and took a little wine with my dinner. At length I found an intimate friend falling into habits of intoxication from using the common Massala wine of Sicily. I then gave up my wine, and so far as I know, all my brethren abstain from the habitual use of it as a temperance measure. In preparing a tract on Temperance for circulation in Syria, we have included *wine with brandy* as one of the causes of intemperance to be avoided." In the East Indies the same change is demanded, as European customs have there spread a wider and more fatal influence in favor of intoxicating drinks. The Rev. Dr. Scudder, of Madras, says: "In India, drunkenness prevails in the higher circles; but it is to be seen in its widest range among the middle classes of Europeans and East Indians. Half of the natives of this city, we have been told, get drunk daily. Probably half of the Europeans who die in the hospitals in Black Town die of intemperance." To counteract this mighty influence for evil, to whom are we to look, under God, but to our missionaries? And while these missionaries bless and dispense the instrument of drunkenness at the Lord's table, it never will be viewed as wrong to be used in moderation on common occasions. The recent forcible imposition of French brandies and other intoxicating drinks upon the Sandwich islanders has met with universal condemnation; yet if the missionaries themselves bless and use the same substance to be administered to their converts at the Lord's table, some one must ship it to them, and why not the French as well as the wine fabricators of Boston or New York? The banishment of intoxicating liquors must be complete, or nothing will be accomplished; the name is nothing, it is the thing that occasions all the evil; it is the alcohol. Let this substance not only have the hatred of the king of these recently Christianized islands, but the missionary also and his converts, and neither the French government nor the cupidity of our own countrymen would find it to their advantage to ship their poisons to these simple-hearted people. Should all our missionaries in all parts of the world, especially in wine countries, at once make this change, the influence would, in my opinion, react most benignly on our churches at home. These unbiased and unsophisticated examples of the followers of the Lamb could not but have its influence on those Christian communities which had by their prayers and contributions been the means, under Providence, in bringing them into the fold of the Redeemer.

To the minds of many, the millennium day is rapidly approaching. The signs of the latter-day glory are not few, and none of the least of these, to my mind, is the present movement in the Temperance cause throughout the world. Since the days of the Apostles, nothing has been known like it. Men are moving in masses under a great moral and irresistible impulse. Those that throw themselves in the way of this mighty enterprise of benevolence, with the hope of arresting it, will either have to yield to this impulse, get out of the way, or lose all influence for good. The millions in Ireland, the hundreds of thousands in England and Scotland, the two millions in this land, and the thousands and tens of thousands of drunkards reforming, all give strong indications that the reign of alcohol is approaching its termination. This great enterprise has already been John the Baptist to millions preparing the way of the Lord; and when the Lord does come, should it not be the earnest prayer of his followers that all his altars should be entirely purified from the cup of intoxication?

Yours, etc., E. C. D.

LETTER XIV.

Dear Brethren—It is a blessed thing that we are permitted to live in a land where no one class has absolute control over another, either spiritual or temporal. All are permitted to worship God according to the dictates of their consciences, and to discuss with entire freedom all matters relative either to their religious or civil liberty. To our Puritan fathers we are indebted for this, and may their children watch with the utmost care every encroachment upon their sacred rights. If an individual Christian feels that there is a practice in the Church with which he is connected injurious in its tendency, it is his duty in every proper way to seek for its abatement. In the question before us, I conclude the officers of churches have much to do. I suppose it is in all our churches their duty to provide the elements to be used at the Sacrament, and as there is no rule laid down, as far as I have heard of, as to the particular kind of wine to be used at the Lord's table, I conclude they will all be disposed to provide the "Fruit of the Vine" of an unexceptionable character when they are perfectly satisfied as to what it should be. Yet the change from the fruit of fermentation to the "Fruit of the Vine" may be so great when the subject has not been discussed or examined, that evil consequences might result from its violent introduction. All this can be avoided by kind and free discussion between the pastor and the people; and if the subject is introduced with an ardent desire to advance the cause of religion and the glory of God, a short time will suffice to bring all to see as one, and act as one.

In the church with which I am connected, the unfermented wine has been introduced; in doing it, some mistakes, I think, were committed, and misunderstanding and unkind feeling for a short time was the consequence, which has occasioned church action.

Yours, etc., E. C. D.

LETTER XV.

Dear Brethren—In concluding these Letters, permit me to express a fear that steps may be taken that will require to be retraced. I am aware that there is a general disgust in many minds on account of the strength and quality of the liquors now in use in our churches, and some seek to relieve their minds by mixing water with these strong drinks. The wines generally used at the Sacrament are about 44 per cent. proof spirit, or nearly half as strong as brandy. Suppose these strong wines should be reduced one half, still the half of the alcohol remains, and in all probability mixed with a due proportion of drugs; and it will appear to any common-sense mind that the argument remains as strong against the half that is left as the half that has been taken away. No holding up of church testimony against the making, vending, or drinking of alcohol, either on common occasions or at the Lord's table, would follow such a half-way measure. It would be as ineffectual to remove the evil in the Church as the ardent-spirit pledge was to remove drunkenness, or cure drunkenness in or out of the Church. The calculation is, that our churches consume about 80,000 gallons at the Sacrament yearly; about 20,000 of it is pure alcohol. So long as the maker and vender can point to the Church as a customer on so large a scale, they will throw back with contempt the charge that they are employed in an immoral trade.

I fear, dear brethren, I have trespassed too long upon your patience; I may attach too much importance to the question, it having occupied my mind for so many years. When I commenced writing, my intention was to have asked the columns of some religious paper, but afterward I concluded that I would give my views in a pamphlet, so as to present what I had to say and what others have to say on the question in a connected form and in one document. I think I can not be mistaken in the belief that the time has now fully come when the Christian community are ready and willing to go into a full, candid, and dispassionate examination of this important question, and that it will be entered upon with a sincere desire to advance the cause of truth. E. C. D.

P. S.—Although I have addressed professing Christians in the foregoing Letters, yet I flatter myself my brethren in the Total Abstinence army all over the world, whether in or out of the Church, with whom I have traveled for so many years, and so prosperously in the Temperance cause, advancing step by step, as light has enabled us to advance, will give this last great question their immediate and dispassionate attention, *remembering that they stand pledged before the world* "in all suitable ways" to promote the cause of Temperance to the fullest extent. Should there be any profits arising from this work, it will all be devoted to the great object we all have in view.

Wherein Consists the Difference?

The GROG-SHOP KEEPER *deals out* the "MOCKER" *for gold* to *his* customers.

CHRISTIANS, as well as others, *keep* the same poisonous "mocker" in their dwellings, *deal* IT *out*, and *give* IT to their families and friends.

CHURCH OFFICERS *purchase* the liquid poison, which "*biteth like a serpent and stingeth like an adder*," and CHRISTIAN MINISTERS *dispense* IT at the *so-called* Table of the Lord, *inviting* ALL TO DRINK OF IT!!!

OFFICERS OF THE

NATIONAL TEMPERANCE SOCIETY

AND

PUBLICATION HOUSE.

President of the Society.

HON. WILLIAM E. DODGE............................New York City.

Vice-Presidents.

E. C. DELAVAN..........................South Ballston, N. Y.
CHAN. R. H. WALWORTH..............Saratoga Springs, N. Y.
GOV. WM. A. BUCKINGHAM............Norwich, Conn.
HON. HORACE GREELEY...............New York City.
REV. DR. HEWITT.......................Bridgeport, Conn.
REV. DR. I. N. WYCKOFF..............Albany, N. Y.
MAJOR-GENERAL HOWARD...........Washington, D. C.
GEO. H. STUART........................Philadelphia, Pa.
REV. H. W. BEECHER..................Brooklyn, N. Y.
JOHN B. GOUGH........................Worcester, Mass.
HON. JAMES HARLAN..................Washington, D. C.
R. W. STEELE...........................Dayton, Ohio.
E. J. MORRIS............................Indianapolis, Ind.
D. R. PERSHING ....Liberty Mills, Ind.
WM. BALLENTYNE.....................Washington, D. C.
JOHN TAPPAN...........................Boston, Mass.
BISHOP E. S. JANES....................21 East 4th Street, New York City.
HON. GERRIT SMITH....................Peterboro, N. Y.
REV. DR. N. S. S. BEEMAN............Carbondale, Ill.
PROF. A. B. PALMER....................Ann Arbor, Mich.
MATTHEW W. BALDWIN..............Philadelphia, Pa.
HON. A. C. BARSTOW..................Providence, R. I.
REV. S. H. TYNG, D.D..................209 East 16th St., New York City.
HON. J. WARREN MERRILL...........Cambridge, Mass.
REV. DR. DOWLING.....................6 Ashland Place, New York City.
GEN. NEAL DOW.........................Portland, Me.
BENJAMIN JOY..........................Penn Yan, N. Y.
GEN. S. F. CARY.........................Cincinnati, Ohio.
REV. DR. ASA D. SMITH................Hanover, N. H.
DR. J. J. BRADFORD....................Augusta, Ky.
PROF. C. A. LEE, M.D..................Peekskill, N. Y.
PROF. YOUMANS........................Saratoga Springs, N. Y.
REV. J. W. CHICKERING, D.D.........Boston, Mass.
CHARLES HATHAWAY.................Delhi, N. Y.
E. REMINGTON..........................Ilion, N. Y.
REV. JOHN MARSH, D.D................5 Beekman Street, New York City.
HON. SAMUEL WILLESTON...........East Hampton, Mass.
B. H. MILLS..............................Upper Alton, Ill.
REV. DR. NELSON......................St. Louis, Mo.
E. S. WELLS.............................Chicago, Ill.

DAVID RIPLEY.......................... Newark, N. J.
S. D. HASTINGS.......................... Madison, Wis.
—— WILLIAMSON..................... Wilmington, Del.
REV. H. C. FISH, D.D................... Newark, N. J.
REV. J. B. WAKELY.................... Sing Sing, N. Y.
WILLIAM H. BURLEIGH............... 104 Wall Street, New York City.
JOHN SHERRY.......................... Sag Harbor, N. Y.
THEODORUS GREGORY................ Poughkeepsie, N. Y.
CHARLES HOPKINS .... New York.
SIMEON MORRILL...................... London, Canada East.
JOHN DOUGALL........................ Montreal, Canada East.
HON. S. L. TILLEY .... Frederickton, New Brunswick.
REV. J. M. CRAMP..................... Wolfville, Nova Scotia.

Treasurer.

WILLIAM A. BOOTH.................... 97 Front Street, New York City.

Assistant Treasurer.

THOS. T. SHEFFIELD................... 91 Wall Street, New York City.

Temporary Corresponding Secretary.

REV. J. B. DUNN........................ 186 19th Street, New York City.

Publishing Agent.

J. N. STEARNS.......................... 172 William Street, New York City.

Financial Agent.

GEORGE E. SICKLES................... 172 William St., New York City.

Board of Managers.

REV. T. L. CUYLER..................... Brooklyn, N. Y.
GEN. JOSEPH S. SMITH................ Custom House, New York City.
REV. DR. W. W. NEWELL............. 66 Second Avenue, " "
REV. PETER STRYKER................ 205 West 31st Street, " "
REV. KENDELL BROOKS............... Philadelphia, Pa.
T. M. SPELMAN.......................... 30 Warren Street, New York City.
JOHN DAVIES............................ 183 William Street, " "
REV. N. E. COBLEIGH.................. Boston, Mass.
J. B. MERWIN............................ 125 Bleecker St., New York City.
REV. EDWIN THOMPSON.............. East Walpole, Mass.
PETER CARTER .... 530 Broadway, New York City.
ALVAN B. PRESTON..................... 69 Murray Street, " "
JAMES BLACK .... Lancaster, Pa.
REV. J. B. DUNN .... 186 19th Street, New York City.
WM. B. SPOONER........................ Boston, Mass.
J. N. STEARNS........................... 172 William Street, New York City.
REV. CYRUS D. FOSS.................. 289 Fourth Avenue, " "
A. S. HUNTER, M.D..................... 363 Broome Street, " "
E. A. LAMBERT........................... 45 John Street, " "
S. B. RANSOM............................. Jersey City, N. J.
T. T. SHEFFIELD........................ 91 Wall Street, New York City.
REV. R. R. MEREDITH.................. Cohoes, N. Y.
A. P. NORTON............................. 117 Nassau Street, New York City.
R. S. DOTY................................ 153 Chambers Street, " "
R. G. PARDEE............................. 92 Broadway, " "
J. W. LESTER............................. 63 Broadway, " "
A. A. ROBINS............................. 193 Chambers Street, " "

*** E. C. DELAVAN, Esq., was elected a member of the Board of Managers and chair man of the Finance Committee, at the organization of the Society, but declined the positions on account of the state of his health. He was then unanimously elected first Vice-President.

No. 8.

A

CONDENSED REPORT

OF THE TRIAL OF THE CAUSE OF

JOHN TAYLOR VS. EDWARD C. DELAVAN,

PROSECUTED FOR AN ALLEGED

LIBEL.

TRIED AT THE ALBANY CIRCUIT, APRIL, 1840.

TRIAL FOR LIBEL.

CIRCUIT COURT, *April Term*, 1840.

Judge CUSHMAN presiding.

JOHN TAYLOR,
vs.
EDWARD C. DELAVAN.

Counsel for plaintiff, Messrs. Stevens, Reynolds, McKown and Van Buren.

Counsel for defendant, Messrs. Beardsley, Taber and Wheaton.

THE PROSECUTION.

TUESDAY, *April* 21, 1840.

Mr. Stevens opened with a brief statement of plaintiff's case, and proceeded to read the alleged libel from the *Evening Journal* of the 12th February, 1835, as follows:

"TO THE PUBLIC.

"The following statement has been made by a respectable and responsible person, in the presence of Chief Justice Savage and E. C. Delavan; (the former took down the testimony.) The individual making the disclosure felt a delicacy in giving his name to the public; but, should his statements be denied, he stands ready, not only to give his name, but make oath to the facts."

"He states, that so long since as six or seven years he was knowing to the fact of Fidler and Taylor's, and Robert Dunlap's malting establishment on the hill in Albany, being supplied with water for malting from stagnant pools, gutters and ditches, often in such a state as to be green on the surface; that such water was collected for several seasons to his knowledge. That he had not only seen the water of this character collected, but deposited in the malting establishment for the use of malting. That no attention was ever paid to cleanliness; the water was often taken from puddles in which were dead animals. When the water was low in the pools, holes were sometimes made, in which the pail was sunk; and he had seen the sides of it come in contact with dead animals in a state of putridity; has seen water carried to the malt houses nearly as thick as cream with filth; saw last winter water passing on carts coming from the direction of the same filthy ponds, and taken to the malt houses. There are several malt houses on the hill, all of which, he believes, rely on water taken from such places as he has described, occasionally. That the facts here stated he believes to be known to hundreds residing in the neighborhood of the malting establishments. He states, also, that seven hogsheads of water are usually placed in a steep-tub at a time, and it is then filled with barley; that he has seen a deposit or sediment of from ten to twelve inches of the most filthy matter settle to the bottom from that quantity of water. This has been from water collected from the places described. That he has no unkind feeling towards any of the brewers; that he is astonished they should deny facts so easily to be proved; that he knows several cartmen who for years have been employed in carting water from the places described to the malt houses. That Mr. Fidler, now Fidler and Ryckman, was recently of the firm of Fidler and Taylor; and that Mr. John Taylor was of the same firm."

Also that of the 17th February, 1835, as follows:

"TO THE PUBLIC.

"The conductors of the *Temperance Press* publish nothing which they do not believe to be entirely true; the statements with regard to impure water made use of by certain malting establishments were furnished by respectable citizens, who have given their affidavits as to the facts. When legal steps are taken by those who feel themselves aggrieved, the public may rest assured that nothing has been stated but what can be most abundantly sustained by proof."

For the publication of these libels Mr. Taylor claimed to recover $70,000 damages. The publications were proved, and the only question was as to their truth or falsity. Mr. Delavan instructed his counsel to put him before the jury on the truth of the matter charged.

The plaintiff's counsel here rested.

Mr. Taber opened the defence to the jury, and thus stated the issue to be tried:

That you may understand this case, and as the counsel for

the plaintiff has not stated what the issue is, it becomes my duty to call your attention to the distinct issue. This case has been before the supreme court, or rather another one by Mr. Fidler, the partner of Mr. Taylor, precisely like this, and the pleadings in that case have undergone the revision of that court. The precise question is thus stated by the Chief Justice :

"That six or seven years ago (that is, previous to the publication,) the plaintiff caused his malting establishment on the hill in Albany to be supplied with filthy, putrid water, such as is taken from pools, gutters and ditches, in which were dead, putrid animals; that the water was often so foul and polluted as to be green on the surface, and nearly as thick as cream with filth; that such water had been used by plaintiff for several seasons in malting for his brewery; and that steep-tubs used for that purpose, which usually contained seven hogsheads, had a deposit of ten or twelve inches of the most filthy matter that settled to the bottom of them. This is the essence of the charge as laid in the declaration, as understood by the general reader, and which the defendant was bound to justify."

THOMAS COULSON (class teacher, Methodist Church) was first sworn for defendant :

Examination direct: I resided on the hill in Albany about nineteen years ; had a glue factory near Willet street ; carried on that glue factory fourteen years ; the malt house of the plaintiff was built previously; I knew the malt house of Fidler & Taylor near me ; there was a pond between my glue factory and this malt house ; the water in this was always bad ; in a putrid state in the fall of the year ; different kinds of animals were floating in the water ; in the warmth of the weather the water was green ; dogs and cats and hogs I've seen ; I have seen a dead horse that died there, pretty near the pond, on the rising ground near it ; the horse remained there ; they don't do anything in summer in malting ; when the fall comes they take the water ; they commenced about October ; there were dead animals in the water ; it would not do to make glue of that water ; it was what I call rotten water ; I have seen it taken in hogsheads into the malt house—poured through at the end of the malt house—into Taylor's malt house, through troughs; the wash of my glue factory ran into the pond; a great many cart loads of this water were carried into the malt house; very often two carts were going at once; as far as I can recollect, they began to dip up and carry this water into the malt house in '26 or '27, and continued until '33 or '34; they drove the cart and horse into it, and dipped it up with a dipper; sometimes with a long handle and sometimes with a short one; have seen Mr. Taylor there.

Cross-examined: Did you at the time know what they were doing with that water? I could not know; saw where it went to; don't know what purpose they put it to; I saw them running it into the house; that is all I can say on the subject; I have seen it dipped when frozen. When you saw it, was it frozen? Sometimes. Sometimes not? In frosty weather it was frozen, in warm weather not.

The Court.—How did you see it? I saw it as they passed me, and as I passed them; the pond was near me.

Direct resumed: My glue factory was distant from the pond perhaps seven or eight hundred feet; from my house, about five hundred feet; the pond and the malt house were in plain sight from the glue factory and the house.

Cross-examined: Hardly ever saw the time in the fall when there were not dead animals in the pond.

HENRY RECTOR, sworn.—*Examination direct:* Resided in this city nearly twenty-seven years; am a surveyor and architect; drew this map; [map shown] it is substantially a correct representation of the relative position of objects; from the nature of the ground I should think the pond was stagnant water; saw dead animals there a few days ago.

JOHN SAVAGE, (late Chief Justice,) sworn.—*Examination direct:* I resided in Albany in 1835; I lived here from 1822 to 1837; I lived on the hill; had occasion to observe, previous to 1835, the pond spoken of; saw it frequently, from 1827 to 1837; being out of health, I was in the habit of riding by it with my family; the water was always dirty; never saw it otherwise; it was not fit for food or drink; my horse refused to drink it; I have seen dead animals there; and I believe I have seen dogs and cats and hogs; observed this for several years, between 1827 and 1835.

Charles W. Harvey, sworn.—*Examination direct:* I am a surgeon dentist; resided in Albany from 1811 up to 1829; returned to the city in 1832; resided from 1824 to 1828 with John Quinlan, my brother-in-law; he was a gardener; sometimes employed as a cartman; have assisted him in drawing water for the plaintiff's malt house, prior to 1835; we got it mostly from the big pond; the pond south of the plaintiff's malt house, on Lark street; the water was let into the building from the bottom of the hogsheads, by a conductor, through a trough; sometimes into a well or a steep-tub; I think in a well; either one or the other; when let into the well, it was pumped out into a steep tub; I assisted in drawing this water, I think, from fifteen or twenty places; from the big pond; that was always a standing source; and then, after rains, from whatever points were nearest the malt house; from puddles on the surface, and from Poor House creek, and from the vicinity of Judson's slaughter house; that was located, I think, on Orange street, north of the Schenectady turnpike; there were puddles in front of the grave yards that we got water from; part of the offal of the slaughter house drained into the pond from which water was taken, near the slaughter house; I drew water from the big pond four or five seasons—the pond in the vicinity of the malt house; the character of the water in that pond was very bad; bad, from the fact that it was receiving almost all the offal from the hill; dead hogs and dogs and cats and horses all drawn very near the pond; many in the pond, and with the sun on them, making it exceedingly foul, so that in drawing it frequently made me sick; on the banks of the pond there were dead animals; almost always more or less dead animals in the water; I have seen dead cats and dogs while dipping, and I think hogs; not sure, however; seen dead horses up towards the glue factory; they were left there to decay; commenced dipping the first cold weather; I think in October or thereabouts; these four or five seasons that I spoke of, I began to draw water for this malt house, I should think, in the commencement of the season—of the malting season; this continued as long as the cold weather continued; they required cold weather for malting; I dipped water in the winter, when it was frozen—cut a hole through the ice; I have frequently seen dead animals there in the winter; they would come to the hole from the wash of the water; I have drowned cats in these holes myself; it was the ordinary way to drown cats in these holes; they came to the hole frequently, so as to be troublesome; the water was green in the fall; not so green as I have seen it before; I suppose from the decomposition of animal matter and filth; there were some privies on the ravine, leading directly down to the pond; seven hogsheads of water were put into a steep-tub at a time; the barley was then let in; I believe usually after the water is put in; it is suffered to remain forty-eight hours; the water is then drawn off; I have seen barley taken out after being soaked; the sediment at the bottom was very thick; after the water is let off, and it has drained some time, the maltsters throw it out with scoops, and as they approach the bottom it is frequently discolored—in other malt houses more than in this—the barley and sediment settling together, and the mass being cleaner as you get up to the top; sometimes more sediment than others, depending on the cleanliness of the water from rains or other causes; have seen the plaintiff about the malt house about the period I speak of; I think I have seen Mr. Fidler there more than Mr. Taylor, but I have seen them both there; there was no other purpose for which water was needed in that malt house, except for malting; the water was not all used in the steep tubs; it was used in sprinkling the barley after it was thrown out; but it was all used for the purpose of malting.

ISRAEL SMITH, (elder in Rev. Mr. Kirk's church,) sworn. —*Examination direct:* Witness knew the pond called the big pond; heard the testimony of Judge Savage as to the charac-acter of the water; generally when witness had seen it, the water looked filthy; had frequently seen dead animals in it as he was riding by—dogs, hogs and cats; had frequently seen carcasses of dead horses lying on the margin of it. Witness spoke of a period some sixteen years ago, when he owned a dyeing establishment at Norman's kill. Fifteen years before, and including 1835, witness passed the pond frequently; sometimes three or four times a week. The character of the water during the fifteen years spoken of was very much the same, differing with the different seasons of the year.

The court here adjourned until Wednesday, April 22.

GARRET MIDDLETON, sworn.—*Examination direct:* Witness lives in Spring street, on the hill; knew the malt house on the corner of State and Lark streets; believed it used to belong to Fidler and Taylor; is acquainted with the pond south of it, or with the pond that used to be there; it is partly filled up now; witness drew water from that pond some years ago—twelve or fourteen years ago; drew it to Mr. Taylor's malt house, corner of State and Lark; drew at different times; witness let it run out of the hogsheads into the steep tub; they had a gutter to run it from the hogshead to the steep tub; saw it go in through the gutter to the steep tub; it was very dirty water, stagnant, all turned green; have seen dead dogs and cats in this pond; think I have seen dead pigs; not positive about that; but I have seen dead dogs and cats in it; the water was such as I have described when I was drawing it.

THOMAS A. HUGHES, sworn.—*Examination direct:* Reside in Washington street, on the hill; am acquainted with the malt house on the corner of State and Lark streets, and the pond near it; have assisted in drawing water from this pond some time ago; should think from ten to twelve years ago; have drawn it to this same malt house; can't tell how many hogsheads; have drawn there a number of times—a number of steeps; I worked for Mr Butler, off and on, four seasons; it ran right from the hogsheads to the steep tubs; it was green, filthy looking water when I drew it; I have seen dogs and cats and hogs in it when drawing it; it had a green looking filthy look.

JAMES D. WASSON, (late alderman,) sworn.—*Examination direct:* Have been a resident of Albany since 1811, with the exception of four years; know the pond in Lark street, and the malt house on the corner of Lark and State; have passed it very often for a great many years—perhaps at all seasons; I should think the water in the pond unwholesome, bad water generally; I think I have seen in it cats and dogs and hogs—dead and alive; I have seen live hogs wallowing there in the summer season; no recollection of ever seeing anything on the banks.

AMOS FASSETT, (elder in Rev. Dr. Campbell's church,) sworn.—*Examination direct:* Am acquainted with the pond and malt house in question; have seen water drawn from the pond to the malt house previous to '35; seen it deposited in the malt house, at the north end; the water I should call very impure; it has always been bad; I have known it for a great number of years; it was a place of general deposit for all kinds of dead animals, at all seasons of the year; I have known the pond twenty-five years; the water has been growing less every year, the pond gradually filling up; when it was deep, the water was not so impure as now, though it was always a receptacle for dead animals; I have seen dead dogs and cats and hogs there—dead cows on the ice in the winter—dead horses; I have seen the water at different times, when passing, put into the malt house; I should think more seasons than one.

Patrick Rooney, sworn.—*Examination direct:* Previous to 1835 lived on the hill with Mr. Delavan, and still live in his family; been with him since 1828; when employed as a coachman, and in driving the cow to pasture morning and night, two seasons, frequently passed the malt house and pond; these seasons were either '31 and '33, or '32 and '34, not successive seasons; saw water taken from the pond to the malt house; not often, once in a while; they put it into the north end of the malt house, through a trough, as near as I could judge; I have seen this done more than one season; it was taken on a cart in a hogshead.

John Lossing, sworn.—*Examination direct:* Have resided in the city twenty-eight years; I am acquainted with the malt house and pond spoken of; have observed the water in the pond at different times for five and twenty years, I suppose; live not far from it in Washington street; I should call the water impure; it was a place of deposit for dead animals; it was not fit to be used for drink or cooking; I have seen dead horses, hogs and dogs, cats, various things in it; Mr. Gibson had a slaughter house that led right into it; it has been moved from there some years; can't tell how long; the filth from the slaughter house went right into the ravine; stood as Wilson's does in regard to the creek; all the slaughter houses on that route ran into the creek—Mr. Perry's, Mr. Wilson's and another; in fact there are four—for, besides these, Mr. Hartness occupied one; I should think all these emptied into the creek previous to 1835.

The court here took a recess until three o'clock, P.M.

Laban W. Keith, sworn.—*Examination direct:* I have resided in the city about twenty-one years; have known the malt house in question ever since it was built, and the pond near it ever since I have been here; the water in the pond has always been pretty poor; I have seen dead animals in there of all descriptions almost, cats, dogs, hogs, and have seen one dead cow in there; of course there was a bad smell about the pond when these creatures were in it; I certainly have smelt it; recollect a drain or ravine from the rear of the buildings on Washington street, before the railroad was built, and that water ran in it into the pond; there was a spring in Spring street, and considerable ran from that through the same ravine into the pond; when there was a freshet it washed everything into this ravine—all kinds of filth I suspect.

ROBERT HARVEY, sworn.—*Examination direct:* Reside in the city; have resided here thirty-nine years; have been nine years out of the city in that time; I was here previous to '35, and am acquainted with the pond and malt house on Lark street; the water in the pond was bad—stagnant water—dirty water; recollect seeing carrion about there in 1818, '19, '20 and '21; am acquainted with the strangers' burying ground it drains into a branch of the Poor House creek; some of the places where they dig graves are quite steep; I was here in the time of the cholera, in 1832; witnessed quite a number of burials; witness spoke of three corpses lying in the Potters' Field unburied at one time, and of three hundred and fourteen buried in the hollow; don't know of more than one buried in the same grave; have not seen the Potters' Field for three or four years; was there in '33 or '34; saw then the edge of the coffins sticking out into the ravine; that was where the water runs; I am the brother of Dr. Harvey.

JOSEPH MANUEL, sworn.—*Examination direct:* Am acquainted with the creek that runs just back of the burying grounds; as I passed I have seen blood and water come from the north, pass under the railroad and down the creek; I think this was about five years ago; have lived here eight years—ever since '32; I have seen blood coming down this stream from, I think, Mr. Perry's, and from another source that joins it just before it passes under the railroad; the blood and water ran separate some distance before they mingled; this was in the fall of the year; and I have seen, day after day, a cart carrying this bloody water to the malt house.

LAMBERT CLARK, sworn.—*Examination direct:* I know the pond and malt house on Lark street; have helped to draw water from the pond for the malt house; commenced working for Calvin Butler ten years ago; have worked for him, off and on, every winter except one — sometimes a month or two; worked for him in '32, '33 and '34; drew some of the water to the malt house; and, if I found it any ways clear, I carried it for washing. What did you do with the water for the malt house? Put it in the gutter that ran into the steep tub. Did not go into the malt house? I have gone into the kiln to warm myself; could see where the water went; it went into the steep tub; I have let it run out while I went in and warmed myself; have seen dead hogs, cats and a horse in the water—almost anything you could wish for; the frame of a horse, I meant. Ever drawn any into it? Yes, and I have carried a bag full of kittens and thrown them in.

THE PROSECUTION.

LAUNCELOT HOWARD, (one of the prosecutors,) sworn.—*Examination direct:* I was a partner of Mr. Taylor in 1832; the malt house was built in 1823; I believe I may consider myself as having the entire control of the malting business from 1823 until 1832—Mr. Taylor seldom interfering—hardly asking me a question about it; this witness testified in substance that the water for malting was drawn from a small spring and well; and that there was never any water from this pond used for the purpose of malting, to his knowledge; I have not known any of it being put into the malt house and used for malting; my connection with the malt house closed in 1832, when our business was closed; Mr. Taylor had the sole management afterwards; I have had nothing to do with it since.

Cross-examined: I am plaintiff in one of the suits against Mr. Delavan for this publication.

[Witness was here asked the number of suits commenced against Mr. Delavan on account of this publication, and of his knowledge of a concert among the brewers to raise money to prosecute them, but denied any knowledge of such an arrangement to raise money.] Did you apply to Robert Dunlap to commence a suit? I did not put myself in his way. [The question was varied several times, and a similar answer given, when the court directed the witness to answer.] Did you urge or ask Mr. Dunlap to commence a suit? I think it probable such a conversation passed; I don't recollect it; I have been in company where he has been urged; I might have done it in conversation in company; might have asked him such a question.

William C. Helse, sworn.—*Examination direct:* Have known the pond between thirteen and fourteen years; it covered, when I first knew it, from three-fourths to an acre; I have seen carts drawing from it; can't tell where they went with it; went in different directions; have seen thirty or forty at a time in there swimming; it is fed principally by a stream; but there are springs that come out from the bank on the northwest corner; found the barrel always full there, ever since I have known it; people round used to go to the barrel to get water; there were others besides that; it was as pure water as could be got from any spring or stream that could be found; I used it in my family when I resided there, for culinary purposes—for drinking too, or coffee, or anything of that kind. The pond water I used always for washing. I lived then on the corner of Lark and Washington streets, 50 or a hundred rods from the pond. Lived there about a year and a half, or two years; there used to be an outlet; never saw a dead cow or horse in the pond; seen plenty on the other side of the road; that was a general depot for them; it is lower that side than the pond is; never saw dead dogs, or cats or hogs in the pond; I have seen the water colored after a storm—riley; never saw it when it could be said with truth that it was as thick as cream with filth; have seen boys swimming in it in hot weather in summer.

Cross-examined.—First went to live in Washington street 14 years ago; lived there a year and a half; I have seen a little green on the south-west corner of the pond; never saw it so bad but what cattle would drink it.

The court here adjourned to

THURSDAY, *April* 23.

CHARLES HOWE, *sworn.—Examination direct:* Never lived nearer the pond than Lydius street, 400 or 500 yards off; had occasion to be at the pond two or three times a day; used to drive through there to water, probably for six, seven or eight years; don't recollect having seen dead animals in it; I have seen dead horses thrown east of the road, down the hollow there; I know there are springs around the pond, where barrels are sunk to get water to use; always supposed it was fed by springs, because there was nothing but the wash of the hills that could come in; it appears to me I did see a dead dog once on the bank; I saw dogs, and horses and hogs in the hollow below; never saw one in the water to my knowledge; in common seasons it was as clear as common water; in the fall not quite so healthy—the pond would be lower; it could not run off about that season.

NICHOLAS RULL *sworn.—Examination direct:* Lived within half a mile of the pond for twelve years; I pass it frequently; I know of but one spring emptying into it that is running water; it has a barrel into it; the water in the pond, in some parts of the season, spring and fall, is pretty clear; in dry weather, in summer, it is pretty riley; it then had a riley, muddy look; don't know that I have seen dead animals in it before 1835; previous to 1835, have seen boys bathing in it.

JOTHAM HANCOCK, *sworn.—Examination direct:* Have

known the pond over 20 years; I live now within five rods of it; the rest of the time within 40 rods. Can't speak of more than one spring; that I know very well. Prior to 1835, was along by the pond almost daily; don't recollect ever seeing dead animals in the pond before that year. The water was stagnant in a dry time in summer; but spring and fall, it was fed by springs and passed off at the outlet; it was generally muddy; when very low, the hogs, geese, &c., resort there and keep it muddy. Can't say that I ever discovered any green on the surface; if it was, I never took particular notice of it. Since the repairs on Lark street—some three to five years ago—it has been pretty much filled up; I should call it a mud-hole now. Have seen women washing there in a dry season.

Cross-examined.—There was a ditch in State street formerly, that ran down and joined this ravine before it got to the pond; there was generally a little water running in it, even in a dry season. Certainly, I have often seen hogs wallowing, and geese washing themselves in and about the pond; one family raised a great many geese; I have seen 20 and 50 in a flock, belonging to one family; you can judge as well as I, as to the neatness of that animal. I think the pond has continued to diminish from the time I first knew it, twenty years ago.

EDWIN SCACE, *sworn.*—*Examination direct:* Have known the pond 16 or 17 years; when I first knew the pond, I should think when full, it would cover pretty near an acre and a half; when down to the drain, probably an acre or an acre and a quarter; I have seen the pond, some years, look pretty well through the season; other years, in summer, I have seen it thick and muddy—unfit for use; in the spring and fall it generally appeared pretty good; it always was until it got below the drain; then it looked more riley. I considered it good to use, when it was high enough to run through the drain, for cooking, &c. I believe I have drank the water of the pond once or twice. Could not say that I have known of its being used, when it was high enough to run through the drain, for cooking, &c. There were persons drawing it for different places. Think I have seen dead animals in the pond—dead hogs; have seen numbers of dead animals in the hollow on the other side of the road.

George Couchman, *sworn.—Examination direct:* I am a malster; I was in Mr. Taylor's employ, in the season of 1831 and '30; worked for him again in '35, in the malt-house on the hill; got the water for malting, principally, from a well in the malt-house; got none from the pond to my knowledge.

John G. White, (brewer and prosecutor,) *sworn.—Examination direct:* My first acquaintance with the pond was in 1827; continued to know it intimately until 1830, or the spring of 1831; I was there, on an average, once a week perhaps from fall to spring, sometimes oftener; can't say that I ever saw any dead animals in the pond; don't know whether the pond is supplied by springs or not; don't know that I could say it was fit for any purpose; I would not drink it if I could get better.

Cross-examined.—Don't know but I am one of the malsters on the hill that has sued Mr. Delavan for this publication; a suit has been entered. I have known the pond since 1831, not as familiary as before; my business has been ever since on the hill; I am still a malster; don't know that I ever examined the pond particularly in summer and fall; never had occasion to go to it in the fall; I think I have seen it when there was not a stream running out of it. Did not get all or the principal part of the water I used in malting and brewing, from the pond, between '30 and '31; quite a small proportion of it; did not get any after '31; not sure that we got any in the spring of 1831; In the fall and winter of '30 we got some; and we might have got it in the spring of '31, but I am not positive. Very likely I have seen Mr. Taylor about his malt-house; no question but that I have seen him; I have frequently seen him about the malting season, about the malt-house.

Mr. HANCOCK, *re-called.*—*Cross-examined*—by defendant's counsel: I think I have seen the water of the pond carted to the plaintiff's malt-house—wont be positive; I have seen it carted to different malt-houses, and I think I have seen it carted to Mr. Taylor's; I have seen them letting the water run into his malt-house at the north end; I don't know that the water was taken from this pond; I thought they might use better water; I have seen water taken from the pond, which I supposed was going to the malt-houses, which was not bad; I do not say it was suitable for malting; it was water that families would use for washing; don't know what water is fit for malting; it was not fit for drink or food.

Direct resumed: I have seen water taken from this pond at different times; and I have seen them running water into Mr. Taylor's malt-house.

WILLIAM AMSDALE, *sworn*—*Examination direct:* I was frequently at Fidler and Taylor's malt-house on the hill, from 1829 up to and including the fall of '34; it was my business to see how they went on; I was the brewer; am acquainted with that and the business of malting; within the period mentioned I have not seen a great deal of water rode; but I have seen water rode there; I have seen this water very clear, and I have seen it somewhat riled, probably by the rain.

ROBERT CLAWSON (colored), *sworn*—*Examination direct:* For about 12 years I have been in the habit of passing the pond on Lark street, four or five times a week; I have drawn water out of the pond; I moved out to Mr. Van Vechten's farm about 12 years ago, and used to pass this pond going back and forth; I drew water from it about 10 years ago; at that time the water was as clear as you could expect such water as that to be; saw no dead animals in the pond—not one; don't know whether the water was used for washing.

Jonathan Sharp, *sworn.—Examination direct:* I guess I have known the pond on Lark street 16 or 18 years; have drawn water there summer and winter, both; after a heavy rain, it would be muddy; I have drawn it for malt-houses and to wash with, and for other purposes—making mortar; the water looked clear enough, unless after a rain; couldn't say that I ever did see dead animals in the pond; have seen dead dogs and hogs, and horses down on the other side of the bank.

Jonathan Gay, *sworn.—Examination direct:* Have known the big pond about eleven years; lived within ten rods of it part of that time; there is one spring, where the barrel is put into the ground, on the west side of the pond, in the bank; there are frequently small springs on the side. Before '36, the water in the pond was good; in the winter, clear and clean, and in the spring and fall, except in freshets, when it was riley; don't recollect seeing any dead animals in it; plenty of them on the other side of the road; have seen plenty of horses drink there; up to '35 do not recollect to have seen the water green.

John Anderson, *sworn.—Examination direct:* Have known the pond 30 years; lived exactly opposite to it on Knox street; I think it is all of 10 or 12 years since it began to fill up; have often been there; have bathed in it; don't recollect any dead animals about it; the water was clear and pure; I have used it in my family for washing; don't know that my folks ever cooked any thing with it; I know of two springs there; helped to sink the barrel for one myself; there was an outlet to it; have seen horses drink out of it.

The Defence resumed.

William White, *sworn.—Examination direct:* I am a brewer and malster; I am one of those in whose name a suit has been brought against Mr. Delavan for this publication. I commenced malting and brewing on the hill in the fall of '26;

continued up to the spring of '30, when I moved the brewing apparatus down, after the brewing season ended, to the dock; we continued our malt-house on the hill up to '35. I am a brother of John G. White, and of the other White sworn in this case; we were all in partnership on the hill. I was acquainted with the pond on Lark street from '26 to the spring of '30; after that I was not so much on the hill, and, of course, don't know so much about it. I have seen dead animals in the neighborhood of the pond. Have you seen them on the banks sloping down towards the pond? Inclined—yes, sir. What kind of animals? I could not say—a variety of them; don't think I could name any particular animal I had ever seen there. Could you have seen animals if they had been in the water? I think it never was transparent enough to see any thing that was in it, if it was under the water. Do you know of malting having been done with water out of that pond, in the condition you have described? Yes, sir, I have done it myself. Have you manufactured beer from that water? Yes, and malt too. Was the beer, made of such malt and water, marketable, saleable beer? Yes, sir, we have sold it.

The Court.—It was marketable, saleable beer? Yes. Do you mean good beer? Yes.

The court here took a recess until three o'clock P. M.

Examination continued.—You stated you had seen this water taken from the pond to the plaintiff's malt-house; did you see it going into the malt-house? I have seen carts frequently putting water in there. Did you see if it went into the vessels within? I have seen it go into the steeps; seen carts unloading water there frequently. What was going on in the malt-house, when this water was going into the steep tubs? They were busy malting when I saw this water rode, I believe. Were they making mortar or plaster at that time? No, sir. How frequently have you seen Mr. Taylor about there? I have seen him there frequently—not so frequently, though, as I have seen Mr. Fidler. About what time have you seen water poured in there? I could not say the particular time; it was during the season of '29 and '30, probably. Two or three seasons? Yes, I would put it at two seasons—'29 and '30—because in the spring of '30 I moved from the hill.

Dr. HENRY GREEN, *sworn.—Examination direct:* I have resided in the city twelve years, on the 1st of May; am a practicing physician; am acquainted with the pond on Lark street; whenever I have seen the water there (it is sometimes dried up) it has been dirty, filthy water; when low, it was still more turbid, and it looked very thick; I recollect once seeing a dead hog lying partly on the margin and partly in the water.

BARENT P. STAATS, (late Alderman,) *sworn.—Examination direct:* I reside in the city. Have known the pond on Lark street since 1814; I don't think it covered over half an acre then; I had occasion to pass it frequently from '21 to '32—a considerable portion of that time as Alms-house physician; I used to be out there sometimes three times a week; it was a dirty pool of water. I have seen dead hogs in it—dead geese; it is a goose pond; I have seen boys swimming in it—and I have seen geese and ducks; I have seen twenty or thirty geese at a time in it. The wash of the bones thrown out from the glue factory would drain off into the pond. Never examined it as minutely as I did in '32, (during the cholera,) when I was health officer; the neighbors supposed it contributed to the disease; it was stagnant, filthy water then—in fact, has always been; it was in July or August of that year that I examined it particularly; I thought that it had a bad smell at the time; at that time, I believe, the drain was three or four feet above the bottom of the pond, and, if I recollect, we ordered it to be lowered. Whenever there was a hard shower, and the pond filled up to the drain, it would run off; it never could run off except after a shower, for there was no

11

supply above that I could perceive; being lower than the hills around, which are clay principally, the water that falls runs down into it, of course. The principal sources of supply are from towards the burying grounds, from Spring street, from State street, and the road ditch from towards Paul Clark's; there may be springs there; I don't say there are not. There is a small stream from a little north of the glue-house, where the collection of bones is; I examined the creek in '32, near Buttermilk falls; I thought it infected then from the slaughter-house, which then stood on the Poor-house lot; at that time the water was bad; in a dry time the water is stagnant, standing in pools.

The Prosecution Resumed.

George Apply, *sworn.—Examination direct:* I worked in Mr. Taylor's malt-house eight or nine months in '33—from September or October to the latter part of April or May; the water for malting was got, exclusively, from the well in the malt-house; none was carted that season, to my knowledge.

Sanford Cobb, *sworn.—Examination direct:* I am acquainted with Mr. Delavan. What is he estimated to be worth? I have heard a great many estimates—I should say, safely, from 3 to $500,000.

The testimony, on both sides, here closed, and Mr. Wheaton summed up on the part of the defendant, when the court adjourned to Saturday, April 25.

Mr. Beardsley closed the defence to the jury, and Messrs. Reynolds and Stevens summed up on the part of the plaintiff.

The court, at 6 o'clock, took a recess until 7 o'clock P. M.

The Charge.

Judge Cushman then addressed the jury in substance as follows:

This action, gentlemen, is brought for two publications in the Evening Journal, in the month of February, 1835. They are alleged by the plaintiff to contain libellous matter, and he comes into court and asks, at your hands, a verdict for the injury he may have sustained. I need not go into a definition of a libel further, than to say that it consists in publishing or causing to be published anything calculated and designed to single out an individual, and to present him to the public in a ridiculous or odious light, or which imputes to him bad actions, or which tends to diminish his comforts or respectability.

For such a publication an action lies; and the plaintiff is entitled to damages without proof of any injury; the law implying that the act was done maliciously, or with intent to injure.

The law affords to every citizen the free use of the press to publish for the information or protection of the public; but it restrains this liberty by requiring an adherence to truth; and without this qualification this liberty cannot be exercised with impunity. But if a defendant is called upon to answer for any published statement, it is a perfect defence to show that the allegations complained of are true.

The publications in this case set forth, having been proved, the defence relied upon is that the published statements are true; and the proof on both sides has been chiefly directed to that point. As regards the libel itself, I have looked particularly through it with a view to see what are the substantial charges. And here I would remark, that in order to sustain a justification of a libel, the party defendant must verify the specific charges he has made. If he imputes acts calculated to hold up an individual to public odium, it is not enough that he proves upon the plaintiff other acts of a similar character. The identical charge made is the one to which he is confined, and which he must sustain substantially.

In looking through the declaration, I find that these are substantially the allegations upon which the suit is founded. That so long as six or seven years ago the plaintiff's malt-house was supplied with water from stagnant pools, gutters and ditches; often in such a state as to be green on the surface; that such water for several seasons was collected and deposited in the malt-house for malting; that no attention was ever paid to cleanliness; that the water was often taken from puddles in which were dead animals; that when the water was low in the pools, holes were sometimes made in which a pail was sunk to get the water of which the malt was made; and that the sides of the pail sometimes came in contact with dead animals in a state of putridity; that water was carried to the malt-house which was nearly as thick as cream with filth; that the plaintiff relies on water taken from such places occasionally; that seven hogsheads were used in a steep-tub; and that ten or twelve inches of filth will settle on the bottom from that quantity of water. And the declaration sets forth that the defendant meant to charge that impure, dirty and filthy water, taken from stagnant pools, gutters and ditches, had, for years, been carried to the malt-house of the plaintiff; and that he had been guilty of using that water in preparing barley for malt.

The counsel here called on the court to state to the jury to what extent the defendant is bound to go to make out his justification. The defendant having charged that water was taken from pools, gutters and ditches, the point has been raised whether, if he adduces proof only of water having been taken from pools, it is a justification. Gentlemen, it would be a justification, provided the quality of the water, as to foulness, was such as to meet fully the description given of it in the publication in question. If the water is proved to be of that character, then—whether taken from one pool or two—whether from ditches or gutters—would make no difference; because, substantially, the entire allegation that is of any importance would be proved. So, as regards the hole charged to have been made, it is of no importance whether it was made through the ice or into the ground, particularly as the libel does not state which. The minutiae of the description are not material. If the allegations made, be all substantially proved, the defence is sustained without the proof of immaterial circumstances in the statement. At the same time, all the allegations as to the offensive character of the water that was used, must be made out by the defendant to sustain his defence.

It is for you to say, upon the evidence adduced, whether the defendant has proved the allegations made in the publications on which the declaration is founded. I shall not detain you by canvassing, particularly, the testimony in relation to the water from the Poor-house creek. It seems from the description given of the map, that there are two ravines meeting below the bridge. The northern ravine receives the wash of the burying grounds principally, and of certain establishments of a character to make the water foul. The southern ravine comes from near Wilson's slaughter-house; and these two form the junction below the bridge. Of course, as regards any evidence of water taken above the bridge in either ravine, (there being no communication above, between the waters of the two,) nothing in the one could affect the other. The proof is, that the principal part of water taken from the creek was taken above the bridge, from the south ravine; some of the witnesses took it from below. But where the testimony is confined to the taking of the water from the creek, without reference to either branch, it will be for you to say, whether the proof of the quality of the water sustains all the charges made by the defendant in the publications in question, as to the degree of its impurity.

Your attention, then, will be more particularly drawn to the state of what is called the big pond or pool. In relation to this, you perceive a very marked difference between the evidence on the part of the defendant and that on the part of the plaintiff. The defendant's witnesses in regard to the condition of that pool and the taking of water there, have been named to you, and elaborate and ingenious comments have been made by the counsel upon this branch of the evidence.

I, however, deem it proper to recapitulate a portion of the testimony, and to make some remarks as to its general character.

The publication being proved, the defendant calls witnesses for the purpose of showing that the publication is true, by proof that the water of the big pond, as it has been termed, was of the offensive character in every substantial particular described in the publications. That point the defendant is bound to establish in order to maintain his defence; and it is for the jury to say whether in this he has succeeded.

The witnesses called have been those who have lived in the neighborhood, or in the immediate vicinity of the pond; or who, residing in the city, have more or less frequently passed it; and, with greater or less opportunity, minutely observed the state of the pool and the drawing of the water. First, as regards the character of the water, the defendant has introduced Mr. Coulson, Judge Savage and others—some 16 or 18 in all. Mr. Coulson's testimony is distinct as to the offensive character of the water. His opportunities of observing he has stated to you. He had the glue factory mentioned. He described the water as what he called rotten water. In the fall, he said, the water in the pool was always bad and in a putrid state in warm weather. That during the whole year it was bad, except after showers. That the water would get green; and that putrid animals would be floating in it. That he has seen dogs and cats and hogs there; and a dead horse on the rising ground in the vicinity of it. That is his general description of it. Judge Savage states that he was in the habit of riding by this pond for several years prior to 1835. His statement is, that the water was always dirty—never saw it otherwise; that it was not in a condition to be used for food or drink; and that his horse refused to drink there. That he has seen dead animals there—dogs, hogs and cats, as Mr. Coulson had represented; and that he had observed this for several years, between 1827 and 1835. That is his representation of the condition of the pool. I have no desire to go through and state what each witness has said; but substantially each of the witnesses, Mr. Green, Mr. Middleton, Mr. Hughes, Mr. Wasson, Mr. Fassett, Mr. Lansing, Mr. Keith, Mr. Harvey, Mr. Ten Eyck, Mr. Clark, Mr. White and Mr. Staats, have stated that they have noticed there the dead animals mentioned, such as dogs, cats, hogs, and agree in the general description of the character of the water, slightly varying the language. Some describe it as stagnant, green, very dirty; others as green and nasty; green and filthy. Very impure, always (is Mr. Fassett's) at all seasons. That of Keith is, "pretty bad always." Harvey says, stagnant, dirty. Ten Eyck says, there was a good deal of stagnant water in the pool; has seen it very green; has seen dead animals there. Mr. Clark says, yellow, riley and muddy. Dr. Green says, dirty and filthy. Dr. Staats says, it was a dirty pool; when low, more thick and muddy. These are the general descriptions given by the defendant's witnesses of the water in the pool. Added to this you have the fact of the construction of Lark street across the ravine; thus, making a dam to catch the water that falls, or that comes from the melting of the snow during the year. You have heard the position of the ground described, and the testimony in relation to the question, whether the pond is supplied with springs, of the manner in which it is visited by travelers with their teams—by the hogs that were about, of the fact in relation to its being the receptacle of the filthy matter above ground washing into it—a depository for dead animals—a place where they were sometimes drowned. As to the quantity of water in the pond, the estimates vary. Some say a half acre; others, an acre and a half. Originally, it appears to have been a very deep pool; but subsequently to have filled up until now, it would seem to be entirely filled. After the street was made, a sewer was formed to carry off the water after rising to a certain height. The water passed off there in great freshets; and you have heard the testimony as to its passing off at other times.

The principal witness relied upon by the defendant to prove, particularly, the facts charged as to the use of the water, and whose testimony is more minute than that of others, is Chas. W. Harvey. You have heard his testimony fully commented on. It will be for you to say whether he has not described the water taken to the malt-house in all the terms mentioned in the publications. The particular term "as thick as cream," has been presented and urged as the language of the libel. It is not precisely that. The term cream is used; but the precise language is, "nearly as thick as cream;" and that is the language the defendant is bound to meet. The representation is, that water was carried to the malt-house nearly as thick as cream with fifth. The fact that water of this description was carried there, is to be made out in order to sustain the defence. You are then to look at the testimony as regards the taking of this water from this pool; (and Harvey testifies as to the fifteen or twenty pools,) and say whether its character, as described by Harvey and the other witnesses, presents to your minds, substantially, the same character of water as that described in the published statement. Harvey states that the water, where he obtained it, was at times offensive; that it made him almost sick; that he obtained it in winter and in the fall; that for three or four years he was thus employed at times; assisting his brother-in-law; that he went with the wagon to the malt-house where it was poured into the tub. Other witnesses state the fact, that water was carried from this pool to the malt-house; this witness more particularly describes the time. Mr. White and some of the plaintiff's witnesses testify that this water was taken to the malt-house, and during malting season. One of the witnesses states that he ran into the kiln to warm himself while the water was running in. The defendant relies on this testimony as evidence that water was taken from this pool and other places of the description set forth in the paper on which the trial is brought.

As to the putridity of the animals, the substance of the allegation is, that the water was sometimes taken from beside a dead body in a state of putridity. Harvey states that after cutting holes in the ice and dipping up the water, the animals would be drawn to the hole, and would come pretty near getting into his pail; and that when thrust off they would come up again. You are to judge whether this would be a natural movement, supposing the water to contain dead animals; whether the dipping of water from a hole in the ice would have a tendency to cause floating matter to be attracted to the hole; whether, if floating, the animals were probably in a putrid state. These are matters which you will weigh and decide for yourselves.

The plaintiff has called a number of witnesses to show that such is not the character of the water; and a larger number, it has been said, have been sworn on the part of the plaintiff than on the part of the defendant. The number of witnesses, gentlemen, is never to be the governing consideration in such a case. You are to look at the character of the witnesses for intelligence and integrity; how far they may be under the influence of bias or interest; the relation in which they stand, and their opportunities of observation. Hence the value of an open examination; that the candor of a witness may be noted, the manner in which he testifies, and his willingness to tell the whole truth. While, therefore, you are not to lay out of view the number of witnesses, you are to look to the circumstances mentioned rather than to the number, to decide upon the weight which is to be given to the evidence adduced.

Mr. Howard is called to meet this evidence. He was a co-partner of the plaintiff down to '32. You have heard his examination, direct and cross; and it is for you to say what is the bearing of that testimony upon the character of the water. His general representation is, that this was water that he did not intend to use. His effort was to get other water; and you have heard the testimony as to the preparations made with that view; the syphon, the arrangement with McNab, the pipes for the collection of rain water. He states that there was some water drawn in '23 from a distance. He, however, testifies that he did not know of any water being drawn from this pool. The most he has said that would indicate that he understood it to be so, is, that he had heard that some trifle had been brought, but did not know it to be the fact. Ward's testimony is a general negative, as regards his knowledge of, or direction concerning, getting water from the pool. The testimony of Mr. Helse, Mr. Lowe, Mr. Watson, Mr. Rull, Mr. Hancock, Mr. Scace, Mr. Toomay, Mr. Hood, Mr. Shufelt, Mr. Couchman, Mr. White, Mr. Haswell, Mr. Hilton, Mr. Clawson, Mr. Sharp, Mr. Bradt, Mr. Waugh, and Mr. Anderson, has been adduced, principally bearing on this subject. These, with three or four exceptions, state that they have had opportunities of observing, (some of them having lived just in the vicinity,) and affirm, generally, that they have never seen any dead animals in the pond. Scace says he has seen dead hogs there; others have seen none. Mr. White, I think, states that he has seen them there. Some of them state that they have drank the water; one or two state they have used the water.

Plaintiff's counsel insisted that there were five.

The Court.—I mean for family use. There are not five that state they used it, except for washing.

Plaintiff's counsel named five or six.

The Court.—I do not find it so on my minutes. I have condensed the testimony to ascertain the facts as regards the general character of the water. You, gentlemen, will recall and scrutinize the testimony given, and regard the opportunities of the witnesses for observation, and their descriptions of the water. One of them, Mr. Scace, spoke of it as pretty good water in the spring and fall; and several of them, as clear; especially in the spring. Several say they would not use it, except in case of extremity. Others say they have seen it taken away in a tea-kettle, and in pails, and for washing. Several have taken it for washing. Cattle drink there; and travelers very frequently drive in to water. Now, gentlemen, you are to take all this testimony, give it its full weight and consideration, and exercise your own good sense in relation to it.

There is also the further evidence of several witnesses who swear there are springs there. One speaks of three, others of two; some speak of them as living springs. Others say there was water enough flowing from one spring to fill an inch bore. Some testify that barrels were sunk there. One witness places it as high on the bank as ten feet above the surface of the pond. The pond is described as having a bottom of clay. You are to say, looking at all the testimony as to the condition of the pond in drought and in freshet, whether the water was supplied by springs in whole or in part during the period when used; or whether by the water that falls. For if the pool was supplied by springs, and water was constantly running from it, the quality of the water would be very different from what it would be in the other case. The witnesses testify that in dry weather the water in the pond falls below the drain. More of the plaintiff's witnesses speak of the continuance of the flow of water, and of the supply from the ravines, than of those on the other side. You are to ascertain the character of the water from the testimony, whether supplied from springs below or from water above ground. If the water contained the bodies of dead animals, left there to decompose, you are to judge what effect it would have upon its quality, either standing or running off. And you must find it to be of the character set forth in the libel to sustain the defence.

The testimony of Harvey, (who states the strong points as to the character of the water on which the defendant relies,) the plaintiff says should not be credited. The testimony insisted on as discrediting Harvey, is that of Mr. Ryckman and Dr. Hinckley; and Judge C. here went into an examination and comparison of the testimony of these witnesses and that of Dr. Harvey; pointing out wherein they differed or appeared to differ—leaving it to the jury to say what weight was to be given to the testimony of the latter in view of the fact that he was corroborated as to many of the main facts to which he testified by other witnesses, who must be discredited if he was.

As to the point whether the plaintiff was cognizant of the fact, that water of the description charged, was used at his brewery in malting; the Judge charged that the allegation, substantially, was, that the plaintiff, by himself or his agent, used such water in making malt; and that the defendant must show enough to prove the plaintiff cognizant of the fact that it was so used. It is not necessary (said the Judge) to prove that he saw the water put there, or directed it to be put there. You are to have testimony that satisfies you that the plaintiff knew that this water was used in malting. You are to look to the fact of the plaintiff's presence there, and his opportunities of knowing what was going on. It appears that the plaintiff was not as much at the malt-house as his partner. Mr. Coulson says he had seen him about the malt-house; Mr. White had seen him there; and Mr. Couchman had seen him there, he thinks, oftener than his partner, Mr. Fidler. This is the testimony relied upon by the defendant to satisfy you that the plaintiff knew what quality of water was used in preparing malt, and whence it was procured.

The plaintiff also urges that the fact is undeniable, that pure air and pure water are indispensable in making good malt as well as good beer; and that this should be regarded in weighing the evidence as to the fact of the use of foul water and of his knowledge of it. You have heard the testimony on this point and the comments upon it. The witnesses on the part of the plaintiff, with one exception upon this point, have testified that pure water and pure air are indispensable. One of the witnesses, Mr. White, used it to make malt and beer from the necessity of the case. From the evidence the plaintiff urges the improbability of the use of foul water with his knowledge, as the effect would be to injure his malt.

The testimony, gentlemen, is too voluminous to justify me in going through it all with minuteness; and the hour admonishes me that I should bring my remarks to a close. The question for you to decide is one of fact; and you are carefully to weigh and compare all the evidence when you retire to deliberate. The plaintiff alleges that the publications in question are calculated to do him great injury. The proof is, that the defendant is a man of large wealth. These are facts proper to be urged in reference to the amount of damages to be given by your verdict. It is also the rule, when the defendant in pleading, gives notice that he will justify the libel by showing it to be true; that this recharging the libel, if the defence fails, is an aggravation of the injury, and a ground for giving enhanced damages.

In every libellous publication the law implies that it was done with malice; and the plaintiff is not bound to show an injury in fact sustained, to entitle him to a recovery of damages. A reiteration of the libel in these pleadings if the defence fails, is a deliberate repetition of the injury, and justifies the claim for a greater amouut in damages.

Upon the whole proof, you, gentlemen, are to say whether the defence has been made out. If you are satisfied that it has, then the defendant will be entitled to your verdict; for any citizen is at liberty to publish truth, although it may injuriously affect his neighbor; and especially should this right be sustained, when the facts published, if true, ought to be known to the community at large. If the facts published are proved true, the law presumes the motive good. If these publications are false, a deep injury has been inflicted upon the plaintiff in his business and his character; and the pecuniary situation of the defendant should be taken into consideration in deciding upon the amount of your verdict.

In view of all the testimony in this case, you will make up your verdict; and I am persuaded that in coming to the result you will be guided by the single purpose of awarding justice between these parties.

The jury retired at 9 o'clock P. M.; and after a consultation of about an hour agreed upon a verdict, which (under the previous direction of the court) was sealed up, and handed in on Monday. The verdict was FOR THE DEFENDANT, WITH COSTS.

No. 9.

LETTER TO THE PRESIDENT

OF THE

WOMAN'S NATIONAL COVENANT.

SOUTH BALLSTON, *May*, 1864.

TO MRS. GENERAL JAMES TAYLOR,
President of the Woman's National Covenant,
Washington, D. C.

MADAM: The whole country is responding to the patriotic design in forming the "*Woman's National Covenant.*" In your admirable address, as president of the national organization, you state that in 1770, ladies occupying the highest social position signed a pledge to abstain from tea, as an example, and from patriotism. The present movement is more particularly confined to dress. Could the "Woman's National Covenant" now step forth on the platform of entire abstinence from *all that can intoxicate,* and add *it* to its pledge, and recommend to all classes of both sexes to adopt and practice it, can there be any doubt that a vast number would comply, and that manifest benefits to them and the country would result, in an economical, moral and religious point of view?

My especial object in addressing you is to call your attention to some extracts, given below, from an address of the Rt. Rev'd Alonzo Potter, D. D., LL. D., Bishop of Pennsylvania, as applicable to the question to which I have taken the liberty to call your attention; the perusal of which may influence your mind to consider this subject, and perhaps lead you to the decision that it may be an act of high Christian duty as well as lofty patriotism in pledging to abstain from all alcoholic drinks, whether pure or adulterated, imported or domestic, and by precept and example, kindly urging all others to do the same.

I remain, Madam, with great respect,
Your obedient serv't,
EDWARD C. DELAVAN.

P. S.—The chapter on CHARITY, by the great English poet, COWPER, in which he treats of the *World's Commerce*, is deeply interesting and instructive. (See extract at the close.)

ON THE DRINKING USAGES OF SOCIETY.

BY ALONZO POTTER, D. D., LL. D., *Bishop of the Diocese of Pennsylvania.*

"But what is the CAUSE of moderate or temperate drinking? Is it the force of *natural* appetite? No. Nine-tenths of those who use alcoholic stimulants, do it, in the first instance, and often for a long time, *not from appetite, but from deference to custom or fashion.* Usage has associated intoxicating drinks with good fellowship—with offices of hospitality and friendship. However false and dangerous such an association may be, it is not surprising that, when once established, it continually gathers strength; with some through engendered appetite, with others through sordid interest. It is in this way that *drinking usages* have become incorporated with every pursuit in life, with the tastes and habits of every grade and class. In the dining room of the affluent, in the public room of the hotel, in every place of refreshment, in the social gatherings of the poor, in the harvest field and in the workshop, alcoholic liquor was at one time deemed essential. Too often it is deemed so still. Many a host and employer, many a young companion, shrinks even now from the idea of exchanging the kind offices of life without the aid of intoxicating liquors, as he would shrink from some sore offence against taste and propriety. *Not to put the cup to your neighbor's lip is, in one word, to sin against that most absolute of earthly sovereigns,* FASHION.

Here, then, lies the gist of the whole difficulty. Fashion propagates itself downward. Established and upheld by the more refined and opulent, it is soon caught up by those in less conspicuous walks. It thus spreads itself over the whole face of society, and, becoming allied with other principles, is planted deep in the habits and associations of a people. It is pre-eminently so with DRINKING USAGES. Immemorial *custom;* the *example* of those whose education or position gives them a commanding sway over the opinions of others ; *appetite* with them who have drunk till what was once but compliance with usage is now an imperious craving ; the *interest* of many who thrive by the traffic in intoxicating drinks, or by the follies into which they betray men — here are CAUSES which so fortify and strengthen our drinking usages, that they seem to defy all change. But let us not despair. We address those who are willing to think, and are accustomed to bring every question to the stern test of utility and duty. To these, then, we appeal.

Drinking usages are the chief cause of intemperance; and these derive their force and authority, in the first instance, wholly from *those who give law to fashion.* Let this be considered. Do you ask for the treacherous guide, who, with winning smiles and honied accents, leads men forward from one degree of indulgence to another, till they are besotted and lost ? Seek him not in the purlieus of the low grog-shop; seek him not in any scenes of coarse and vulgar revelry. He is to be found where they meet who are the observed of all observers. There, in the abodes of the rich and admired; there, amidst all the enchantments of luxury and elegance; where friend pledges friend; where wine is invoked to lend new animation to gaiety, and impart new brilliancy to wit; in the sparkling glass, which is raised even by the hand of beautiful and lovely women,— *there* is the most dangerous decoy. Can that be unsafe which is thus associated with all that is fair and graceful in woman, with all that is attractive and brilliant in man ? Must not that be proper which has the deliberate and time-honored sanction of those who stand before the world as the 'glass of fashion,' and 'rose of the fair state ?'

Thus reason the great proportion of men. They are looking continually to those who, in their estimation, are more favored of fortune, or more accomplished in mind and manners than themselves. We do not regulate our watches more carefully or more universally by the town-clock, than do nine tenths of mankind take their tone from the residue who occupy places towards which all are struggling.

Let the responsibility of these drinking usages be put, then, where it justly belongs. When you visit, on some errand of mercy, the abodes of the poor and afflicted; when you look in on some home which has been made dark by drunkenness, where hearts are desolate and hearths are cold; where want is breaking in as an armed man; where the wife is heart-broken or debased, and children are fast becoming demoralized,— friends! would you connect effect with cause, and trace *this* hideous monster back to its true parent, let your thoughts fly away to some abode of wealth and refinement where conviviality reigns; where, amidst joyous greetings and friendly protestations, and merry shouts, the flowing bowl goes round, and *there* you will see that which is sure to make drinking everywhere attractive, and cannot fail to make drunkenness common.

Would we settle our account, then, with the *drinking usages of the refined and respectable?* We must hold them answerable for maintaining corresponding usages in other classes of society; and we must hold them answerable, further, for the frightful amount of intemperance which results from those usages. We must hold them accountable for all the sin, and all the unhappiness, and all the pinching poverty, and all the nefarious crimes to which intemperance gives rise. So long as these usages maintain their place among the respectable, so long will drinking and drunkenness abound through all grades and conditions of life. Neither the power of Law aimed at the Traffic in liquors, nor the force of Argument addressed to the understandings and consciences of the many, will ever prevail to cast out the fiend Drunkenness, so long as they who are esteemed the favored few, uphold with unyielding hand, the practice of drinking.

Hence the question, whether this monster evil shall be abated, resolves itself always into another question. *Will the educated, the wealthy, the respectable, persist in sustaining the usages which produce it?* Let them resolve that these usages shall no longer have their countenance, and their insidious power is broken. Let them resolve that, wherever they go, the empty wine glass shall proclaim their silent protest; and Fashion, which now commands us to drink, shall soon command us with all potential voice, to abstain.

When Paul appeared before the licentious Felix, he *reasoned* with him on *Temperance*. It is the only appeal I desire to make. I might invoke your passions or your prejudices; but they are unworthy instruments, which he will be slow to use who respects himself; and they are instruments which generally recoil with violence on the man that employs them. There is enough in this cause to approve itself to the highest reason and to the most upright conscience. Let us not be weary, then, in calling them to our aid. If we are earnest, and yet patient; if we speak the truth in love, and yet speak it with all perseverance and faithfulness, it *must* at length prevail. But few years have passed since some of us who are now ardent in this good work, were as ignorant or sceptical as those we are most anxious to convince. We then thought ourselves conscientious in our doubts, or even in our opposition. Let our charity be broad enough to concede to those who are not yet with us, the same generous construction of motives which we then claimed for ourselves. And let us resolve that, if this noble cause be not advanced, it shall be through no fault of ours; that our zeal and our discretion shall go hand in hand; and that fervent prayer to God shall join with stern and indomitable effort to secure for it a triumph alike peaceful and permanent.

It was a glorious consciousness which enabled St. Paul, when about to take leave of those amongst whom he had gone preaching the kingdom of God, to say, "*I take you to record this day, that I am pure from the blood of all men.*" May this consciousness be ours, in respect, at least, to the drunkards! May not one drop of the blood of their ruined souls be found at last spotting *our* garments! Are we ministers of Christ? Are we servants and followers of Him who taught that it is more blessed to give than to receive? Let us see to it that no blood-guiltiness attaches to us here. We *can* take a course which will embolden us to challenge the closest inspection of our influence; which will enable us to enter without fear, on this ground at least, the presence of our Judge. May no false scruples, then, no 'fear of man which bringeth a snare,' no spirit of self-indulgence, no unreasoning prejudice, deter us from doing that over which we cannot fail to rejoice when we come to stand before the Son of Man!"

WESTMINSTER REVIEW, LONDON, ETC.

This influential Review, in 1855, defended the moderate use of alcohol in health, as necessary, indeed, as food for the body. Prof. Youmans, and others, of the United States, and learned writers in Great Britain, exposed the fallacy of this position.

Now, in 1860, this same Journal magnanimously acknowledges that recent scientific French investigators of the highest rank, have exploded this doctrine, asserting that alcohol *is a poison*, and always pernicious as a beverage, in health. By the use of alcohol, they say, "*The pathological* alterations are *very vivid inflammation of the mucous membrane of the stomach.*"

"Very lately," says Dr. James McCulloch, of Scotland, "Messrs. Lallemand, Perrin and Duroy, in France, and Dr. Edward Smith, LL. D., F. R. S., in London, have published a number of carefully conducted experiments, and most important discoveries, proving that alcohol undergoes *no change in the body*, it being expelled unchanged by the lungs, skin and kidneys;" and that, in the words of Dr. Smith, "it *should be prescribed medicinally as carefully as any other poisonous agent.*"

The *British Medical Journal*, lately, in a leader, appears willing to accept the improved scientific *status quo* as touching alcohol. It says, "The subject of the use of alcohol is daily becoming one of more importance. The question of its influence on the body in health is being daily canvassed by the chemist and physiologist; and, *as far as their lights reach*, it would seem that not only is alcohol not of service to the body, but is actually injurious."

"That alcohol is poison, is an admitted fact."—*Rev. Dr. E. Nott, President of Union College.*

That alcohol, whether found in rum, brandy or wine, is "poison," is conceded on all hands. It is classed among poisons, because, says a learned writer, it is one of "those substances which are known by physicians as capable of altering or destroying, in a majority of cases, some of the functions necessary to life."—*Dr. Romeyn Beck's Medical Jurisprudence.*

The ancient Greeks, instead of saying "the man is drunk," were in the habit of saying "the man is poisoned." Our word intoxication is derived from the Greek word toxicon, which signifies poison. That eminent French physician, Broussais, about fifty years since discovered that, by the use of alcoholic wine, a diseased state of the stomach was produced. The late eminent physician, Dr. Sewall, of Washington, after deep study and numerous dissections, prepared a drawing of the moderate drinker's stomach, showing conclusively that such drinking brought on an incipient disease of the stomach, and if continued would induce diseases of various kinds, and ultimately, in many cases, death by delirium tremens. Those celebrated anatomists, Drs. Warren, Mott and Horner, of this country, at the time sustained Dr. Sewall in his position; God, the highest of all authorities, says "wine (intoxicating) wine is a *mocker*," not much, or little, but, "*it is a* mocker." No one can drink this mocker in health without being mocked by it, in the degree he permits himself to use it. The London Times says wine (alluding to weak French wine) is less poisonous than gin.

REV. DR. E. NOTT, LL. D. (*President of Union College*), ON THE ADULTERATION OF LIQUORS.

"Wine indeed, 'falsely so called,' we have in abundance, but names do not alter the nature of things. The extract of logwood is not less the extract of logwood, nor is the sugar of lead less the sugar of lead, because combined with New England rum, Western whisky, sour beer, or even Newark cider, put up in wine casks, stamped Port, Champagne or Madeira, and sold under the imposing sanction of the collector's purchased certificate, passed from hand to hand, and perhaps transmitted from father to son, to give the color of honesty to cool, calculating, heartless imposition.

"O! it was not from the vineyards of any distant grape-bearing country, that those disguised poisons, sent abroad to corrupt and curse the country, were derived. On the contrary, the ingredients of which they are composed were collected and mingled, and their color and flavor imparted, in some of those garrets above, or caverns beneath, the observation of men; caverns fitly called 'hells,' where, in our larger cities, fraud undisguised finds protection, and wholesale deeds of darkness are securely and systematically performed.

"I do not say this on my own authority. I had a friend who had been himself a wine dealer; and having read the startling statements made in public in relation to the brewing of wines and the adulteration of liquors generally, I inquired of that friend as to the verity of those statements. His reply was: 'GOD FORGIVE *what has passed in* MY OWN *cellar, but the* STATEMENTS MADE ARE TRUE, TRUE, I assure you.'

"That friend has since gone to his last account, as have doubtless many of those whose days on earth were shortened by the poisons he dispensed. But I still remember, and shall long remember, both the terms and tone of that laconic answer.

"Another friend informed me that the executor of a wine dealer, in a city named, assured him that in the inventory of articles for the manufacture of wine found in the cellar of that dealer, and the value of which amounted to many thousand dollars, there was not one dollar for the juice of the grape! And still another friend informed me, that in examining, as an assignee, the papers of a house in that city which dealt in wines, and which had stopped payment, he found evidence of the purchase during the preceding year, of hundreds of casks of cider, but none of wine. And yet it was not cider, but 'wine,' which had been supposed to have been dealt out by that house to its confiding customers."

Since the foregoing was forwarded to the printer, I have received the N. Y. Observer of June 2d. I make the following extract:

"THE LADIES' COVENANT.—A friend in Boston sends me a letter by Mr. Everett to Mrs. Quincy, in which the eloquent orator encourages the ladies to go onward with their retrenchment and economy, that they may be able to do more for the country. My Boston friend begs me to say a few words to help on the movement. Others have asked me how to discriminate between foreign and domestic goods; and this leads me to the only point worth coming to: and that is the duty of avoiding extravagance. Mr. Everett hits the nail on the head when he says:

'A reform is needed, on the part of both sexes, and in many things besides foreign luxury. Extravagance in the general style of living, in building, furniture, equipage, entertainment, amusements, hotels, watering places,—***extravagance often as tasteless as it is otherwise reprehensible***,—is growing upon us, and consuming, worse than unproductively, the substance of the country. The waste at a fashionable private entertainment would support three or four men in the ranks of the army for a twelvemonth, and provide for the relief and comfort of a hundred wounded soldiers in a hospital.' The Observer states:

"This is the doctrine. It is of little account for the women to retrench unless the men hold up, and *vice versa*. It is of little account to economize in foreign goods and waste money on domestic; and *vice versa*. Dress is not the only or chief matter about which we are to be frugal now. It is wise and patriotic to husband all our resources, and bring what we have, and what we can save, and lay it on the altar of God and the country."

Permit me to add: the patriotic ladies who have organized the "NATIONAL COVENANT" have set a ball in motion, which, I hope and believe, will roll on for good, until its influence shall be felt in every family, and by every individual having responsibility, whether in the dwellings of the lowly or wealthy, and until a judicious economy is adopted by all classes, by which alone, as I fear, can the national honor in its credit be finally established and repudiation prevented. The war ended, the Union restored, we shall soon have a population of thirty-five millions of people.

One cent saved a day by each in retrenchment amounts in a year to				$124,750,000
Two cents	do	do	do	249,500,000
Three cents	do	do	do	374,250,000
Four cents	do	do	do	499,000,000
Five cents	do	do	do	623,750,000

E. C. D.

EXTRACT FROM COWPER'S ESSAY ON CHARITY.

"Again—the band of commerce was design'd
T' associate all the branches of mankind;
And if a boundless plenty be the robe,
Trade is the golden girdle of the globe.
Wise to promote whatever end he means,
God opens fruitful nature's various scenes:
Each climate needs what other climes produce,
And offers something to the gen'ral use;
No land but listens to the common call,
And in return receives supply from all.
This genial intercourse, and mutual aid,
Cheers what were else a universal shade,
Calls nature from her ivy-mantled den,
And softens human rock-work into men.
Ingenious Art, with her expressive face,
Steps forth to fashion and refine the race;
Not only fills necessity's demand,
But overcharges her capacious hand:
Capricious taste itself can crave no more
Than the supplies from her abounding store:
She strikes out all that luxury can ask,
And gains new vigour at her endless task.
Her's is the spacious arch, the shapely spire,
The painter's pencil, and the poet s lyre;
From her the canvass borrows light and shade,
And verse, more lasting, hues that never fade.
She guides the finger o'er the dancing keys,
And gives difficulty all the grace of ease,
And pours a torrent of sweet notes around,
Fast as the thirsting ear can drink the sound.
These are the gifts of Art, and Art thrives most
Where Commerce has enriched the busy coast.
He catches all improvements in his flight,
Spreads foreign wonders in his country's sight.
Imports what others have invented well,
And stirs his own to match them, or excel.
'Tis thus reciprocating, each with each,
Alternately the nations learn and teach;
While Providence enjoins to ev'ry soul
A union with the vast terraqueous whole.
Heav'n speed the canvass, gallantly unfurl'd
To furnish and accommodate a world,
To give the pole the produce of the sun,
And knit th' unsocial climates into one.—
Soft airs and gentle heavings of the wave
Impel the fleet, whose errand is to save,
To succour wasted regions, and replace
The smile of Opulence in Sorrow's face.—
Let nothing adverse, nothing unforseen,
Impede the bark, that ploughs the deep serene,
Charg'd with a freight, transcending in its worth
The gems of India, Nature's rarest birth,

That flies, like Gabriel on his Lord's commands,
A herald of God's love to pagan lands.*
But ah! what wish can prosper, or what pray'r,
For merchants rich in cargoes of despair,
Who drive a loathsome traffick, gauge, and span,
And buy the muscles and the bones of man?
The tender ties of father, husband, friend,
All bonds of nature in that moment end;
And each endures, while yet he draws his breath,
A stroke as fatal as the scythe of death.
The sable warrior, frantick with regret
Of her he loves, and never can forget,
Loses in tears the far-receding shore,
But not the thought, that they must meet no more;
Deprived of her and freedom at a blow,
What has he left, that he can yet forego?
Yes, to deep sadness sullenly resign'd,
He feels his body's bondage in his mind;
Puts off his gen'rous nature; and, to suit
His manners with his fate, puts on the brute.
O most degrading of all ills, that wait
On man, a mourner in his best estate!
All other sorrows Virtue may endure,
And find submission more than half a cure.
Grief is itself a med'cine, and bestow'd
T' improve the fortitude that bears the load,
To teach the wand'rer as his woes increase,
The path of Wisdom, all whose paths are peace;
But slav'ry!—Virtue dreads it as her grave:
Patience itself is meanness in a slave;
Or if the will and sov'reignty of God
Bid suffer it awhile, and kiss the rod,
Wait for the dawning of a brighter day,
And snap the chain the moment when you may.
Nature imprints upon whate'er we see,
That has a heart and life in it, Be free:
The beasts are charter'd—neither age nor force
Can quell the love of freedom in a horse:

*The "Ladies Covenant" pledge against the use of foreign productions of certain descriptions and under certain circumstances.—Foreign nations exchange their commodities for ours, and the exchange is for mutual benefit; let our retrenchments be dictated by the most expansive benevolence, let us consider also the nations of the earth as belonging to one great community, and mutually dependent on each other. The laborers abroad (they are our friends and deeply sympathise with us in our present gigantic struggle,) toil at the loom, the forge, and bobbin, to prepare for us those commodities we want and they can make cheaper than we can, and let us in return pay them in our surplus of food, &c., &c., which we can produce cheaper than they can.

Should foreign nations combine against us, and agree to look elsewhere for *our surplus food*, what would be the consequence? that surplus would be almost without value. and so reduce the price of *what would be needed for our own wants*, that labor would not be rewarded, and universal stagnation, and panic would pervade the country, until *time* could remedy the evil, by an entire change in the application of labor. Let us put our faces like a flint, against all use of every article whether foreign or domestic *injurious in itself*, and without distinction between foreign and domestic, retrench in every proper way to meet the necessities of our country, now in its day of trial, and great peril

He breaks the cord, that held him at the rack;
And conscious of an unencumber'd back,
Snuffs up the morning air, forgets the rein;
Loose fly his forelock and his ample mane;
Responsive to the distant neigh he neighs;
Nor stops till, overleaping all delays,
He finds the pasture where his fellows graze.
Canst thou and honour'd with a Christian name,
Buy what is woman born, and feel no shame;
Trade in the blood of innocence, and plead
Expedience as a warrant for the deed?
So may the wolf, whom famine has made bold
To quit the forest and invade the fold:
So may the ruffian, who with ghostly glide,
Dagger in hand steals close to your bedside;
Not he, but his emergence, forc'd the door,
He found it inconvenient to be poor.
Has God then giv'n its sweetness to the cane,
Unless his laws be trampled on—in vain?
Built a brave world, which cannot yet subsist,
Unless his right to rule it be dismiss'd?
Impudent blasphemy! So Folly pleads,
And Av'rice being judge, with ease succeeds." *

* The traffic in intoxicating drink, as a beverage, always has been, and still may be, more disastrous to the human family in its wide spread influences and results, than the slave trade or slavery. The Rum Dealer not only holds the body of his victim in cruel bondage, but crushes out his heart—Slavery chains the body, but leaves the gates of Heaven wide open for the soul of the slave to enter—even tho' his body is striped all over, by the thonged lash of his task-master.

COMPARISON

BETWEEN THE

DANGERS ARISING FROM RAIL ROAD TRAVEL AND THE LIQUOR TRADE, ETC., ETC.

The English railways in 1863 covered 8,568 miles of rails and conveyed nearly a hundred and seventy-four millions of passengers, besides an enormous quantity of coal, cattle, &c. The money paid by passengers was £12,262,416; for goods traffic, £13,950,406—a total of £26,212,822. But in the same period the English people (assigning to them two-thirds of the expenditure of the United Kingdom) paid for intoxicating liquors upwards of fifty millions sterling—twice as much as the total receipts of all the railway companies—and then did a far more foolish thing by swallowing what they had paid for! Taking the railway system of the United Kingdom, it appears that upwards of two hundred million fares were paid by travelers in 1863 (of course the same persons often paying several fares), and yet only one person was killed in every six million of these journeys, and of these fatalities only one in every fifteen million journeys was caused other than by the fault of the traveler. There was one accident to every five hundred thousand personal journeys. If, as Mr. Buxton calculates, there are half a million drunkards in the United Kingdom out of a population, exclusive of young children, of fifteen millions, and if the losses by death (say three per cent) are made up by those who pass from the class of moderate drinkers into drunkards, a comparison of the risks incurred by railway traveling and by drinking will be instructive. The risk of being killed on a railway is as 1 to 6,000,000 journeys, and of being injured as 1 to 500,000 journeys; but the annual risk of becoming a drunkard in any given year is six thousand times greater than of being killed on a railway, and five hundred times greater than of being injured on the same in cases of conveyance.

No. 10.

TEMPERANCE OF WINE COUNTRIES.

To the Rev. Dr. E. Nott, LL. D.,
President Union College, Schenectady, U. S. A.

Paris, *May* 1*st*, 1860.

My Dear Sir : Since I last wrote you, I have had an interesting interview with Cardinal Wiseman, in Rome. I found him entirely posted up with regard to the adulterations of liquors, and the *baneful* influences they were exerting on the world, especially the laboring classes, and he approved a plan, which, if sanctioned by the Roman Catholic bishops in America, he said he would second at the Vatican. Other ecclesiastics in Rome, of high station, have promised to aid the measure also.

You will perceive by the English press, that the Chancellor of the Exchequer is making an effort to introduce weak, cheap wine into England, at a low duty, and then fill the land with additional licensed places to sell it, and this *as a temperance measure.* The total abstainers, as well as many others, are up in arms to prevent this, and they are bringing up their arguments and statistics to prove that, in their opinion, in place of being a "temperance measure," it will increase intemperance to a frightful extent.

The same idea prevails in England, as in many minds in the United States, that by the introduction of cheap and weak wines, intemperance would by degrees die out. Nothing, in my opinion, can be more delusive ; let the love of weak wine be established, then it will not satisfy, stronger will soon take the place of the weak, and then ardent spirits will follow as a matter of course.

On thorough examination, facts and arguments have established the truth, that all use of alcohol as a beverage, whether in large or small quantities, is opposed to health and life : the question is only one of degree.

Cardinal Wiseman, in writing on the subject, remarks :— "Though compared with other nations, the Italians cannot be considered as unsober, and the lightness of their ordinary wines does not so easily produce lightness of head as heavier potations ; they are fond of the *osteria* and the *bettola*, in which they sit and sip for hours, encouraged by the very sobriety of their drinks. There, time is lost, and evil conversation exchanged ; there stupid discussions are raised, whence spring noisy brawls, the jar of which kindles fierce passions, and sometimes deadly hate. Occasionally even worse ensues. From the tongue sharpened as a sword, the inward fury flies to the sharper steel lurking in the vest or the legging ; and the body pierced by a fatal wound, stretched on the threshold of the hostelry, proves the deadly violence to which a quarrel over cups may lead."

This statement of the Cardinal coincides with my examinations, and the experience of thirty years. Science and the Bible fully sustain the same great doctrine. Science and the Bible, when rightly understood (the Author of both being the same), are always in harmony. If the Bible sanctions the use of alcohol, or intoxicating drinks, as a beverage in health, then there should be an end of the movement in favor of total abstinence as a duty ; but I believe, and think you are of the same opinion, that the Bible *throughout*, is a total abstinence book, as far as intoxicating drinks are concerned as a beverage in health. If this view of the scriptural doctrine of temperance is true, is it not time that the Church of Christ should be governed by it? If not true, let the error be exposed, and the moderate use of alcohol, as a common beverage, be henceforth considered true temperance by true temperance men.

Rev. Sydney Smith declared :—" If you wish to keep your mind or body healthy, abstain from all fermented liquors."

Sir Henry Holland (his son-in-law) says :—" All men should, for health's sake, make at least one fair trial of abandoning the use of wine and all intoxicating drinks."

Lord Acton, while Supreme Judge of Rome (afterwards Cardinal), stated in a letter addressed to me on the subject : " I beg leave to state my opinion upon the proportion of crimes which in this country may be traced, for their origin, either to the immoderate use of wine, or to the too great frequenting of public houses. I think I may fairly record one-third under this head."

Lord Bacon wrote :—"Of all things known to mortals, wine is the most powerful and effectual for exciting and inflaming the passions of mankind, being common fuel to them all." Of course Lord Bacon doubtless alluded to bad wine—wine "the mocker"—not the wine of the cluster, the press, and the vat; and before "the mocker" had been formed by fermentation.

Milton asks—"What more foul and common sin among us than drunkenness? and who can be ignorant that, if the importation of wine, and the use of all strong drinks were *forbidden*, it would rid the possibility of committing that odious vice, and men might afterwards live happily and healthfully, without the use of these intoxicating drinks."

I find the following in a letter addressed by the Rev. D. Burns, of London, to the Chancellor of the Exchequer :—"The Archbishop of Cambray, in his 'Telemachus,' composed for the instruction of that young Prince, whose early death was considered a providential judgment on France, sought to convey those principles of government and moral conduct which should bless the French nation with a wiser sovereign than Louis XIV."

International peace and free trade, are doctrines of which Fenelon was an early apostle; and as to wine, what was his sentiment, founded on all he saw around him? There are two passages which answer to this inquiry. Adoam had described the happy state of the people of Bœatica; and in answer to the question of Telemachus, whether they drank wine, Adoam answered :—"They care so little for drinking it that they never wish to make it. Not because they are without grapes, for no soil produces more delicious ones, but they are satisfied with eating the grape, as they do other fruits, and they dread wine as the corrupter of mankind. It is a species of poison, they say, which causes madness. It does not make man die, but it degrades him into a brute. Men may preserve their health and vigor without wine; with wine they run the risk of ruining their health and losing their morals."

Quite as remarkable is the advice given by Mentor to Idomeneus :—"I believe, too, that you ought to take care never to allow wine to become too common in your kingdom; if too many vines are planted, they must be rooted up. Wine is the source of the greatest evils among communities. It causes diseases, quarrels, seditions, idleness, aversion to labor, and family disorder. Let wine, then, be preserved as a kind of restorative, or as a very rare liquor, not to be used except for sacrifices, or for extraordinary festivities; but do not hope to cause the observance of so important a rule, if you do not yourself set the example."

How surprisingly the evidence here recorded of the teachings of Fenelon, coincides with the opinions of Louis Philippe, and his son, the Duke of Orleans, as expressed to me in the presence of General Cass, our most worthy minister here in 1838.

I see that the Rev. D. Burns has recorded the conversation, in part, that took place at this interview. This important testimony has often been published, but in this communication it may not be out of place to give it again. I take it in the main from his letter to the Chancellor of the Exchequer :—

"How matters stand in France, more facts will show; and the authorities cited shall be the late King of the French, Louis Philippe, and his much-loved son, the Duke of Orleans. I was anxious, on the 19th instant, to place before you the printed statement relating to this circumstance, but it will be enough now to explain that, in the November of 1838, Mr. E. C. Delavan, a gentleman of New York State, visited France, and obtained an interview with the King, who, says Mr. Delavan, "stated expressly that the drunkenness of France was occasioned by wine; that in one district of his empire, there was much intemperance on gin, but he considered wine the great evil. I took the liberty of asking him if I understood him to say that his opinion was that wine occasioned most of the evils of intoxication in France, and was answered in the same words :—'The drunkenness of France is on wine.'

"I stated to the King that I had been outside the barriers, where the common people resort to drink wine, because there it is free of duty. 'Oh,' said he, 'there you will see drunkenness,' and truly I had seen it there, in all its horrors and debasing effects, and chiefly on wine. I told him my guide said that he thought one-eighth of the adult male population of Paris were drunkards. His Majesty thought this too great a proportion." The Duke of Orleans, in a conversation with the same gentleman, remarked, as the King had done, that he had no doubt that all intoxicating drinks are injurious as a beverage to men in health, and that the intemperance of France was on wine.

"He also stated that in those districts where most wine was made, there also was the greatest wretchedness, and the most frequent appeals to government for aid; and also, that so large a proportion of the soil was now cultivated for wine, that the raising of stock and grain was diminished to an alarming extent, and *that he looked to the diminution in the use of wine in other countries as a source of hope to France,* that failing of a market for her wines, the fields of France might be cultivated to greater advantage, to produce more abundant food and clothing for the people." I will add to the above statement, that the Duke of Orleans told me that the drinking of a single bottle of wine a day, by the soldier, it being weak, would do but little injury; but the use of this bottle stimulated the appetite, and the pay went to purchase more, the use of which caused breach of rules—and disorders of all kinds—then followed court-martials and punishments.

Louis Philippe, or his son, told me that raw silk, to the value of 100,000,000 of francs was yearly imported into France, which might be produced in the country, were not the soil monopolised to so great a degree by the vine.

How wise it would be in the Emperor of the French to discourage the replacing of the diseased grape vines with new ones; indeed, to discourage the cultivation of the grape vine altogether, except for food and other allowable purposes.

Such a course would, in my opinion, add greatly to the wealth, health, morals, and general prosperity of the nation.

Some articles in "Household Words," in 1854, on the workmen of France, described the lamentable influence of the wine shops; and in 1855, the Times' Paris correspondent stated, that on the 30th of October, the Prefect of the Department of the Sarthe had issued a circular to all the mayors of his department, in which he declared "the resorting to wine houses is deplorable in every respect, for there the

Government is villified, the health impaired, and the resources of the family foolishly squandered, to the detriment of morality and religion."

In the words of De Quincey, "Preparations of intoxicating liquor, even when harmless in their earlier stages, are fitted to be stepping-stones for making the transition to higher stages that are not harmless."

Smollett, the historian and novelist, found about a hundred years since, in the course of his travels, "that all wine districts are poor, and the French peasantry were always more healthy when there was a scarcity of wine."

The Count de Montalembert (and he a Frenchman, *ought* to know,) said in his place in the French National Assembly, 1850, "Where there is a wine shop there are the elements of *disease*, and the frightful source of *all* that is at emnity with the interests of the workmen."

In an article in the Magazine, called "The Work-a-day World of France," the following alarming picture is drawn of the condition of the French industrial centres :—

"Drunkenness is the beginning and end of life in the great French industrial centres. Against this vice what can the salaries of women and children do? The woman's labors help the drunken husband on his road to ruin. The child is born with disease in his bones, and with evil example before him."

"There are manufacturing towns (Lille for instance), where the women have followed the example of the men, and have added drunkenness to their other vices. It is estimated that at Lille, 25 out of every 100 men, and 12 out of every 100 women, are confirmed drunkards. Here there are even women's wine shops, where the unfortunate frequenters drink coffee and spirits, while their babes lie drugged at home with a '*dormant*,' as the popular infant's narcotic is called."

Well may the talented editor of the "Alliance Weekly News," say "this is a terrible picture ; and of France, too, the land of light wines, where Mr. Gladstone's Temperance drink is the cheap and abundant popular beverage. It is no surprise to us to learn that the mayors of manufacturing towns in France have begun to turn their eyes towards prohibition, as the only available remedy."

In 1833, Judge Platt, one of the Supreme Judges of the State of New York, stated in a public address, "*that when the public mind was properly enlightened, grog shops would be indictable at common law as public nuisances.*"

Chancellor Walworth, about the same time, in his annual address before the New York State Temperance Society (of which he was their first President), stated "that it was his opinion that the time would come, when men would as soon be engaged in poisoning their neighbor's wells, as dealing out to them intoxicating drinks to be used as a beverage."

Horatio Greenough, the eminent American sculptor, in a letter to me from Florence, in 1838, said:—"Many of the more thinking and prudent Italians abstain from the use of wine; several of the most eminent of the medical men are notoriously opposed to its use, and declare it a poison. When I assure you that one-fifth, and sometimes one-fourth of the earnings of the laborers are expended in wine, you may form some idea as to its probable influence on their health and thrift."

He also stated that the dealers in the weak wines, did not hesitate to adulterate them in order to add a trifle to their gains.

J. Fenimore Cooper, the American novelist, said:—"I came to Europe under the impression that there was more drunkenness among us than in any other country, England, perhaps, excepted. *A residence of six months in Paris changed my views entirely.*"

"Light wines," says Sir Edward Bulwer Lytton, "nothing so treacherous! They inflame the brain like fire, while melting on the palate like ice. All inhabitants of light wine countries are quarrelsome."

"Oh thou invisible spirit of wine, if thou hast no name to be known by, let us call thee DEVIL."—[*Shakespeare.*

In a former communication I described Piquette, or the ordinary wine (so called) of the country, as being a mere "decoction" leeched from grape stalks, skins, &c., after being drenched with water, and after all the wine had been trodden out by the feet.

In answer to an inquiry with regard to the *average* value of Piquette, &c., Messrs. Barton, Guertier & Co., wrote me from Bordeaux, 27th of April, 1860:—

"The wine vats of Medoc, produce, on an average, 40 hhds. of wine; each 63 American gallons, or 48 English Imperial gallons.

"The average value of Piquette in Medoc, and about Bordeaux, has varied, like the wine, 150 per cent. within the last five or six years.

"The Imperial gallon, without the cask, in 1853, was 31 centimes (about 6 sous), in 1860, 38 centimes (about 8 sous). Piquette pure, however, is hardly to be met with, and is replaced by mixtures of cider, rum and water, and all sorts of artificial beverages."

It appears from this that even the mild wines are used up by fabrications, and mixed with all sorts of artificial substances, and then palmed off upon the public and the nations of the world, as pure healthful wines. This statement agrees with that of the sculptor Greenough.

The French drink wine as we in America drink tea and coffee. No wonder that the great physician, Broussais, found the stomachs of most of the adults he dissected, in a state of disease, and that he came to the conclusion at last, that *that* disease was occasioned by the use of heating liquors. No wonder, too, that Dr. Sewall, of Washington, in his dissections, found the stomachs of even regular moderate drinkers of intoxicating liquor in a state of inflammation, and so recorded them in his admirable drawings of their stomachs. How could it be otherwise? Alcohol is as sure to make an impression on the stomach as on the face.

In walking the streets of Paris for weeks past, I have been much struck with the difference in appearance of the middle-aged and more advanced among the higher classes here and in Italy. There the use of strong drink of any kind is limited, and it is rare to meet a face among the class specified, indicating intemperance; here such faces meet you at every turn, faces not bearing the hue of health, but that hue which indicates the ravages of the poison alcohol.

"Alcohol," says Liebig, "is a bill drawn on the laborer's health (every man should be a laborer of some sort), which he is incessantly compelled to renew, as he has not funds to meet it; the bankruptcy of the body is the inevitable result."

Dr. Romeyn Beck, in his Medical Jurisprudence, says:

"'That alcohol, whether found in rum, brandy or wine, *is* 'poison,' is conceded on all hands. It is classed among poisons, because, says a learned writer, it is one of 'those substances which are known by physicians as capable of altering or destroying, in a majority of cases, some of the functions necessary to life.'"

I have no doubt the surface of the stomach of the regular moderate drinker of alcohol is always in a state of disease, and diseased in proportion to the alcohol used. It must be so, or Liebig and Dr. Beck are in error as respects the qualities of alcohol.

The diminished production of pure wine on the continent, and consequent increase of price, and the fear of being poisoned by fabrications, may have had some influence, not only in checking consumption, but in lessening crime and poverty to the like extent.

Then again, the recent great extension of the barriers here has brought all the drinking of the inhabitants within them; before this extension the laboring classes of Paris were in the habit of resorting to wine shops outside the barriers, where they could drink free of duty. Now these same drinking places are brought within, and when resorted to for intemperance, the city tax on the liquor is added to the price.

Having a letter of introduction to one of the most extensive vendors of pure wine here, he stated very frankly that wine was not a necessary article, but that, like Adam and Eve, we were all prone to do that which was *forbidden*. He told me that the wine introduced into Paris was not Piquette, but heady wine; that the fabrications took place in the city, and that he believed that full one-half of the liquor drank as wine in Paris was fabricated.

I have learned from another source, that pretty much all the common wine sold in the shops is manufactured in the city, and is of the most injurious quality, from the materials used in the manufacture, aside from its contained alcohol.

Families purchasing directly from makers of known integrity, are alone partially safe from drugged wine; and even *they* should be watchful as to the channel through which they receive it. The honest dealers find it difficult to carry on their trade in competition with the fabricators.

The wine merchant above referred to, stated that being ill, his physician recommended him to take his own Burgundy as a medicine. In place of taking his advice, he drank nothing but water for six weeks, and recovered. The physician was well pleased with the recovery of his patient, and that his remedy had been so effectual; but when told that water had been substituted for wine, he looked blank enough. Still no temperance movement opposes the cautious use of pure intoxicating drink as a medicine ; but, when used as a medicine, it should be abandoned like other medicines the moment it has effected the object for which it was used.

A gentleman told me that he drank strong beer at dinner by advice of his physician. I asked him, "How long have you been taking this medicine at dinner?" "Two years," was his reply. I remarked that I thought it rather a singular habit to take medicine for so long a time at the dinner table. After a moment's reflection he laughed outright, and said, "I will own up, I love it." Another gentleman of the same city called on me while here in 1838, and remarked, "I am 74 years old; I was in the habit of taking two glasses of wine a day as a medicine ; I gave it up because I wished to give my entire example to the cause of temperance, and much to my surprise, I found the disease left me I had been taking wine to cure." While in Rome I saw it announced that he had died at the age of 94. I know men sometimes live to a great age using alcohol, but they live on in spite of alcohol, and probably would have lived much longer without it. Let one case in a thousand exist like this, and it is constantly quoted in opposition to the only safe principle—total abstinence from all that can intoxicate as a beverage in health.

"Out of a caravan of eighty-two persons, who crossed the great desert from Algiers to Timbuctoo, the present summer, all but fifteen used wine and other liquors, as a preventive against African diseases. Soon after reaching Timbuctoo, these all died, save one; while of the fifteen who abstained all survived."

This wine merchant directed me to where I could see the results of wine drinking in all its debasement. I visited one wine shop with my guide last evening (Monday) ; I saw the proprietor, and told him that I was curious to see his establishment; he was very polite, and sent a person round with us.

At the lowest, five hundred persons were already assembled, and the people were flocking there in droves; men women and children, whole families, young girls alone, boys alone, taking their seats at tables ; a mother with an infant on her arm came reeling up one of the passages.

It was an immense establishment, occupying three sides of a square, three or four stories high, and filling rapidly with wine votaries. I saw hundreds in a state of intoxication, to a greater or less degree. All, or nearly all, had wine before them.

The attendant stated to me that the day before (Sunday) at least 2,000 visited the establishment, and that the average consumption of wine was 2,000 bottles per day.

This place was considered a rather respectable wine shop. My guide then took me to another establishment, not ten minutes' ride from the Emperor's Palace.

The scene here beggars description. I found myself in a narrow lane, filled with men and women of the lowest grade. The first object which met my sight was a man dragging another out of the den by the hair, into the lane. Then commenced a most inhuman fight ; at least fifty people were at hand, but not a soul attempted to part the combatants ; at last one fell against the curb-stone, I thought him dead, but he soon got up again, and at it they went.

I then entered into the outer room of the establishment, which was packed full of the most degraded human beings I ever beheld, drinking wine, and talking in loud voices. I did not dare to proceed further. It was much worse than the wine shops I visited in Rome, in 1839, when I was sent by Cardinal Acton, to see the result of wine drinking there. It is rather a remarkable fact, that in starting on my expedition last night, as I was entering my cab for the purpose, the very man who took me to that Roman wine shop, in 1839, was standing at the door of my hotel.

I asked him if he remembered the circumstance. "Oh, well," said he. "It was bad enough ;" and well do I recollect his having said to me at the time, "Let us go, our lives are in danger here."

I was informed by the cabman, that in the establishment last visited, he had seen from 80 to 150 lying drunk at a time ; that they frequently drank to beastly drunkenness, and remained until the fumes passed off, for if found drunk in the streets the police take them in charge.

Mr. Gladstone's plan of inundating Great Britain with French liquor called wine, at a low rate of duty, as a temperance measure, is calling forth extensive and thorough information with regard to the effect of the use of wine on the inhabitants of mis-named *temperate* drinking France. An intelligent Englishman, now engaged in making examinations with regard to this important question, has written a long letter to his correspondent in England, giving some of the results. I make a brief extract from his letter :

"That men—any men—can sit for hours drinking wine, of ever so moderate a percentage of alcohol, without perceptible effect, no one can believe. When, however, we find that the wine is not so moderate as is commonly supposed, and that the stronger liquors are pretty freely used, the effort to maintain a calm exterior becomes a more difficult matter. Anyhow, even within the early hours, the effect is apparent on not a few; while, as evening advances, the reign of Bacchus becomes more conspicuous.

"If not (in appearance) drunk, they are excited. If stupefied, they would be comparatively harmless. If maddened, they would be shunned. The simple Boor sleeps after his pot, and is wheeled to his bed. The whisky-loving Irishman flourishes his stick, and makes a clear course with all except another inspired one. The wine-elevated Frenchman is raised to the *dangerous point*—dangerous to himself and others. His passions are not drowned or enfeebled, but developed and intensified. He has had sufficient to *silence conscience;* but not to subdue reason. He is not bestialised but devilised. Such a man requires not to be placed within the sphere of temptation to commit sin; he carries with him a defiled moral atmosphere, and becomes himself the tempter. The principles of true honor are forgotten, and the claims of friendship and society are disregarded. He is prepared to execute any evil to gratify his own unholy feelings, provided he does not place himself in danger. Burning with base passions, he is not so lost by the drink as to hazard his own person, or fail to win his object by incautious haste. He is thus truly drunk in the worst possible degree—in the most dangerous sense. As I shall be hereafter able to prove, in my subsequent communications, the sad moral state of France and other continental countries, is more owing to alcoholic liquors, mild as they may be, than to all other causes put together."

I add from another reliable source :

"With regard to intemperance, it has almost become an accepted fact, that it is more prevalent in England than in any other country. *But we have only wanted accurate and reliable statistics to dispel this fallacy.* Mr. Jules Simon shows us that in the manufacturing towns of France, that hitherto accepted model of a temperate country, the working classes who inhabit the squalid lodgings of the back slums, are as violently addicted to liquor, as the most degraded of the same class in England. We can find no parallel in London to the picture drawn by M. Simon, of a Rouen wine shop. The workmen are no sooner let loose from the factory than they rush in a mass to the cabaret, while a crowd of weeping wives may be seen waiting for them for weary hours outside the doors. The apprentices, at the early age of twelve, may be seen drinking the coarse brandy, which they very aptly call the "cruel." As a body, these workmen and their families are feeble and sickly They die at a terrible rate."

Cardinal Acton stated to me in 1839, the Government of Rome had more to fear from the wine shops, than from any other source.

I am convinced that the Emperor of the French has more to fear from the wine shops than all other sources united. They furnish the material for riot and revolution, and the wine drank in them is the stimulant to every vice. Americans and others, visiting the fashionable walks of Paris and other continental cities, seeing but few staggering men in the streets, suppose, and honestly suppose, that wine countries are, in a great measure, free from the vice of intemperance, but it is a great mistake. I was told there were hundreds of such places in Paris as I visited last night.

I do hope that hereafter my countrymen interested in the question, when in Paris, will devote an hour or two on some Monday evening to the examination I went through last night. By so doing, they would, like Mr. Greeley, of the *Tribune*, help to correct a great mistake. I could not but wish last evening that Mr. Gladstone had been with me. Had he seen what I saw, I think we should hear no more of his Wine Bill, unless immediate income has more weight with him than public morals, which I do not believe.

Solomon seems to have understood this matter better than some good men of the present day, when he says :—" Wine is a mocker, strong drink is raging, and whosoever is deceived thereby is not wise." " Who hath woe ? Who hath sorrow ? Who hath contentions ? Who hath babbling ? Who hath wounds without cause ? Who hath redness of eyes ? They that tarry long at the wine ; they that go to seek mixed wine." And it would seem that Isaiah had witnessed scenes somewhat similar to those described, when he said :—" But they also have erred through wine, and through strong drink are out of the way ; the priest and the prophet have erred through strong drink ; they are swallowed up of wine ; they are out of the way through strong drink ; they err in vision, they stumble in judgment. For all tables are full of vomit and filthiness, so that there is no place clean."

If such facts and opinions as the above, from men who could have no motive to mislead, will not satisfy the intelligent mind of the fallacy of introducing cheap and weak wines into any country, as a *temperance measure*, I do not know what will.

BRUSSELS, *Belgium, May 4th*, 1860.

Being in this city for a day or two only, I have had no time to make any personal examination, but while visiting the Parliament House, I met with a very intelligent person, who gave me some information on the drinking usages of the people.

He stated that the principal beverage is strong beer, of which, at least 200 tuns are consumed daily in Brussels, each tun containing from 250 to 300 litres. Besides this beer, much French wine is drank, most of which is very bad, being falsified. He stated that a large proportion of the deaths here are occasioned by these drinks. Many will drink from ten to twelve large glasses of beer at a sitting.

LONDON, *May 9th.*

When in this city, in 1838, I attended a vast meeting of the friends of temperance from all parts of the kingdom, at Exeter Hall. After a severe and exciting contest, the pledge of the American Temperance Union was adopted by a vote almost unanimous. The Queen was *then* at the head of the movement opposed to the use of ardent spirits.

Since the adoption of the total abstinence pledge, I believe no organization favoring any other exists, either in this country or any other. The name is of little importance, the *thing* is everything; alcohol is the same poison, whether found in the wine decanter or the gin flask.

When alcohol in the wine cup was assailed, although the same poison as alcohol in the whisky jug, many, as you well know, walked no longer with us. I could give a tragical history of some who halted, while you and others went right on. Not a day has passed over my head since I was here, in 1838, that I have not felt deep regret that Her Majesty could not have seen it to be her duty at that time, to continue in the movement, and sanction total abstinence from the use of alcohol in fermented drinks, as she has from alcohol in ardent spirits. I pray she may yet see it to be her duty to take the step.

I have had a long conversation with one of Her Majesty's household; he spoke of the habits of the Queen and the heir to the throne, and as extremely moderate in the use of strong drink. I asked him what he thought the effect upon the world would be, should they adopt *entire* abstinence: his reply was, "mighty."

Last night was one of deep interest to me. At an early hour, I was placed, by the politeness of a member, in one of the best seats for listening to the debates on the floor of the House of Commons. The great discussion of the night was the Chancellor of the Exchequer's wine bill, to extend licenses to vend wine to all persons selling refreshments. The object of the bill was to bring eating and wine drinking into an indissoluble union. Had the bill passed in the shape it was introduced by Mr. Gladstone, I have no doubt there would have been 100,000 licensed drinking shops added to those already in existence.

The opposition to the measure was very powerful, and I suppose, for the first time, the principle of total abstinence was broached in Parliament. Very feeble, indeed, was the advocacy in its favor. One member remarked, "should the bill be passed, the drunkenness of Paris will be superadded to that London."

How I did wish men could have been there like Bishop Alonzo Potter of Pennsylvania, General Cary, Chancellor Walworth, and many others I could mention, to shed light upon this great subject; but, as it was, the Chancellor of the Exchequer trembled for his measure, and had he not promised to amend it in many important particulars, it never could have reached (I have been assured) its third reading. I send you the London *Times* containing the discussion.

The Chancellor of the Exchequer acknowledged that the whole question of license was involved in the discussion. I think, with him, that the question now before Parliament "does involve the whole license system"—a system honestly designed to check intemperance, but its *effect* ever has been to legalize and make respectable a traffic which, in fact, is a most intolerable nuisance, and the parent of every crime known to the courts. When the public mind shall be properly instructed with regard to the *results* of this system, pure minded law makers will as soon license men to go forth with poisoned daggers, to stab their fellow-creatures, as license them, with poisonous liquors to execute, and with unrelenting vengeance, on like unsuspecting victims, the same work of death.

Lord Chesterfield, in his address before the House of Lords, 125 years ago, touched the point exactly. He said: "luxury, my lords, is to be taxed, but vice prohibited, let the difficulty of the law be what it will. Luxury, or that which is pernicious by excess, may very properly be taxed, that such excess, though not unlawful, may be made more difficult; but the use of those things which are simply hurtful in their own nature, (intoxicating drinks as a beverage are always so), and in every degree, is to be prohibited."

I must in candor say that it is my belief that, from the peculiar government and stability of the laws in Great Britain, the rich blessings to flow from the total prohibition of the liquor traffic will be enjoyed there much sooner than with us in America.

I am rejoiced to find that the labor of instructing the public mind on this question is in the hands of men who will never relax their efforts until the work be accomplished.

The belief is becoming more and more diffused, that intoxicating liquors are never necessary or beneficial as a beverage in health. Their sale for such use is at war with the best interests of the people, under every government and in every land.

Physicians are greatly in the way of the total abstinence movement. I have hardly conversed with a moderate drinker, who has not opposed me by saying, "I drink by order of my physician." Even Mr. Gladstone, in defence of his own wine bill, read a note from Dr. Ferguson in favor of it, and remarked also that the same celebrated physician recommended wine to him in "no illiberal potations." (Now this same Dr. Ferguson signed a certificate, with hundreds of the most distinguished medical men in the country, giving it as their opinion that the use of even fermented drinks was never necessary, but injurious as a beverage in health, and millions of copies of this certificate were circulated in the United States.) Doctors ought, it should seem, to know better. Look back, my dear sir, to the end of many of the greatest statesmen in our own, as well as in this country. In how many instances have they been betrayed by the fallacy of the assumption that wine is a healthful beverage, into a practice which has proved fatal alike to their happiness and their virtue.

Surely it cannot be desirable to superadd to the miseries occasioned by beer drinking in England, the intense miseries inflicted by the drinking of the fabricated wines of France.

The more wealthy classes will not drink the kind of wine now about to be introduced; the object is to induce the middle classes to take to wine drinking as a temperance measure.

If the Emperor of the French really entertains malicious designs against England, to wipe out the recollection of Waterloo, and the thoughts which St. Helena naturally calls forth, I do not see how he could have his feelings more gratified than by deluging the English nation with his fabricated drinks.

I have no doubt, should Mr. Gladstone's plan be fully carried out, there would be more people destroyed by it yearly in this country than fell on the field of Waterloo.

It is a well ascertained fact, that there is not enough pure wine produced in France to supply the tables of the wealthy of that country, so that shipments of the "decoctions" called wine, as a general rule, will be of the most disgusting and poisonous character, unfit to be used by man or beast. Forty years ago, and before science had taught the secret of transmutation of drinks, and when alcohol was the only poison in them to be contended with, a man *might* live-on using them, "with all becoming moderation," for twenty years or so, without becoming a staggering drunkard; but now, since these scientific discoveries, it is a well ascertained fact in the United States, that on the *average* a man does not live over three years after the love of these fabricated intoxicating drinks has gained an ascendency over him.

Of all the humbugs by which the good people of England and America are taken in, there is none quite equal to the wine humbug. I find the following in the London *Times*, in relation to the individual who negotiated the Commercial Treaty with France (I only apply to the wine part of it)—"*To use a good old word, which in the days of Queen Anne was classical English, the Emperor has completely 'bubbled' him*"

The *Times* remarks that the object of the bill is to introduce a drink "*less poisonous*" than gin. Why in the name of common sense should Government desire to introduce a "poisonous" drink at all, and then commission men to sell it as a common beverage?

What are to be the remedies for the appalling evils, flowing from the use of alcohol as a beverage? for alcohol is the poison which causes the drunkenness of the world. Alcohol is, indeed, a good creature of God, but misapplied when used as a beverage in health, as really as laudanum or prussic acid would be.

The doctrine that the Bible sanctions the use of intoxicating drinks, as a beverage, has been the bane of the church, and has already caused the downfall of millions upon millions within its Pale, and is still leading other millions on to the same impending judgment.

The delusive doctrine, that the moderate use of intoxicating drinks as a beverage, is safe, and excess is only to be avoided, has caused most of the drunkenness of the world; this delusion must be expelled, or intemperance will continue to the end of time. The use of alcohol, as a beverage in health, is at all times, and in all cases, a violation of the laws of life, which are the laws of God; and so long as such moderate use of intoxicating poison is sanctioned, or winked at by the church, drunkenness will (though unwittingly) be sanctioned.

Temperance organizations have, through their presses and lectures, furnished the world with facts and arguments to show that there can be no cure for the mighty evil in question, but TOTAL ABSTINENCE; by doing which they have cleared the way for the church to come to the rescue, and carry forward the glorious work to its final consummation. This done, the church having spoken, and the national conscience quickened by her voice, the right kind of legislation will follow, and an end be put to the sale of poisons, which now (under sanction of law) is producing an amount of disease, poverty, taxation and crime, under the weight of which the nation, especially our cities, groan.

Even now the people of the United States are fully prepared for stringent laws against the vending of fabricated liquors.

Let *Congress* enact a law to have trustworthy chemists appointed in all our ports of entry, to test imported liquors, and if found to be adulterated, *condemned.* Let State legislators enact laws to prevent the sale of adulterated liquors, and to inflict severe punishment on those infringing such laws, and a step would be taken in the right direction; a step which, by the blessing of God, might prove the inception of measures destined to lead to the removal of the curse of intemperance, to the renovation of the world.

The use of tobacco in Europe is becoming as general as in America, and its effects are most manifest; the evil is second only to the use of alcohol, and if not arrested will, in time, reduce the people of Europe and America to the present condition of China and Turkey, through their use of opium.

The testimony of Lord Brougham is of great value with regard to the wine question. He has an estate on the Continent; he resides thereon a part of the year, and can speak from personal observation. I visited his Lordship in his castle in England; we exchanged views on the Temperance question generally; his mind is tending to prohibition. He asked me whether I thought strong beer injurious; I replied, "just so far as it contains alcohol and drugs; just so far I consider it injurious as a beverage in health." He gave three very significant nods to my reply; I concluded he understood the science of alcohol as well as Liebig. In an address before the society for the promotion of social science, delivered at Glasgow, speaking of the Maine Liquor Law, he says, and I think with great truth and justice: *

"At our last Congress, great attention was given to the important subject of temperance, and especially to the necessity of preparing public opinion for those *repressive* measures which experience daily proves more and more clearly to be required for lessening the consumption of spirituous liquors The great source of pauperism and of crimes has hitherto only been attacked by *palliatives,* and although these have had a certain success, yet if there be

* This letter was published in England, and a copy placed before each member of the House of Lords and Commons, before Mr. Gladstone's wine bill came up for discussion. Lord Brougham in his place sustained me as to the effects of the use of wine in wine producing countries.—E. C. D.

any means not exposed to serious objections, by which the evil may be extirpated, the gain to society would be incalculable. Remember the memorable expression of that great philanthropist, our eminent colleague, the Recorder of Birmingham, 'Whatever step I take,' says Mr. Hill, 'and into whatever direction I may strike, the drink demon starts up before me, and blocks the way.'

"This is a subject which, happily with us, has never in any respect, been brought within the dominion of party, either civil or religious. Such, however, has been its lot in the New World; and it affords the most remarkable illustration of the evils which afflict the United States from the practice of their constitution, maintaining in every part of the country an incessant canvass, caused by the distribution of patronage and change of offices. Every subject of a nature to interest the community, and thus to create a difference of opinion, becomes the ground of controversy to contending parties, and so the Maine Liquor Law becomes a question upon which Governors were chosen and removed. The evils which the suspension of that law occasioned in the great increase of pauperism and crimes which had, under its beneficent operation, been reduced within an incredibly narrow compass, but which now rapidly revived, so seriously impressed men's minds with the mischief of having made it a party question that a resolution was passed at the State convention against ever so treating the subject hereafter. Nothing can redound more to the honor of the American people than their thus firmly persevering in their just and righteous determination. But it is impossible to avoid feeling how great is our happiness in this country to be free from the influence of such disturbing forces upon our most important measures. We discuss them freely on their own merits, and apply to the consideration of them those principles which, on mere matters of science—but science reduced to practice—should guide the inquiry and dictate the conclusions. We are removed above the storms raised by popular fury, nor are ever stunned by the noise which the psalmist compares to that of the raging sea; and our vision is not obscured by the clouds which faction drives together."

Yours very truly, EDWARD C. DELAVAN.

No. 11.

[From the Albany Atlas.]

A THRILLING SCENE,

ILLUSTRATING MODERATE DRINKING.

Permit me to illustrate my views of moderate drinking, by relating substantially a thrilling scene, which occurred in a town in a neighboring State, while the people were gathered together to discuss the merits of the license question, and decide informally, whether neighbors should any longer be permitted to destroy each other by vending alcoholic poisons.

The town had suffered greatly from the sale and use of intoxicating liquors. The leading influences were opposed to total abstinence. At the meeting, the clergyman, a deacon, and the physician, were present, and were all in favor of continuing the custom of license—all in favor of permitting a few men of *high moral character* to sell alcohol—for they all agreed in the opinion, that alcohol in moderation, when used as a beverage, was a good creature of God, and also, to restrict the sale or moderate use, was an unjust interference with human liberty, and a reflection upon the benevolence of the Almighty. They all united in the belief, that in the use of alcohol as a beverage, *excess* alone was to be avoided.

The feeling appeared to be all one way, when a single teetotaller,* who was present by accident, but who had been a former resident of the town, begged leave to differ from the speakers who had preceded him. He entered into a history

* The *facts* contained in this article were furnished by this teetotaller.

of the village from its early settlement; he called the attention of the assembly to the desolation moderate drinking had brought upon families and individuals; he pointed to the poor-house, the prison-house, and the grave-yard, for its numerous victims; he urged the people by every consideration of mercy, to let down the flood gates, and prevent, as far as possible, the continued desolation of families, by the moderate use of alcohol. But all would not do. The arguments of the clergyman, the deacon, and the physician, backed by station, learning and influence, were too much for the single teetotaller. No one arose to continue the discussion or support him, and the president of the meeting was about to put the question—when all at once there arose from one corner of the room, a miserable female. She was thinly clad, and her appearance indicated the utmost wretchedness, and that her mortal career was almost closed. After a moment of silence, and all eyes being fixed upon her, she stretched her attenuated body to its utmost height, then her long arms to their greatest length, and raising her voice to a shrill pitch, she called upon all to look upon her. "Yes!" she said, "look upon me, and *then* hear me. All that the last speaker has said relative to moderate drinking, as being the father of all drunkenness, is true. All practice, all experience, declares its truth. All drinking of alcoholic poison, as a beverage in health, is *excess.* Look upon *me.* You all know me, or *once* did. You all know I was once the mistress of the best farm in this town. You all know, too, I once had one of the best—the most devoted of husbands. You all know I had five noble hearted, industrious boys. Where are they now? Doctor, where are they now? You all know. You all know they lie in a row, side by side, in yonder church-yard; all—every one of them—filling the drunkard's grave! They were all taught to believe that moderate drinking was safe,—*excess* alone ought to be avoided; *and they never acknowledged excess.* They quoted *you*, and *you*, and *you*, pointing with her shred of a finger to the Priest, Deacon and Doctor, as authority. They thought themselves safe under such teachers. But I saw the gradual change coming over my family and prospects, with dismay and horror; I felt we were all to be overwhelmed in one common ruin; I tried to ward off the blow; I tried to break the spell—the delusive spell—in which the idea of the benefits of moderate drinking had involved my husband and sons; I begged, I prayed; but the odds were greatly against me. The Priest said the poison that was destroying my husband and boys was a good creature of God; the Deacon (who *sits under the pulpit there*, and took our farm to pay his rum bills), sold them the poison; the Physician said that a little was good, and *excess* ought to be avoided. My poor husband and my dear boys fell into the snare, and one after another was conveyed to the dishonored grave of the drunkard. Now look at me again—you probably see me for the last time—my sand has almost run. I have dragged my exhausted frame from my present abode—*your poor-house*—to warn you *all*—to warn you, Deacon!—to warn you, false teacher of God's word"—and with her arms high flung, and her tall form stretched to its utmost, and her voice raised to an unearthly pitch—she exclaimed, "I shall soon stand before the judgment seat of God—I shall meet you there, ye false *guides*, and be a swift witness against you all." The miserable female vanished—a dead silence pervaded the assembly—the Priest, Deacon and Physician hung their heads—the President of the meeting put the question—Shall we have any more licenses to sell alcoholic poisons, to be drank as a beverage? The response was unanimous—No! Friends of humanity everywhere, what would have been your verdict had you been there?

ANOTHER.

I was well acquainted with a gentleman in the city of New York, many years since, of high position in the church, and social standing in the community: *he* commenced the habit of moderate drinking at a period of life when the effect was not perceptible to all, while it was to me, still he never went beyond moderation. He had six sons—all but one became drunkards and died drunkards; that one was discharged from a responsible public trust in consequence of his habits; this brought him to his senses, he reformed, and appealed to me to help to procure his restoration. I enquired of him the cause of all this desolation in his family. Oh! said he, "it was the habit of my father to give to his sons, after a certain age, before breakfast, a small quantity of alcoholic bitters, to give them an appetite, and on Sunday to invite each to drink wine to the health of father and mother." Let me ask, who is to answer for all this? E. C. D.

TO TRUTH-SEEKERS.

And does that blessed Book of books, which none
But bold bad men despise, its sanction give
To *poisonous* alcoholic wines? And
Can the Christian plead a Bible charter
For the use of that which history, science,
Reason, and experience, all combined
On amplest scale, have fairly, fully proved
To be inimical to man? Hath God
By inspiration taught frail, erring men,
To venture on an awful precipice,
Where danger lurks at every step? Hath He
Whose workmanship we are, no more regard
Or care paternal for his creature man,
Than thus to jeopardize, on ruin's brink,
The fair and beauteous fabric of his hand,
Whence shine creative wisdom, power and skill,
In lines of brighter hue than all the vast
Of nature's splendid scenery can boast?
Can it be thought that He, whose boundless love
Evolved Redemption's scheme of grace immense,
And laid upon his own all-potent arm
The mighty undertaking—can it be
That He approves the use of that which tends
With constant, uniform, and powerful sway,
To mar, pervert and frustrate all his work?
Did that same Jesus, from Heaven sent
On God-like mission of eternal love,
To spoil the powers of darkness, death, and hell,
And lift from ruin's vortex of despair,
A prostrate, helpless, dying, rebel world—
Did He, by precept or example, stamp
A signature divine upon that cup
Which, as 'a mocker,' sparkles to deceive?

Did He, the famous Galilean King,
When first he showed his wonder-working arm,
And poured the glory of his Father forth
At Cana's holy, blest, connubial feast—
Did He the copious water plenished jars
Defile with *poisonous adder-stinging wine*,
And palm upon that unsuspecting group
A *serpent*, sparkling in a raging cup?
And did the holy, harmless, spotless Lamb
Who gave his life for all, a ransom vast,
And seal'd with blood the cov'nant of his grace—
Did He the parting 'cup of blessing' fill
With *lust-inspiring* wine? Did He command
His loved and loving ones to shadow forth
His dying passion and undying love,
By drinking at his sacred board of that
Which, as a second curse, since the old flood,
Has spread a tide of moral pestilence
O'er all the earth; 'neath whose corrupting stream
PROPHET and PRIEST and SAINT have sunk o'erwhelm'd,
And with unnumbered millions found, alas!
Perdition's deepest, darkest, direst hell?
Nay, Christian! startle not; no sceptic's sneer;
Or scowl of infidel, or jest profane,
Is couch'd beneath the queries now proposed.
WE take with firm confiding trust and love
The sacred volume, and revere the page
Whose hallowed verities unfold to man
His nature, origin and destiny.
WE joyously adore and venerate
The God of Heaven and earth, and lowly bow
Before His throne, as suppliants for His grace;
With faith unfeigned we take salvation's cup,
And call upon the name of Him by whom
Redemption's price was paid for all our race.
It is because we thus revere God's word,
And venerate our Father's holy name,
And cling with faith and love to Jesus' cross,
That we would seek to *wipe away*
The stain, which infidels would be well pleased to view
Upon the mirror of Eternal Truth.—*English Publication.*

SCHOHARIE OYER AND TERMINER:

TRIAL OF JOHN BURNETT

FOR THE MURDER OF

GEORGE SORNBERGER.

Hon. Amasa J. Parker, Circuit Judge.

Solomon Pratt Sworn—I keep a tavern; the prisoner was there on the 24th of March last, George Sornberger was there also. *They drank together at my house;* they left my house together; I saw the body of Sornberger next when they were *holding the inquest; Sornberger staggered some when he left.*

Jacob Sanford. I saw Sornberger fall near Franklinton, and he pulled Burnett over with him.

Michel Sanford, the counsel for the defence, remarked—

"I harbor no enmity against Solomon Pratt, neither would I utter a word of reproach to wound his feelings or injure his character. I have been personally acquainted with him for a number of years, and believe him to be a good citizen and a worthy neighbor, as he is esteemed to be in his own community. But when, hereafter, he deals out to his fellows, *RUM, let him remember that his traffic produced this unhappy result; hastened Sornberger, unwarned, to the tribunal of his Maker—deprived his wife of her chosen companion, her children of their earthly protector, and brought this prisoner, if he be executed, to his untimely doom.*"

"It is an unrighteous law that commissions one class of men to deal out to another class an agent to produce crime, while at the same time it provides prisons, and affixes penalties to punish all such offences committed. *I hate this law*, and its miserable effects have led me for twenty years past to raise my voice in behalf of temperance. THESE LANDLORDS THAT DEAL OUT THE LIQUID POISON, ARE THEMSELVES RESPONSIBLE FOR THE CRIMES OF THEIR VICTIMS, AND IF THEIR LITTLE *BURNING HELLS* WERE SHUT UP, MAN MIGHT GO TO HEAVEN. Yes, the lawyers might plough, the clerks hoe, and the judges preach, if rum was banished from the land. The murderer is drunk—his victim is drunk; and ofttimes the jury and those assigned to try the prisoner are drunk. This mighty source of misery and evil is ghastly apparent every where, and notwithstanding the scene before us, and all that is daily and constantly experienced, there will still be found those disposed to continue its traffic."

Verdict, Guilty; Sentence, to be hung *by the neck* in the jail at Schenectady, on Tuesday, the 14th July next,—AND WAS SO HUNG.

WORDS OF WISDOM FROM GREAT AND WISE MEN.

REV. DR. LYMAN BEECHER, in a letter to me wrote years since: "Alcohol taken as a beverage, is always injurious in proportion to the quantity taken and the frequency of its use.

"Its use is therefore not only inexpedient as an injurious example, but is morally wrong, both as it endangers health, and exposes to the insidious dominion of a deadly habit, and countenances its production and use with all its sweeping desolations and woes.

"The use of alcohol, therefore, as a beverage, is in my judgment, both inexpedient as an example, and morally wrong as a violation of the obligation, to use all lawful means to preserve our own and the life of our neighbor."

President WAYLAND in an address says: "Can it be right for me to derive my living from that which is debasing the minds and ruining the souls of my neighbors? Would it be right for me to derive my living by selling *poison* or propagating the plague around me—or from the sale of a drug which produced misery and madness: from that which destroyed, forever, the happiness of the domestic circle—which is filling the land with women and children in a condition far more deplorable than that of widows and orphans: from that which is known to be the cause of nearly all the crimes which are perpetrated against society: which causes nearly all the *pauperism* which exists, and which the rest of the community are obliged to pay for; and which accomplishes all these at once, and which continues to do it *without ceasing?*

"Do you not know that the liquors you are selling will pro

duce these results? Do you not know that 999 gallons produce these effects, for one that is used innocently? I ask, would it be right, then, for me to sell *poison*, on the ground that there was one chance in a *thousand* that the person would not die of it?

"Do you say you are not responsible for the acts of your neighbors? Is this clearly so? Is not he who knowingly furnishes a murderer with a weapon, considered as an accomplice? Is not he who navigates a slave ship considered as a pirate?

"If these things be so (and that they are who can dispute), I ask you, my respected fellow citizens, what is to be done? Let me ask, Is NOT THIS TRADE ALTOGETHER WRONG? Why, then, should you not abandon it altogether? If any man think otherwise, and choose to continue it, I have but one word to say. My brother, when you order a cargo of intoxicating drink, *think how much misery you are importing into the community.* As you store it up, think how many curses you are heaping up together against yourself. As you roll it out of your warehouse, think how many families each cask will ruin. Let your thoughts then revert to your own fireside, your wife and little ones; look upward to HIM who judgeth righteously, and ask yourself, my brother, in His presence, before whom we must one day be judged, IS THIS RIGHT?"

"THE GREAT DISCOVERY," says a European writer, "HAS AT LENGTH COME FORTH LIKE THE LIGHT OF A NEW DAY, THAT THE MODERATE CONSUMERS OF INTOXICATING DRINKS, ARE THE CHIEF AGENTS IN PROMOTING AND PERPETUATING DRUNKENNESS." On whose mind this great truth first rose, is not known. Whoever he was, whether humble or great, peace to his memory. He has done more for the world than he who enriched it with a continent; and posterity, to the remotest generations, shall walk in the light he has thrown around them. Had it not been for him, Americans and Europeans might have continued to countenance the moderate ordinary use of a substance, whose most moderate ordinary use is temptation and danger; and amidst a flood of prejudice and temptation, urged onward by themselves, they would have made rules against drunkenness like *ropes of sand*, to be burst and buried by the coming wave. "Temperance Societies," he says, "have only made America truly the NEW world."

THE

LITTLE GOLDEN-HAIRED BOY

AND

HIS ELDER BROTHER.

FOUNDED ON FACT.

There were in a once happy family, two brothers — a promising youth approaching manhood, and his brother, a little lad, with golden ringlets falling over his neck and shoulders. They loved each other dearly. The little brother had a patch of ground set off for him in the garden. One day, his elder brother was decoyed into a grog shop near at hand, and persuaded by the keeper to take a drink of his "fire water." This little took immediate effect on his brain, and he was tempted to take a little more and still a little more, and then he turned for his home. Passing through the garden, the first one he met was his little brother with his hoe in hand cultivating his little garden. Prompted by the alcohol within him, the elder brother made some brutal remark, to which his little brother made a reply, which increased the flame rum had already kindled within him. In a fury he wrenched the hoe from the little one's hand, and with a single blow laid him dead at his feet. He too fell, *dead* drunk. The little brother waked up, doubtless in Paradise. The elder brother awakened to find himself in chains. "Why am I here and thus?" was his first exclamation. At the moment, he was unconscious of his crime. It is not necessary to describe the horror and agony of this miserable victim of the rum dealer. He was tried for the murder of his little golden-haired brother, and hung.

Question.—Was this youth the only guilty person deserving punishment? Let the children of District and Sunday Schools decide this question. Judges and Juries may be enlightened by their decision.

DEMORALIZATION OF THE REBEL ARMIES.

Those who study carefully every sign showing the condition of the rebel confederacy, that they may judge better of the time of its approaching downfall, will do well to read attentively the extract which we make prominent here.—*New York Times*, *Oct.* 15*th*, 1864.

[From the *Richmond Enquirer*, *Oct.* 6*th*, 1864.]

"Do you ask for an explanation of these rapidly occurring disasters in a portion of the State where the Confederates until the 19th ult., never suffered defeat? It is simply and easily given. We have two enemies to contend with in the valley, one of whom has never been beaten since Noah drank too much wine and lay in his tent. These enemies are the Federal Army and John Barley Corn. Sherman has been largely reinforced, and the valley is running with apple brandy. Here is the key to our reverses: Officers of high position, yes, of very high position, have, to use an honest English word, been drunk, too drunk to command themselves, much less an army, a division, a brigade, or a regiment. And when officers in high command are in the habit of drinking to *excess*, we may be sure their pernicious example will be followed by those in lower grades. The cavalry forces that had been operating in the valley and flitting hither and thither along the Potomac and Shenandoah, were already demoralized, and since their last visit to Maryland, they have been utterly worthless. They were in the habit of robbing friend and foe alike. They have been known to strip Virginian women of all they had—widows whose sons were in the army—and then burn their houses."

Remarks.—When will the world, especially the Christian part of it, learn the great truth, that all use of intoxicating liquor as a beverage, is abuse. Talk of "excess" in the use

NOTE BY THE EXECUTIVE COMMITTEE

OF THE

NEW YORK STATE TEMPERANCE SOCIETY,

On giving publicity to the controversy called forth by the publication of DR. SEWALL'S PLATES, *exhibiting the effects of intoxicating liquors on the human stomach, from* HEALTH *to death by delirium tremens.*

(See page —.)

The Executive Committee agree with Prof. Dean, that the line which divides temperate from intemperate drinking, "*has not yet been drawn.*"

According to Dr. Sewall, the taking "*a glass of mint sling in the morning, of toddy at night, or two or three glasses of Madeira at dinner, is* (in common parlance), termed TEMPERATE DRINKING, and as connected with Plate 2, in his work.

According to the London Press, the "*Standard,*" the taking of *half a dozen glasses of wine, a glass of brandy and water, or two glasses of ale daily,* IS TEMPERATE DRINKING.

According to Dr. Hun, *the drinking just so much as promotes the comfort and well-being of an individual, at any particular time, of which each person must be his own judge,* IS TEMPERATE DRINKING.

E. C. Delavan maintains (as Dr. Hun remarks), that there is no such thing as temperate drinking; that alcohol in all its forms is poisonous; that alcoholic drinks, when taken (in health), are always injurious; consequently there can be no temperance in the use of these drinks (as a beverage in health,) any more than of arsenic; or in other words, all use (as a beverage in health), is abuse.

Others, there are, whose definition would include a much greater quantity than either the first or second of the preceding definitions predicated on a *fixed* quantity is safer (and safer because the quantity is *fixed,* however frightful that quantity may be), that a definition predicated on a *moveable scale,* capable of a *progressive adjustment,* from the first inceptive sip, to the deep potations of the confirmed drunkard; a definition suited to every stage of inebriety, and which imposes no restraint on either youth or manhood, at any stage through the whole descent of that traveled road from total abstinence, through moderate drinking, quite to drunkenness.

of a poison? How preposterous! How fatal to true temperance is such a belief. About thirty years since, Lieut. Gen. Scott said to me, I had rather march at the head of 5,000 thorough total abstinence men, against 20,000 topers or drinkers of strong drink, than against 20,000 topers, with 20,000 topers. This government now, by laws of Congress, allow no spirit rations in the army or navy. How far our recent victories can be attributed to this prohibition, Lieut. Gen. Grant can tell better than I. EDWARD C. DELAVAN.

October 18th, 1864.

FRANKLIN A WATER DRINKER.

" My companion at the press," says Franklin, speaking of his life as a journeyman printer in London, " drank every day a pint of strong beer before breakfast, a pint at breakfast with his bread and cheese, a pint between breakfast and dinner, a pint at dinner, a pint in the afternoon about six o'clock, and another when he had done his day's work. I thought it a detestable custom, but it was necessary he supposed to drink *strong* beer, that he might be strong to labor. I endeavored to convince him that the bodily strength afforded by beer, could only be in proportion to the grain or flour dissolved in the water of which it was made; that there was more flour in a penny's worth of bread; and therefore, if he could eat that with a pint of water, it would give him more strength than a quart of beer. He drank on however, and had four or five shillings sterling to pay out of his wages every Saturday night for that vile liquor, an expense which I was free from ; *and thus these poor devils keep themselves always under.* (See Dr. Franklin's Life, written by himself.)

Remarks.—Dr. Franklin was not a " *charlatan*," he was not " *a fanatic*," he was not a man to teach "*fallacies*," but great truths. It is said the people of England drink enough strong beer yearly to float the whole British navy. There is no permanent strength gained in the use of strong beer or any kind of intoxicating drink. Their use, even in the greatest moderation, tends to weakness, disease, misery, poverty and premature death. " Perhaps," says the New York Observer, the best definition of the *brink of ruin*, is the *brink of the goblet.*"

E. C. D.

No. 12.

LETTER

FROM

MR. DELAVAN TO GOVERNOR KING.

OFFICE NEW YORK STATE TEMPERANCE SOCIETY,
Albany, N. Y., January 21st, 1857.

To His Excellency, JOHN A. KING,
Governor of the State of New York:

DEAR SIR—Your elevation to the high and responsible station of the Chief Magistrate of the Empire State, so greatly multiplies your influence over all classes and ages of your fellow-citizens, that I confess myself desirous that your sympathies and active co-operation should be enlisted on the side of the cause of Temperance. With this motive, I take the liberty to ask you to read this communication, which cites a part of the proofs that this movement has already achieved very considerable results for the public good. I lay these facts before you with more encouragement and hope, because I am of the impression that, to statements which are honestly submitted, you will listen with candor, even when you are not prepared to endorse the reasoning and inferences which accompany them. It is by calm and kind appeals to the judgments and consciences of men, that so many, both of the humble and the great, have been brought to advocate and support the cause of Abstinence and Prohibition. And it is on such means that the friends of the cause should rely to bring distinguished public men, like your Excellency, among the number.

LETTER FROM MR. DELAVAN

EFFECTS OF PROHIBITION ON CRIME IN NEW YORK.

When some of our opponents survey the field as it is now, they say that there never was more selling in the State than at present, and that therefore all the efforts of Temperance men have wrought no good, but have made even matters worse. But this is not fair. They should revert to the period when the Prohibitory Law was in force, by which the commitments for crime in this State were reduced two-fifths from the number under the License Law. The operations of the Prohibitory Law were such, that during the six months after it came in force, there were in nine counties but 2898 commitments for crime, compared with 4960 in the same counties during the same period under the License Law. The fearful and sudden increase in drunkenness since that law was laid prostrate, so far from proving that the efforts of Temperance men are of no avail, only demonstrates the deplorable effects of thwarting those efforts. For if that law had been sustained by the Court of Appeals, as it had already been by a majority of the Judges of the Supreme Court, what a vast abatement would it by this time have wrought in Intemperance, Pauperism and Crime! And perhaps the disastrous consequences which resulted from annulling that law were necessary to work a complete conviction of the wisdom and policy of Prohibition.

But the enactment, and the temporary enforcement of the Prohibitory Law in this State, and the enactment and permanent enforcement of such a law in Connecticut, Vermont, New Hampshire, and other States, is only one of the fruits of the Temperance Reform.

It was stated by the Executive Committee of this Society, in their Report* to the Meeting on the 18th of December, that "during the twenty-nine years since your Society was organized, such a reformation has been wrought in the habits of the civilized world as has never before been witnessed in the same length of time." I think that facts will fully bear out this statement.

LIQUORS ON THE TABLE AND SIDE-BOARD.

1 When the Temperance Reform began, thirty years ago,

* See *Prohibitionist* for December, 1856, p. 90, vol. iii.

every family who could afford it had intoxicating liquors on the table and side-board. These included not only wine, but brandy and rum. Every guest and every caller was invited to drink, and it was about as uncivil not to drink as not to invite to drink. In this respect the usages of society have undergone a striking change. The family tables which have liquors are now the exception. In many of these cases they are furnished only when guests are present, and the liquors are almost universally limited to wines.

DRINKING USAGES AMONG FARMERS.

2. Hardly a farm in the land was worked without spirits; and such a case was a matter of remark, and was pointed to as an evidence of niggardliness in the owner. It would now be a matter of unfavorable remark, if a farmer should furnish his workmen with intoxicating liquors. Not one in a thousand, if one in ten thousand does it.

3. Every farmer, having an orchard, had a cider mill, or used his neighbor's. Cider was as plenty in the farmer's cellar, as water in his well; and it was drank in place of water by men, women and children. The falling off in the use of cider is, of itself, a striking and conclusive proof of the revolution which the Temperance Reform has wrought in the drinking usages of society.

4. Intoxicating liquors were almost universally brought into our workshops. Now, almost never.

AMONG SAILORS AND TRAVELERS.

5. Time was when nearly every merchant vessel which sailed on the ocean, the rivers or lakes, furnished spirit rations to the men. I doubt if any do so now. This change is very marked as to fishery and whaling ships; a class of facts which, a mutual friend informs me, your Excellency is well acquainted with.

6. When the ocean steamships began to cross the Atlantic, their tables were supplied with spirits as free as water. This was the case in the Great Western, when I crossed in her, in one of her earliest voyages, in 1839. When off Great Britain the passengers held a meeting (Lord Lennox in the chair), and, to the number of one hundred and twenty, signed a petition to the owners, at Bristol, requesting them to discon-

tinue this custom. It happened to the undersigned, to be appointed to present said petition. I did so; and the liquors disappeared thereafter from the table. I believe every steamship now adopts the same rule.

7. At the period referred to, there was not a hotel table or steamboat table at which ardent spirits were not furnished *free*. It would have been considered as unfurnished, as if it was without bread or salt. Now there is not a public table in the land where intoxicating liquor is furnished gratuitously. And probably not one person out of twenty, at our public tables, calls for such liquors.

REFORMATION OF THE DRUNKARD.

8. When the reform began, it was thought that moderation would save the drunkard. Since that time, even temperance advocates have supposed that the avoidance of ardent spirits would save him. Now it is pretty generally admitted, on all hands, that the drunkard is safe only when he abstains entirely from all liquors, wines included. It being admitted that abstinence is of vital consequence to the drunkard, it follows that it is the duty of others to abstain, so as not only to remove every temptation, but to strengthen him by the force of example.

9. The testimony of convicts that their crime began with drink; and of drunkards generally, that they learned the habit from their parents, or from the example of professing Christians, have united with science to impress upon all parents, and all good men, the solemn conviction that as Abstinence is the only safe practice for themselves, so it is the only proper example for others.

PUBLIC SENTIMENT AS TO THEIR HEALTHFULNESS.

10. The belief that all use of intoxicating liquors as a beverage is injurious, and never beneficial, has pretty generally taken the place of the idea that the moderate use of it is safe, and almost entirely of the error that such liquors are essential to health as a beverage.

11. Since the Temperance agitation commenced, the most eminent physicians of this and other countries have declared by thousands that intoxicating liquors are not only unnecessary as a beverage, but positively injurious. That

even in sickness it is rarely necessary; while in health it is always injurious, impairing the functions of the brain, the stomach, and indeed the whole human organism.*

IN CONNECTION WITH RELIGIOUS SOLEMNITIES.

12. Thirty years ago, liquors were brought forward as a matter of course, at weddings, at christenings, and even at funerals. After burial, the friends returned to the house of the mourners to drink. Now intoxicating liquors are the exception at weddings, seldom furnished at christenings, and almost never at funerals.

13. It used to be thought that the Bible favored the use of intoxicating liquors as a beverage. Now the idea is extensively prevalent that where the Bible approves of wine as a beverage, it means the unintoxicating wine of the cluster, the press, and the vat, while intoxicating wine is condemned as "the mocker."

14. When fifteeen years ago I instituted an inquiry as to the kind of wine, intoxicating or unintoxicating, which it was proper to be used at the Communion, great numbers of church members were sorely troubled for fear of harm to the solemn rites of Religion. Very many journals, both religious and political, denounced the movement. Within a few months I have caused, on my own responsibility, some 20,000 pamphlets to be issued on the same subject, and not one word of disapprobation has yet reached me.

HABITS AND SENTIMENTS OF THE CLERGY.

15. An aged Divine, now living, well acquainted with the clergy in Albany and vicinity, once drew my attention to the fact that, some thirty years ago, every clergyman when he

* Since this letter was written, the following resolution, which goes beyond any expression which has heretofore emanated from any large body of the Faculty, was passed unanimously by the Medical Society of the State of New York, 4th February, 1857:

"*Resolved*—That in view of the ravages made upon the morals, health and property of the people of this State by the use of Alcoholic drinks, it is the opinion of this Medical Society that the moral, sanitary and pecuniary condition of the State would be promoted by the passage of a Prohibitory Liquor Law."

For a detailed account of this important event in the Temperance world, and which, strange to say, was not even mentioned in any newspaper report of the society's proceedings, see the *Prohibitionist* for March, 1857, vol. iv., p. 20.

made his pastoral visits was invited to drink. If he visited twenty of his parishioners, he was invited to drink, and sometimes did drink, twenty times. The same Divine found that fifty per cent. of the clergy, within a circuit of fifty miles, died drunkards.* Now it is only a small proportion of the clergy who drink a drop; and those who do drink show themselves extremely sensitive when the fact is alluded to in print, as if they regarded it as a reflection upon their standing as Ministers of the Gospel.

16. It is thirty years since, at a large assembly of the Ministers of the Gospel, in New England, one of their number, impressed with the evils of the Drink-System, urged them to adopt a resolution pledging themselves to abstain—not from wines—but from Ardent Spirits, while at the convention. It failed. These pious and devoted clergymen could not see why they should be called upon to give up a "good creature of God." Now there are vast religious bodies, who, were they to see one of their ministers drink intoxicating liquors, would be affected almost as much as if they were to hear him swear.

FASHION—THE PRESS.

17. Though few of the rich and fashionable have openly professed adherence to the Temperance cause, yet many now express their sympathy with it and are beginning to aid it pecuniarily, as a movement which inures to the public good.

*A writer in the New York *Observer* questions the correctness of the statement of an aged clergyman in Albany to Mr. Delavan, that a minister of former days was exposed in twenty visits in a day to twenty strong drinks, and that fifty per cent. of the ministers in a circuit of fifty miles were drunkards. As to the first, every man living, who was in the ministry in 1820, knows it was true. Good Dr. Fisher said, in conversing on this subject a little before his death, that it was the greatest wonder he was not a drunkard; he was in his early ministry so forced to drink, lest he should, by refusal, offend his parishioners. The mug of cider or brandy sling were brought out at every house. As to the proportion of intemperate ministers, this is, no doubt, in general, incorrect; though it was not, as can be confirmed by men living as far back as 1810, in some of our cities. And there was no reason why it should not be so. Ministers have the same flesh and blood and nerves with other men; and if they will drink poison, why should they not suffer? "Can a minister take fire in his bosom and not be burned? Can he walk on hot coals and his feet not be burned?" Thanks be to Him who takes care of his church, that the ministry have been pulled from the fire; though sad it is, that some are yet trifling with it, and are boasting how strong they are.—*Journal of the American Temperance Union.*

Many of our most distinguished citizens have lately given large social entertainments without wine; and this is not so significant, as that public opinion sustains and applauds it.

18. There was a time when the Temperance movement was the common theme of ridicule with the press. Now there are but few journals, even those which are opposed to Prohibition, which do not approve voluntary abstinence, and which do not compliment private citizens, or public bodies, who give entertainments without intoxicating liquors.

19. The spirit-ration has been abolished in the army. I am of the impression too that it has been diminished in the navy.*

MANUFACTURING ESTABLISHMENTS.

20. Before the Temperance Reform began, and while we were ignorant of the nature and effects of strong drink, Nathaniel Prime, Lynde Catlin, and others, myself among the number, formed a chartered company, with a capital of $300,000, for the manufacture of steam engines and other heavy iron work. Thinking to do good to the workmen, and further the objects of the company, we directed that strong beer should be passed, gratis, to every man two or three times a day. We soon found that our work was badly done, almost every contract was in consequence litigated in the courts, and the company failed; by which failure the company not only sunk the whole capital of $300,000, but (to save their own credit) ten of the stockholders contributed ten thousand dollars each, to pay off further liabilities, of which eight thousand dollars of my contribution (including my whole stock) proved a dead loss. On a review of the whole subject, I firmly believe that this catastrophe is mainly ascribable to the unfortunate drinking habits which, from the best of motives, we ourselves encouraged.

21. Another company, formed to manufacture nearly the same kind of article, and who employed about 100 workmen, had their attention drawn to the evils of strong drink among operatives. One of the partners drew up a Total Abstinence Pledge, signed it, and induced nearly every workman to adopt the same principle. When the step was taken, hardly one of the workmen was beforehand in the world, and many were in debt. After four years upon the Temperance princi

* Now in the navy.

ple, none were in debt, and many had bought lots of land, and erected cottages for their families; and one of the partners told me that the aggregate amount saved by these 100 men during the four years since they abandoned strong drink, would make capital enough to carry on the business operations of the company.

EFFECTS OF THE REFORM ON NATIONAL WEALTH.

22. A manufacturer who employed 300 hands, informed me that after they all, or nearly all, adopted the Total Abstinence principle, the prosperity of the establishment was vastly promoted, and that their improved steadiness, fidelity and style of workmanship were as good to him as a protective duty of twenty-five per cent. At this rate, what sums have accrued to the National wealth from the adoption of Temperance principles by the hundreds of thousands of abstainers!

23. The late Abbott Lawrence, that merchant prince and public benefactor, and late United States Minister to the Court of St. James, was asked before he died, what had occasioned the great increase of wealth and prosperity in the United States? He instantly replied: "Our prosperity, in my opinion, is greatly owing to the Temperance Reformation. The influence of this movement is felt in the workshop, on the farm, and in every branch of human industry. Before the Temperance Reform was started, a vast number of the farms in New England were mortgaged for rum bills,—now hardly one."

24. Until the subject of Temperance was agitated, the frauds of the liquor traffic were not suspected. All liquors were supposed to be what they pretended to be. Now the matter of adulteration, though but partially understood yet, is the theme of common conversation even among drinkers.

25. When the Temperance Reform commenced in this State there were about 1100 flour mills, and more than that number of distilleries. The population has about doubled since that time, and now there are 1464 flour mills and only 88 distilleries. It must be admitted, however, that the distilleries now in operation are on a much larger scale than the average of those of the former period.

CLASSES OF DEALERS WHO HAVE LEFT THE TRAFFIC.

26. Of the great number of native citizens in the United

States who used to sell intoxicating liquors, a vast number have left the business. The Temperance agitation has *educated* them to regard the traffic as immoral and degrading. It is found in the great cities that seven out of eight of all who sell liquor are foreign emigrants. The great majority of those who now sell liquor in America are a proof, not that the Temperance Reform does nothing, but of what the moral sense of our countrymen would have been on this subject, at this time, had this reform never been agitated.

27. Formerly, church members and church officers of all our churches used to be engaged in the traffic; now, vast bodies of them denounce the traffic as an immorality; and the number of church members, American born citizens, who make or sell liquor, is probably not one to five hundred of the former proportion.

28. Witness, as a proof of the effects of the Temperance Reform, the growing idea that liquor when offered for sale, as a beverage, is a nuisance to be abated like any other nuisance.

29. What but the Temperance agitation has changed the policy of so many States; substituting laws aiming at Prohibition, in the place of laws which allowed rum to be sold by the authority of the State?

PROHIBITION APPLIED TO THE DRUNKARD.

30. Not only is the moderation theory now abandoned, and Total Abstinence held to be essential to the reformation of the drunkard, but Physicians,* Clergymen and Judges agree that Asylums should be established by the State for the resort of inebriates, where no strong drinks can be procured—which, as far as the drunkard is concerned (of whom there are over 50,000 in the State of New York), is an emphatic endorsement of the humanity and necessity of prohibition. The advocates of Temperance extend the same principle, and by a general enactment, prohibiting the sale of liquors throughout the State, aim to remove the temptation

* The following resolution was adopted by the Medical Society of the State of New York, on the 4th of February, 1817:

"*Resolved*, That this Society commend the object sought to be attained by the project for an Asylum for Inebriates, to the favor and earnest support, not only of the Legislature of the State but to the public at large."

from all who have this habit partially formed, as well as those who have it fully formed, and so, by the united influence of moral and legal suasion, aim to create such *an asylum in every household in the land.*

These facts and illustrations might be greatly extended, but I forbear. Enough has been said to indicate a vast improvement in the drinking usages of society.

THE NEXT STEP IN THE REFORM.

But it will be said, if the Temperance agitation has done so much, why not go right on in the old way, without a resort to legislation. The same question might be asked of gambling, of lotteries and of duelling. A stage is at last reached, where legislative enactments are essential. Not that moral suasion is to be abandoned, but, in addition to this, the public sentiment regarding these evils must be embodied into statutory enactments. Of this, those who have used moral suasion most, and with the greatest success, are the most profoundly convinced. After obtaining millions of signatures to the Total Abstinence Pledge, Ireland was ripe for Prohibition. But it was not applied. The golden opportunity was lost; and the consequence is, that nearly as much liquor is drank in Ireland now, as before Father Mathew commenced his remarkable labors. The language of this beloved and renowned Apostle of Temperance, penned a year or two before his death, and published in the *Prohibitionist* for July, 1855, should teach a solemn lesson to the world on the subject of Temperance:

"The question of prohibiting the sale of ardent spirits, and the many other intoxicating drinks which are to be found in our country, is not new to me; the principle of Prohibition seems to me *to be the only safe and certain remedy for the evils of Intemperance. This opinion has been strengthened and confirmed by the hard labor of more than twenty years in the Temperance cause.* I rejoice in the welcome intelligence of the formation of a Maine Law Alliance, which I trust will be the means under God of destroying this fruitful source of Crime and Pauperism."

The friends of Prohibition in Great Britain are now making up for lost time; they are pressing on steadily, firmly and perseveringly, and the triumph of Prohibition is only a question of time.

OUGHT NOT EVERY GOOD MAN TO CO-OPERATE?

When the Temperance Societies began, the general view of religious men was, that the work should be done through the churches. I submit that, in the main, what has been done, *has* been done by the churches. The Temperance Reform originated in the churches. If I may refer to myself in this connection, it was a devout and learned minister of the Gospel who converted me to the movement. If, since that time, I have been enabled to do more in my way than some of my fellow citizens, it is only because Providence has placed me in circumstances to do so. But it is the fervent, effectual prayer of the righteous, and the widow's mite, offered in faith, which points to the secret of the success of temperance. Nor can I ever review the history of this benign and arduous enterprise without being deeply and profoundly penetrated with the conviction, that the great motive power, from the first and always, has been the Grace and Spirit of Almighty God, as shed abroad in the hearts of thousands of His pious servants, both men and women, and who are to be found in all religious denominations throughout the Christian world.

It is the religious sentiment of the country; it is the divine principle of self-denial, taught by our blessed Savior, which has wrought whatever has been done for this reform, and which I have ever regarded as the handmaid of Religion. There are good men who still think this work should be restricted to the churches, or perhaps to their own particular church. I put it to their hearts, would they go back to where we were thirty years ago? Would they have undone what has been done? And ought not every believer in Christianity, to whatever particular church he may belong, to unite as one man—in pressing forward with yet greater vigor, with the united energy of faith and prayer and works, by his example, his influence, and by contributions of his substance—the cause of personal Abstinence and legislative Prohibition? And if this is true of the Christian in private life, how important to the poor drunkard, to his wife, his children, and the whole community, do such duties become, when, as in the case of your Excellency, the private citizen is clothed by the people with great authority and official power! So sacred and important are the interests at stake, and so great is now your Excellency's influence for good, that I feel that I have not exceeded the privilege of your humblest fellow-citizen in attempting to enlist your personal and official cooperation on the side of a cause which has been so signally approved and blessed of God, and which redounds so palpably to the physical, the moral and the religious interests of the human family.

I remain, with great respect, your Excellency's friend and obedient servant,

EDWARD C. DELAVAN,
President New York State Temperance Society.

No. 13.

TEMPERANCE LECTURE No. XI.

BY REV. DR. E. NOTT,

PRESIDENT UNION COLLEGE, SCHENECTADY.

RECAPITULATION—GENERAL APPEAL IN BEHALF OF TEMPERANCE.

Appeal to Parents—to Youth—to Women—Conclusion.

In the preceding lectures, we have shown that a kind of wine has existed from great antiquity, which was injurious to health and subversive of morals; that these evils, since the introduction of distillation, have been greatly increased; that half the lunacy, three-fourths of the pauperism, and five-sixths of the crime with which the nation is visited, is owing to intemperance; that there are believed to be five hundred thousand drunkards in the republic, and that thousands die of drunkenness annually. We have also shown that drunkenness results from moderate drinking, and that drunkenness must continue, by a necessity of nature, as long as habitual moderate drinking is continued; that it is not the drinking of water or milk, or any other necessary or nutritive beverage, but of intoxicating liquors only, that produces drunkenness; that as the existing system of moderate drinking occasions all the drunkenness that exists, so that system must be abandoned, or its expense in muscle and sinew and mind, provided for by this, and all future generations; that even moderate drinking is now more dangerous than formerly, because intoxicating drinks are more deadly—to the poison of alcohol, generated by fermentation, other poison having been added by drugging, an *that* alike to intoxicating liquors, whether fermented or distilled. We have enumerated the kinds of poison made use of in the products of the still and of the brew-house, and met the objection that the use of wine was sanctioned by the Bible, by showing that there were different kinds of wine, some of which were good and some bad, and that the former only were commended in the Bible; that though it were allowable to use pure wines in Palestine, it would not follow that it was allowable to use mixed wines here, where intenser poisons exist, and where the use of wine leads to the use of brandy, and the use of brandy to drunkenness: We have shown that even in Palestine it was good not to drink wine, when it caused a brother to offend, and therefore not good elsewhere, and especially here, and at the present time, when the tremendous evils of intemperance in some classes of community render total abstinence befitting in all classes, in conformity to that great law of love which Jesus Christ promulgated, and in conformity to which the apostles of Jesus Christ acted, and the disciples of Jesus Christ are bound to act.

We have shown that the books of Nature and Revelation both proceeded from God, and both contain, though with unequal degrees of clearness, an expression of his will: that the import of the one is discovered by reading and meditation, of the other by observation and experiment; that in this latter oracle mankind are distinctly taught, that aliments restore the waste of the human organism, but that stimulants impair the sensibility on which they operate, and hence that the latter are not intended for habitual use, that they who so use intoxicating liquors violate an established law of nature, and that the drunkenness, disease and death, which result from such use, are the penalty which follows, by the appointment of God, the violation of that law; that God wills the happiness of his creatures, and when the authority of the Bible is plead in behalf of any usage that leads to misery, it may be known that the Bible is plead in error in behalf of such usage; that in the present instance, and so far as the wines of commerce are concerned, to appeal to the Bible as authority, is absurd; that the Bible knows nothing and teaches nothing directly, in relation to these wines of commerce—the same being either a brandied or drugged article, never in use in Palestine; that in relation to these spurious articles the book of nature must alone be consulted, and that being consulted, their condemnation will be found on many a page, inscribed in characters of wrath.

In the view of these and other truths, we have addressed ourselves to the manufacturer and vender of these legalized poisons; and there are yet others to whom, in the view of the same truths, we would, in conclusion, address ourselves.

Fathers, mothers, heads of families, if not prepared at this late hour to change your mode of life, are you not prepared to encourage the young, particularly your children, to change theirs? Act as you may, yourselves, do you not desire that they should act the part of safety? Can you not tell them, and truly tell them, that our manner of life is attended with less peril than your own? Can you not tell them, and truly tell them, that however innocent the use even of pure wine may be, in the estimation of those who use it, that its use in health is never necessary; that excess is always injurious, and that in the habitual use of even such wine there is always danger of excess; that of the brandied and otherwise adulterated wines in use, it cannot be said, in whatever quantity, that they are innocent; that the temptation to adulterate is very great, detection is very difficult, and that entire safety is to be found only in total abstinence? Can you not truly tell them this? Will you not tell them this? And having told them, should they, in obedience to your counsel, relinquish at once the use of all intoxicating liquors, would their present condition, you yourselves being judges, would their present condition be less secure, or their future prospects less full of promise, on that account? Or would the remembrance, that the stand they took was taken at your bidding, either awaken in your bosoms misgivings now, or regrets hereafter? Especially, would it do this as life declines, and you approach your final dissolution and last account? Then, when standing on the verge of that narrow isthmus, which separates the future from the past, and connects eternity with time; then, when casting the last lingering look back upon that world to which you are about to bid adieu forever, will the thought that you are to leave behind you a family trained to temperance not only, but pledged also to total abstinence, will that thought, then, think you, plant one thorn in the pillow of sickness, or add one pang to the agonies of death? O! no, it is not this thought, but the thought of dying and leaving behind a family of profligate children, to nurture other children no less profligate, in their turn to nurture others,—thus transmitting guilt and misery to a remote posterity; it is this thought, and thoughts like this, in connection with another thought, suggested by those awful words, "For I, the Lord thy God, am a jealous God, visiting the iniquities of the fathers upon the children, to the third and fourth generation, of them that hate me;"—it is thoughts like these, and not the thought of leaving behind a family pledged to total abstinence, that will give to life's last act a sadder coloring, and man's last hour a denser darkness. Between these two conditions of the dying, if held within our offer, who of us would hesitate?

Ye children of moderate drinking parents; children of so many hopes, and solicitudes and prayers; the sin of drunkenness apart, the innocence of abstinence apart, here are two classes of men, and two plans of life, each proffered to your approbation, and submitted for your choice: The one class use intoxicating liquor, moderately indeed, still they use intoxicating liquor, in some or many of its forms; the other class use it in none of them: The one class, in consequence of such use of intoxicating liquor, furnish all the drunkenness, three-fourths of all the pauperism and five-sixths of all the crime, under the accumulating and accumulated weight of which our country already groans. Yes, in consequence of such restricted use of intoxicating liquors, the one class pays an annual tribute in muscle and sinew, in intellect and virtue, aye, in the souls of men; a mighty tribute, embodied in the persons of inebriates, taken from the ranks of temperate drinkers and delivered over to the jail, the mad-house, the house of correction, and even the house of silence!

The other class pays no such tribute; no, nor even a portion of it. The other burthens of community they share indeed, in common with their brethren; a portion of their earnings goes even to provide and furnish those abodes of woe and death, which intoxicating liquors crowd with inmates; but the inmates themselves are all, all trained in the society, instructed in the maxims, moulded by the customs, and finally delivered up from the ranks of the opposite party—the moderate drinking party.

Now, beloved youth, which of these two modes of life will you adopt? To which of these two classes will you attach yourselves? Which think you is the safest, which most noble, patriotic, Christian? In one word, which will insure the purest bliss on earth, and afford the fairest prospect of admission into heaven?

For the mere privilege of using intoxicating liquors moderately, are you willing to contribute your proportion annually to people the poor-house, the prison-house, and the grave-yard? For such a privilege, are you willing to give up to death, or even to delirium-tremens, a parent this year, a wife, a child or brother or sister the next, and the year thereafter a friend or neighbor? Are you willing to do this, and having done it, are you further willing, as a consequence, to hear the mothers', the wives', the widows', and the orphans' wailings, on account of miseries inflicted by a system deliberately adopted by your choice, sustained by your example, and perpetuated by your influence? Nor to hear alone; are you willing to see also the beggar's rags, the convict's fetters, and those other and more hideous forms of guilt and misery, the product of intemperance, which liken men to demons, and earth to hell?

That frightful outward desolation, apparent in the person and the home of the inebriate, is but an emblem of a still more frightful inward desolation. The comfortless abode, the sorrow-stricken family, the tattered garments, the palsied tread, the ghastly countenance and loathsome aspect, of the habitual brutal drunkard, fill us with abhorrence. We shun his presence, and shrink instinctively from his polluting touch. But what are all these sad items, which affect the outer man only, in comparison with the blighted hopes, the withered intellect, the debased propensities, the brutal appetites, the demoniac passions, the defiled conscience; in one word, in comparison with the sadder moral items which complete the frightful spectacle of a soul in ruins; a soul deserted of God, possessed by demons, and from which the last lineaments of its Maker's image have been utterly effaced; a soul scathed and riven, and standing forth already, as it will hereafter stand forth, frightful amid its ruins, a monument of wrath, and a warning to the universe.

Be not deceived, nor fear to take the dimensions of the evils that threaten, or to look that destroyer in the face, which you are about to arm yourselves against. Not the solid rock withstands forever the touch of water even, much less the living fibre that of alcohol, or those other and intenser poisons mingled with it, in those inebriating liquors of which a moiety of the nation drinks. The habitual use of such liquors in small quantities prepares the way for their use in larger quantities, and yet larger quantities progressively, till inebriation is produced. Such is the constitution of nature; it is preposterous, therefore, to calculate upon exemption. Exceptions indeed there may be; but they are exceptions merely. The rule is otherwise. If you live an habitual drinker of such liquors, you ought to calculate to die a confirmed drunkard: and that your children, and your children's children, should they follow your example, will die confirmed drunkards also. And if life shall be prolonged to them, and they so live, they will so die, unless the course of nature shall be changed.

In the view of these facts and arguments which the subject before you presents, make up your minds, make up your minds deliberately, and having done so, say whether you are willing to take along with the habitual moderate use of intoxicating liquors, as bought and sold, and drank among us, the appalling consequences that must result therefrom. Are you willing to do this? and if you are not, stop,—stop while you may, and where you can. In this descent to Hades there is no half-way house, no central resting place. The movement once commenced, is ever onward and downward. The thirst created is quenchless, the appetite induced insatiable. You may not live to complete the process—but this know, that it is naturally progressive, and that with every successive sip from the fatal chalice, it advances, imperceptibly indeed, still it advances towards completion. Yon demented sot, once a moderate drinker, occupied the ground you now occupy, and looked down on former sots, as you, a moderate drinker, now look down on him, and as future moderate drinkers may yet look down on you, and wonder;

"Facilis decensus averni."

Let it never be forgotten that we are social beings. No man liveth to himself; on the contrary, grouped together in various ways, each acts, and is acted on by others. Though living at a distance of so many generations, we feel even yet, and in its strength, the effect of the first transgression.

Now, as formerly, it is the nature of vice, as well as virtue, to extend and perpetuate itself. Now, as formerly, the existing generation is giving the impress of its character to the generation which is to follow it—and now, as formerly, parents are by their conduct and their counsel, either weaving crowns to signalize their offspring in the Heavens, or forging chains to be worn by them in hell.

Hearer, time is on the wing; death is at hand; act now, therefore, the part that you will in that hour approve, and reprobate the conduct you will then condemn.

It has not been usual for the speaker, as it has for some others, to bespeak the influence of those who constitute the most numerous, as well as most efficient part of almost every assembly, where self-denials are called for, or questions of practical duty discussed. And yet, no one is more indebted than myself to the kind of influence in question.

Under God, I owe my early education, nay, all that I have been, or am, to the counsel and tutelage of a pious mother. It was, peace to her sainted spirit, it was her monitory voice that first taught my young heart to feel that there was danger in the intoxicating cup, and that safety lay in abstinence.

And as no one is more indebted than myself to the kind of influence in question, so no one more fully realizes how decisively it bears upon the destinies of others.

Full well I know, that by woman came the apostacy of Adam, and by woman the recovery through Jesus. It was a woman that imbued the mind and formed the character of Moses, Israel's deliverer—it was a woman that led the choir, and gave back the response of that triumphal pro cession, which went forth to celebrate with timbrels, on the banks of the Red Sea, the overthrow of Pharoah—it was a woman that put Sisera to flight, that composed the song of Deborah and Barak, the son of Abinoam, and judged in righteousness, for years, the tribes of Israel—it was a woman that defeated the wicked counsels of Haman, delivered righteous Mordecai, and saved a whole people from utter desolation.

And not now to speak of Semiramis at Babylon, of Catharine of Russia, or of those Queens of England, whose joyous reign constitute the brightest periods of British history, or of her, the young and lovely, the patron of learning and morals, who now adorns the throne of the sea-girt Isles; not now to speak of these, there are others of more sacred character, of whom it were admissable even now to speak.

The sceptre of empire is not the sceptre that best befits the hand of woman; nor is the field of carnage her field of glory. Home, sweet home, is her theatre of action, her pedestal of beauty, and throne of power. Or if seen abroad, she is seen to the best advantage, when on errands of love, and wearing her robe of mercy.

It was not woman who slept during the agonies of Gethsemane; it was not woman who denied her Lord at the palace of Caiaphas; it was not woman who deserted his cross on the hill of Calvary. But it was woman that dared to testify her respect for his corpse, that procured spices for embalming it, and that was found last at night, and first in the morning, at his sepulchre. Time has neither impaired her kindness, shaken her constancy, or changed her character.

Now, as formerly, she is most ready to enter, and most reluctant to leave, the abode of misery. Now, as formerly, it is her office, and well it has been sustained, to stay the fainting head, wipe from the dim eye the tear of anguish, and from the cold forehead the dew of death.

This is not unmerited praise. I have too much respect for the character of woman, to use, even elsewhere, the language of adulation, and too much self-respect to use such language here. I would not, If I could, persuade those of the sex who hear me, to become the public, clamorous advocates of even temperance. It is the influence of their declared approbation; of their open, willing, visible example, enforced by that soft, persuasive, colloquial eloquence, which, in some hallowed retirement and chosen moments, exerts such controlling influence over the hard, cold heart of man, especially over a husband's, a son's or a brother's heart; it is this influence which we need;—an influence chiefly known by the gradual, kindly transformation of character it produces, and which, in its benign effects, may be compared to the noiseless, balmy influence of Spring, shedding, as it silently advances, renovation over every hill, and dale, and glen, and islet, and changing, throughout the whole region of animated nature, Winter's rugged and unsightly forms, into the forms of vernal loveliness and beauty.

No, I repeat it, I would not, if I could, persuade those of the sex who hear me, to become the public clamorous advocates of temperance. It is not yours to wield the club of Hercules or bend Achilles' bow. But, though it is not, still you have a heaven-appointed armour, as well as a heaven approved theatre of action. The look of tenderness, the eye of compassion, the lip of entreaty, are yours; and yours, too, are the decisions of taste, and yours the omnipotence of fashion. You can therefore,—I speak of those who have been the favorites of fortune, and who occupy the high places of society,—you can change the terms of social intercourse and alter the current opinions of community. You can remove, at once and forever, temptation from the saloon, the drawing-room and the dining-table. This is your empire, the empire over which God and the usages of mankind have given you dominion. Here, within these limits, and without transgressing that modesty which is heaven's own gift and woman's brightest ornament, you may exert a benign and kindly but mighty influence. Here you have but to speak the word, and one chief source of the mother's, the wives', and the widow's sorrows, will, throughout the circle in which you move, be dried up forever. Nor throughout that circle only. The families around you and beneath you will feel the influence of your example, descending on them in blessings like the dews of Heaven that descend on the mountains of Zion; and drunkenness, loathsome, brutal drunkenness, driven by the moral power of your decision, from all the abodes of reputable society, will be compelled to exist, if it exist at all, only among those vulgar and ragged wretches, who, shunning the society of woman, herd together in the bar-room, the oyster cellar and the groggery.

This, indeed, were a mighty triumph, and this, at least, you can achieve. Why, then, should less than this be achieved? To purify the conscience, to bind up the broken-hearted, to remove temptation from the young, to minister consolation to the aged, and kindle joy in every bosom throughout her appointed theatre of action, befits alike a woman's and a mother's agency,—and since God has put it in your power to do so much, are you willing to be responsible for the consequences of leaving it undone?

Are you willing to see this tide of woe and death, whose flow you might arrest, roll onward by you to posterity, increasing as it rolls forever?

O! no, you are not, I am sure you are not; and if not, then, ere you leave these altars, lift up your heart to God, and, in his strength, form the high resolve to purify from drunkenness this city. And however elsewhere others may hesitate, and waver, and defer, and temporize, take you the open, noble stand of ABSTINENCE; and, having taken it, cause it by your words, and by your deeds, to be known on earth and told in Heaven, that mothers here have dared to do their duty, their whole duty, and that, within the precincts of that consecrated spot over which their balmy, hallowed influence extends, the doom of drunkenness is sealed.

Nor mothers only; in this benign and holy enterprise, the daughter and the mother alike are interested.

Ye young, might the speaker be permitted to address you, as well as your honored parents, and those teachers, their assistants, whose delightful task it is to bring forward the unfolding germs of thought, and teach the young idea how to shoot—might the speaker, whose chief concernment hitherto has been the education of the young, be permitted to address you, he would bespeak your influence, your urgent, persevering influence, in behalf of a cause so pure, so full of mercy, and so every way befitting your age, your sex, your character.

O! could the speaker make a lodgment, an effectual lodgment, in behalf of temperance, within those young, warm, generous, active hearts within his hearing, or rather within the city where it is his privilege to speak, who this side of Heaven could calculate the blessed, mighty, enduring consequence? Could this be done, then might the eye of angels rest with increased complacency on this commercial metropolis,* already signalized by Christian charity, as well as radiant with intellectual glory;—but then lit up anew with fire from off virtue's own altar, and thus caused to become, amid the surrounding desolation which intemperance has occasioned, more conspicuously than ever, an asylum of mercy to the wretched, and a beacon light of promise to the wanderer.

Then from this favored spot, as from some great central source of power, encouragement might be given and confidence imparted to the whole sisterhood of virtue, and a redeeming influence sent forth, through many a distant town and hamlet, to mingle with other and kindred influences in effecting throughout the land, among the youth of both sexes, that moral renovation called for, and which, when realized, will be at once the earnest and the anticipation of millennial glory.

O! could we gain the young,—the young who have no inveterate prejudices to combat, no established habits to overcome; could we gain the young, we might, after a single generation had passed away, shut up the dram-shop, the bar-room and the rum selling grocery, and, by shutting these up, shut up also the poor-house, the prison-house, and one of the broadest and most frequented avenues to the charnel house.

More than this, could we shut up these licensed dispensaries of crime, disease and death, we might abate the severity of maternal anguish, restore departed joys to conjugal affection, silence the cry of deserted orphanage, and procure for the poor demented suicide a respite for self-inflicted vengeance.

* Philadelphia.

This, the gaining of the young to abstinence, would constitute the mighty fulcrum on which to plant that moral lever of power, to raise a world from degradation.

O! how the clouds would scatter, the prospect brighten, and the firmament of hope clear up, could the young be gained, intoxicating liquors be banished, and abstinence with its train of blessings introduced throughout the earth.

No. 14.

EXTRACT

FROM

PRESIDENT NOTT'S LECTURE No. IX.,

In which he calls attention to DR. SEWAL'S DIAGRAMS, which will be found on page 20 of this work, closing with "the frightful ravings of a poor inebriate who died of the delirium tremens."

Think not that God is heard only in the book of revelation. The book of nature, as well as the book of revelation, is a book of God. Both were written by him, and hence David bound them up together, and in the 19th Psalm you will find a summary of both.

"The heavens," saith he, "the heavens declare the glory of God," and having said this, he adds in unbroken continuity, "the law of the Lord is perfect, converting the soul."

These two books, which David more than thirty centuries since bound up together, have not yet been separated, and are both, with reverence, now, as formerly, to be consulted; and both, consulted on the question now at issue, return the same answer. It is the book of nature, however, with which chiefly we are now concerned. Let us examine its contents. Let us obey its teachings.

Whatever obscurity there may be elsewhere, here there is no obscurity; here there are no opposing phenomena to explain—no contradictory testimony to reconcile. After a lapse of six thousand years, the original law of God, concerning intoxicating poisons, with its awful and unchanged penalty, stands out to view, written, on the living organism of those who drink it, in characters so broad and bold, and plain, that he who runs may read.

In view of this recorded prohibition of those poisons, talk not of temperate use; such use belongs to authorized healthful beverage—to water, milk and wine; I mean good, refreshing, unintoxicating wine, such as might have been drank in Palestine, such as was drank at Cana; even such wines, when used, are to be used temperately; and there may be times, and I think the present is such a time, when from motives of humanity as well as religion and expediency, their use should be dispensed with.

But poisonous beverage, even poisonous wine, wine that intoxicates, wine the mocker; that serpent's tooth, that adder's sting, against which the book of revelation warns, and to which warning the book of nature in accents long and loud responds; of such wine there is no temperate use. Such wine is poisonous, and is therefore to be everywhere and at all times utterly rejected. The chalice that contains it, contains an element of death. It is not even to be received, or, having been received, is to be rejected; and happy the youth—the man—who dashes it untasted from his hand.

This is not declamation—it is not the speaker, BUT THY MAKER, hearer, that counsels thus. That counsel, as we have said, is made apparent in ruins stamped by the ordination of Jehovah in every age, in every clime, and on every organ of every human being who transgresses his published law in regard to poisons. Yes, in ruins, stamped from their first inception in the moderate drinker, to their final consummation in the death of the drunkard by delirium tremens.

The shadowing forth of these ruins, as seen in a single organ, transferred by the pencil from the dissecting-room of the surgeon* to the canvass of the painter, I shall now proceed to exhibit and very briefly to illustrate.

The organ in question is the human stomach, with its triple coatings, with its inlet for food, its outlet for chyme, its mysterious solvent for converting the former into the latter, and

* Dr. Thomas Sewal. See page 20 for diagrams.

its contractile power for transmitting the same (when so converted), through other viscera, to be absorbed in the repairing of the wastes of an ever-perishing and renovated organism.

Fig. I represents the inner surface of this organ, exposed to view in its natural and healthy state—the state in which it was created, and in which it would ordinarily continue through life, but for those elements of ruin with which, by the indiscretion of man, it is so early and often brought in contact.*

Fig. II represents the changed aspect of this same organ, as it appears in the person of the temperate drinker. You perceive how that delicate and beautiful net-work of blood-vessels, almost invisible in the healthy stomach, begins to be enlarged—how the whole interior surface, irritated and inflamed, exhibits the inception of that progressive work of death about to be accomplished.

This change is effected by a well known law of nature, to wit, the rushing of the blood to any part of a sensitive texture to which any irritant is applied. You know what is the effect produced by even diluted alcohol when applied to the eye; you know what the effect is, of holding even undiluted brandy in the mouth; what, then, must be the effect of pouring such an exciting and corrosive poison into that delicate and vital organ, the human stomach?

Fig. III represents the stomach of the habitual drunkard, with its thickened walls, its distended blood-vessels, and its livid blotches, visible at irregular intervals to the eye, like the unsightly rum blossoms that overspread the countenance, in token of the havoc which disease, unseen, is making with the viscera within

Fig. IV exhibits the ulcerated stomach of the habitual drunkard—with its loathsome corroding sores, eating their way through its triple lining, and gradually extending over the intervening spaces: all bespeaking the extent of the hidden desolation which has already been effected.

Fig. V represents the frightful stomach of the habitual drunkard, rendered still more frightful by the aggravation of a recent debauch. Its previously inflamed surface has become still more inflamed, and its livid blotches still more livid.

* When this lecture was delivered, Dr. Sewal's drawings of the human stomach were exhibited, and the text is the explanation of them severally, as then given.

Grumous blood is issuing from its pores, and its whole putrid aspect indicates that the work of death is nearly consummated.

Fig. VI represents the cancerous stomach of the drunkard, or rather a cancerous ulcer in such a stomach, the coats of which stomach, as the surgeon who performed the dissection affirms, were thickened, and schirrous, and its passages so obstructed as to prevent for some time previous to death the transmission of any nutriment to the system.

Fig. VII represents a stomach in which this progressive desolation is completed—it is the stomach of the maniac, the drunken maniac—as seen after death by delirium tremens, than which there is no death more dreadful,—signalized as it ever is by unearthly spectres, hydras and demons dire.

It may have been the lot of some of you to have witnessed such a death scene; if it has, you will bear me out in saying that no language can express its horrors.

The following lines convey but a faint idea of the frightful ravings of a poor inebriate who died of delirium tremens in an asylum to which he had been removed, and who, amazed at the situation in which he found himself placed, conceived the idea that, though sane himself, the friends who had placed him there were deranged. Excited to phrenzy and haunted by this illusion—

Why am I thus, the maniac cried,
Confined 'mid crazy people? Why?
I am not mad—knave, stand aside!
I'll have my freedom, or I'll die.
It's not for cure that here I've come—
I tell thee, all I want is rum—
I must have rum.

Sane? yes, and have been all the while;
Why, then, tormented thus? 'Tis sad!
Why chained, and held in duress vile?
The men who brought me here were mad.
I will not stay where spectres come—
Let me go hence; I must have rum,
I must have rum.

'Tis he! 'tis he! my aged sire!
What has disturbed thee in thy grave?
Why bend on me that eye of fire?
Why torment, since thou canst not save?
Back to the churchyard whence you've come!
Return, return! but send me rum,
O! send me rum.

Why is my mother musing there,
  On that same consecrated spot
Where once she taught me words of prayer?
  But now she hears—she heeds me not.
Mute in her winding sheet she stands—
Cold, cold, I feel her icy hands—
    Her icy hands!

She's vanished; but a dearer friend—
  I know her by her angel smile—
Has come her partner to attend,
  His hours of misery to beguile;
Haste! haste! loved one, and set me free;
'Twere heaven to 'scape from hence to thee,
    From hence to thee.

She does not hear—away she flies,
  Regardless of the chain I wear,
Back to her mansion in the skies,
  To dwell with kindred spirits there.
Why has she gone? Why did she come?
O God, I'm ruined! Give me rum,
    O! give me rum.

Hark! hark! for bread my children cry—
  A cry that drinks my spirits up;
But 'tis in vain, in vain to try—
  O give me back the drunkard's cup:
My lips are parched, my heart is sad—
This cursed chain! 'twill make me mad!
    'Twill make me mad!

It wont wash out, that crimson stain!
  I've scoured those spots, and made them white—
Blood reappears again,
  Soon as morning brings the light!
When from my sleepless couch I come,
To see—to feel —— O! give me rum,
    I must have rum.

'Twas there I heard his piteous cry,
  And saw his last imploring look,
But steeled my heart, and bade him die—
  Then from him golden treasures took:
Accursed treasure—stinted sum—
Reward of guilt! Give—give me rum,
    O! give me rum.

Hark! still I hear that piteous wail—
  Before my eyes his spectre stands,
And when it frowns on me, I quail;
  O! I would fly to other lands!

But, that pursuing, there 'twould come—
There's no escape! O! give me rum,
O! give me rum.

Guard! guard those windows—bar that door—
Yonder I armed bandits see;
They've robbed my house of all its store,
And now return to murder me;
They're breaking in, don't let them come;
Drive—drive them hence—but give me rum,
O! give me rum.

I stake again? not I!—no more,
Heartless, accursed gamester! No!
I staked with thee my all, before,
And from thy den a beggar go.
Go where? A suicide to hell!
And leave my orphan children here,
In rags and wretchedness to dwell—
A doom their father cannot bear.

Will no one pity? no one come?—
Not thou! O come not, man of prayer
Shut that dread volume in thy hand—
For me damnation's written there—
No drunkard can in judgment stand!

Talk not of pardon there revealed—
No, not to me—it is too late—
My sentence is already sealed;
Tears never blot the book of fate.
Too late! too late these tidings come;
There is no hope! O give me rum,
I must have rum.

Thou painted harlot, come not here!
I know thee by that lecherous look—
I know that silvery voice I hear—
Go home, and read God's holy book.
For thee there's mercy—not for me;
I'm damned already—words can't tell
What sounds I hear, what sights I see!
I'm sure it can't be worse in hell!

See how that rug those reptiles soil!
They're crawling o'er me in my bed!
I feel their clammy, snaky coil
On every limb—around my head—
With forked tongue I see them play;
I hear them hiss—tear them away!
Tear them away!

A fiend! a fiend! with many a dart,
  Glares on me with his bloodshot eye,
And aims his missiles at my heart—
  O! whither, whither shall I fly?
Fly? no! it is no time for flight!
  I know thy hellish purpose well—
Avaunt, avaunt, thou hated sprite,
  And hie thee to thy native hell!

He's gone! he's gone! and I am free;
  He's gone, the faithless braggart liar—
He said he'd come to summon me—
  See there again—my bed's on fire!
Fire! water! help! O haste! I die!
  The flames are kindling round my head!
This smoke! I'm strangling! cannot fly—
  O! snatch me from this burning bed!

There! there again—that demon's there,
  Crouching to make a fresh attack!
See how his flaming eye-balls glare—
  Thou fiend of fiends, what's brought thee back
Back in thy car? For whom? For where?
  He smiles—he beckons me to come—
What are those words thou'st written there?
"IN HELL THEY NEVER WANT FOR RUM!"
          In hell they never want for rum.
Not want for rum! Read that again—
  I feel the spell! haste, drive me down
Where rum is free! where revelers reign,
  And I can wear the drunkard's crown.

Accept thy proffer, fiend? I will,
  And to thy drunken banquet come;
Fill the great cauldron from thy still
  With boiling, burning, fiery rum—
There will I quench this horrid thirst!
  With boon companions drink and dwell,
Nor plead for rum, as here I must—
  There's liberty to drink in hell.

Thus raved that maniac rum had made—
  Then starting from his haunted bed—
On, on, ye demons, on! he said,
  Then silent sunk—his soul had fled.

Scoffer beware! he in that shroud
  Was once a moderate drinker too,
And felt as safe—declaimed as loud
  Against extravagance, as you.

*The rum maniac varied.

And yet ere long I saw him stand
  Refusing, on the brink of hell,
A pardon from his Savior's hand,
  Then plunging down with fiends to dwell.

From thence, methinks, I hear him say,
  Dash, dash the chalice, break the spell,
Stop while you can, and where you may—
  There's no escape when once in hell.

O God, thy gracious spirit send,
  That we, the mocker's snare may fly,
And thus escape that dreadful end,
  That death eternal, drunkards die.

No. 15.

SKETCH

BY THE

HON. WILLIAM H. SEWARD,

SECRETARY OF STATE, WASHINGTON.

The following brief sketch, from the pen of the Hon. William H. Seward, appeared in the English edition of Dr. Nott's celebrated Temperance Lectures. In re-publishing a part of the ninth and the whole of the eleventh and last of the series, in this volume, it appears to be appropriate that the following just tribute by his pupil, should be published also.

E. C. D.

Dr. Nott has lived nearly a century. The period of his life comprises the whole of our national history, and even his matured and publicly active years have been more than "three score years and ten." Gifted with rare versatility of talent and industry of habit, he has impressed himself upon the country and the age in many ways, as deeply as other men only aspire to impress themselves in one.

Were any historian of our times to begin to catalogue the names of the eminent divines of our country, perhaps the first name that would occur to him would be that of Dr. Nott. Were he to go on and add those of its noted instructors of youth, again the name of Dr. Nott would first suggest itself. Were he then to add those of its Biblical expositors, the same name would again present itself among the foremost. Were he to continue with those of its philosophers and reformers, still the same honored name would recur with like pre-eminence.

The pulpit has long counted him as one of its most impressive orators. Union College, over which he has so long presided, owes to his organization and management its high prosperity. Thousands who were once his pupils, and are now scattered throughout the Union and the world, useful and prominent in every walk of public and professional life, look back to him with almost filial affection, and are, unconsciously even to themselves, disseminating and perpetuating the influences of his teaching. Science has been enriched by his researches; art owes to him more than one valuable invention. Literature has received from him contributions which will endure with the language itself.

No great political or moral reform has taken place during the century which is not indebted for a part of its success, to his sagacious and efficient support. A life of irreproachable purity, Christian benevolence and virtue has made him at once a teacher and an exemplar of his generation.

His remarkable influence over men, individually or in masses, is in part attributable to keen perception of character and careful study of human nature, but more perhaps to the tendency of his mind toward the examination of subjects in their practical rather than their theoretical bearing. Thus in religion his attention has been given to ethics, rather than polemics; in science, to the practical application of laws rather than abstruse investigations of their origin; in politics, to measures and results, rather than theories or controversy; in literature, to its instruction rather than its recondite studies or its elegant pleasures.

Few men have in their lives done so much to guide the lives of others in accordance with the dictates of philosophy, and the teachings of Christian revelation.

WM. B. CARPENTER, M. D., F. R. S., ETC., ETC.,

ON THE

USE AND ABUSE OF ALCOHOLIC LIQUORS IN HEALTH AND DISEASE.

Space will not allow of lengthy extracts from the writings of this distinguished English physician. He states:

"Experience has proved that the Temperance Reformation cannot be carried to its required extent, without the coöperation of the educated classes, and that *this* influence can only be effectually exerted by *example*. There is no case in which the superiority of *example* over mere *precept*, is more decided than it is in this. 'I PRACTICE TOTAL ABSTINENCE MYSELF,' is found to be worth a thousand exhortations; and the lamentable failure of the advocates who cannot employ *this* argument, should lead all those whose position calls upon them to exert their influence to a *serious* consideration of the claims which their *duty to society* should set up in opposition to their individual feelings of taste or comfort. * * * *I believe it to be in the power of the* CLERICAL *and* MEDICAL *professions combined with the educated classes*, to promote the spread of this principle among the '*masses*' to a degree which no other agency can effect."

Dr. Carpenter adds:

"In his general view of the case, he has the satisfaction of finding himself supported by the recorded opinion of a large body of his professional brethren; upwards of *two thousand* of whom, in all grades and degrees, from the court physicians and leading metropolitan surgeons, who are conversant with the wants of the upper ranks of society, to the humble country practitioner, who is familiar with the requirements of the artisan in his workshop and the laborer in the field, have signed the following certificate:

'We, the undersigned, are of opinion,

'1. That a very large proportion of human misery, including poverty, disease and crime, is induced by the use of alcoholic or fermented liquors as beverages.

'2. That the most perfect health is compatible with total abstinence from all such intoxicating beverages, whether in the form of ardent spirits, or as wine, beer, ale, porter, cider, &c.

'3. That persons accustomed to such drinks may, with perfect safety, discontinue them entirely, either at once, or gradually after a short time.

'4. That total and universal abstinence from alcoholic beverages of all sorts would greatly contribute to the health, the prosperity, the morality and the happiness of the human race.'

"No medical man, therefore, can any longer plead the *singularity* of the total abstinence creed as an excuse for his non-recognition of it; and, although a certain amount of moral courage may be needed for the advocacy and the practice of it yet this is an attribute in which the author cannot for a moment believe his brethren to be deficient."

LORD BYRON.

He died at Missolonghi, Greece, April 19, 1824: Lord Macaulay said of this great but misguided man, whose wisdom would have been to act on the proverb, "Wine is a mocker," without exemplifying its truth: "An imagination polluted by vice, a temper embittered by misfortune, and a frame habituated to the fatal excitement of intoxication, prevented him from fully enjoying the happiness which he might have derived from the purest and most tranquil of his many attachments. Midnight draughts of ardent spirits and Rhenish wines had been ruin to his fine intellect. His verse lost much of the energy and condensation which had distinguished it." Byron learned by sad experience the falseness of his own line, that "In the goblet no deception is found." The serpent whose praises he sang struck deep into his own breast its envenomed sting.—*Spectator*.

No. 16.

CHIPMAN'S REPORT.

A. Champion, Esq., of Rochester, N. Y., engaged, over thirty years since, Samuel Chipman of the same beautiful city, to visit all the Poor-Houses, Jails, and Orphan Asylums in the State of New York, to ascertain the sources from which they were filled with so many wretched and depraved victims. He was engaged about two years in this duty, and in all cases, his statistics were verified by the heads of those establishments. The manuscript copy of the report was handed to that great and pure-minded statesman, William L. Marcy, then Governor of the State of New York, who expressed great astonishment at these astounding verified statistics, and recommended their being printed and circulated to the greatest possible extent. Over 100,000 were printed and circulated. They were also republished in Paris, France.

The report is now out of print, but a single extract from the statistics of Albany county, is given as a sample of all the counties, and also an extract from Mr. Chipman's letter to Mr. Champion.

Garret Hogan, jailor, certifies, "that in *one* month 114 criminals were received into the jail: 15 temperate, 17 doubtful, 82 intemperate; of the intemperate, at least 20 have been committed for the abuse of their families. During the year at least 100 cases of delirium have occurred. Imprisoned in conse. quence of intemperance, in one year, at least 820; for whipping their wives or abuse of families, not less than 200."

JOHN O. COLE, the police magistrate (yet in office), states, "that he examined into every criminal case brought before him for a *single week:* of 50 cases, 48 clearly originated in intemperance. Over 2500 criminal cases were brought before me in a single year, 96 in the hundred originated in, or were directly connected with intemperance."

"To A. CHAMPION, Esq., Rochester, N. Y.:

"Of the cause of temperance I may just say, that I have not found a spot where it has not made some progress. In the southern tier of counties, parts of which are comparatively new, I was surprised to find that this subject appeared to be as old, was as well understood, and had received as large a share of attention, as in the older counties. In fact, I have at every step seen conclusive evidence that the blessing of God has attended the *means* that have been used to arouse public attention to the desolating evils of intemperance; and that in proportion to the *means* has been the *success.* On this, as on every subject of moral reform, the people need 'line upon line, and precept upon precept'—to have facts and arguments presented—to have them pressed home upon their *consciences* where they have any, and where they have not, the appeal must be made to their self-interest.

"I am fully aware that in the details I have given, there is great sameness, but my object is to show what is the *uniform, legitimate* effect of the use of ardent spirits,* and without going into these details, this could not be fully acomplished. ALCOHOL is on trial—sheriffs, keepers of poor-houses, clerks of supervisors, magistrates, the superintendents and officers of the house of refuge and of the lunatic asylum, &c., are giving testimony. Let them be heard. The greater the uniformity in the testimony they give, the greater the influence it ought to, and will have on the minds of an honest and intelligent jury.

"There is another reason for giving these particulars. Those officers have chosen to insert them in their certificates—they *may* deem them important, especially in their own counties, where their statements will be scrutinized. I will not assume the responsibility of adding or diminishing aught.

* *All kinds* of intoxicating drinks are now regarded as ardent spirits.—ED.

"And now, in view of the facts which the statistics I have exhibited—showing the proportion of pauperism and crime growing out of intemperance, and the expense which it occasions, arising *directly* from the same cause, besides the incalculably larger amount arising from it *indirectly*, in the loss of time, of litigation it occasions; the time of parties, witnesses and spectators; the interruption and derangement of business; the destruction of property; the loss of health, and the bills of physicians—it would seem that men endowed with reason would look around them and inquire for the *benefits* to counterbalance these *evils;* and if none could be found, that the next object of inquiry would be the *remedy*. And this reason and common sense cannot mistake. The evils had existed, had been seen and deplored, and yet had *increased* for centuries, until societies were formed taking for their fundamental principle, *total abstinence*. The success which has followed their organization, and the exertion of their members, can leave no doubt that a complete victory will finally crown their efforts. And notwithstanding I have shown beyond the power of contradiction, that *more* than three-fourths of the ordinary tax is absorbed by the support of the poor, and the administration of criminal justice—that more than *three-fourths* of the pauperism is occasioned by intemperance, and *more* than five-sixths of those committed on criminal charges are intemperate, yet the greatest obstacle in your way is the pecuniary interest of a few individuals—*that of manufacturers and venders*. If the tax-payers will submit to this, we might, looking upon it as a mere matter of pecuniary profit or loss, stand by and laugh at their folly: but when we reflect that the business of the manufacturer and vender involves the temporal happiness of thousands, as well as their eternal interests, this subject assumes an infinitely more serious aspect. In no poor-house that I have visited have I failed of finding the wife or the widow, and the children of the drunkard. In one poor-house, as my certificate will show, of 190 persons relieved there the past year, were NINETEEN wives of *drunken husbands* and SEVENTY-ONE children of *drunken fathers*. In almost *every* jail were husbands confined for whipping their wives or for otherwise abusing their families. In one *nine*, in another fourteen, in another sixteen, had been in prison for this offence the last year: in another, three out of the four who were *then* in prison were confined for *whipping* their *wives*. But when we reflect that but a very small proportion of these brutes in human shape are thus punished, the amount of misery and domestic suffering, arising from this source, exceeds the powers of the human mind to compute; and yet the sale of that which causes all this is not only tolerated but is AUTHORIZED by LAW.

"Could we collect the wives and children of this class in a great amphitheatre—place in an outer circle the manufacturers and the venders, and fix them there until each mother and child had told the history of their griefs—of their downward course from affluence, or competency, from respectability and domestic happiness to poverty, to misery and wretchedness—could the scenes of domestic discord be all acted over—could the blows of the sworn and once loved and cherished protector, now transformed to a madman and a brute, be made to sound in their ears, with the shrieks of these wives and mothers, and the wailings of their innocent children; could they for the occasion be furnished with powers of language to describe their days of toil and misery, and their nights of unmitigated, unmingled and unavailing sorrow and anguish; could they throw into their countenances all the agony which has so often wrung their souls, all the terror and trembling, all the disgust and loathing which the conduct of their husbands and fathers have caused them; could these men hear the prayers of these wives for their husbands, that the temptation which had so besotted and enslaved them might not again be thrown in their way—and finally, could the secret tears which they have shed be made to flow in full view of this circle of makers and dealers that surround them—could all this be done, is there a soul not absolutely in league with the great Adversary and Tempter himself, who could for another day or hour continue in his unholy business!!! Yet all this is seen by the eye of Omniscience, and these groans and wailings, and prayers, have entered into the ears of the God of Sabaoth; and yet these men who are the chief agents in producing all this, would have us consider them as patriots, as philanthropists, or even as *Christians*—yes, men who profess to be governed by the law of *love!*—to feel their paramount obligation to do good to all men;—yet assisting to hoist the flood-gates of intemperance, spreading desolation, and ruin, and death!!—

occasioning misery in all its disgusting and horrid and heart-rending forms;—and crime, which is filling our jails with felons, our mad-houses with maniacs, and our land with widows and orphans, and hastening to the grave and to the judgment, those whom God has said, cannot inherit his kingdom ! ! ! And yet all this is seen in every section of our country at this day, when no man can plead ignorance in regard to this subject.

"You, sir, with every friend of his country, and especially, every friend to the religion of our Savior, cannot but be pained at the bare recital of these facts ; yet you, and all that are engaged in the temperance reformation, may have the pleasing reflection that you are laboring to eradicate these evils, and that all your labors and sacrifices in this cause have thus far been crowned with a measure of success so far beyond your most sanguine anticipations, as to demonstrate that the cause of temperance is under the special protection of Him who can and will cause it ultimately to gain a complete and glorious triumph.

I am, sir,
Very respectfully, yours,
S. CHIPMAN."

Mr. Chipman extended his examinations to other states—Massachusetts, Vermont, &c., &c.—the result was about the same. Deacon Moses Grant, of Boston, says:

"From the establishment of the House of Correction, in 1823, I was seven years one of the Overseers of that Institution; for several years I have been connected with the House of Industry, and I have also been two years one of the Overseers of the Poor, which has led me to examine into the causes of the great amount of pauperism and crime in this city; and I have long since made up my mind, that could ardent spirits be banished from society, three-fourths of the expense attending the institutions referred to would be saved, and an immense amount of misery and wretchedness annihilated.

I am also of opinion, from personal observation, and actual inquiry of the intemperate, that a very large proportion of all the intemperance, which so severely taxes this community, owes its origin to DRAM-SHOPS."

A

SHORT SERMON

FROM THE

OLD TESTAMENT.

TEXT:

LEVITICUS 10 CHAP., 8, 9 AND 10 VERSES.

"And the Lord spake unto Aaron, saying, do not drink wine nor strong drink, thou, nor thy sons with thee, when you go into the tabernacle of the congregation, lest ye die: *it shall be* a statute for ever throughout your generations: and that ye may put difference between holy and unholy, and between unclean and clean."

Remarks.—A short sermon was prepared to follow, but is omitted, illustrating *the universal application* of the prohibitory text, in consequence of the nature of the substance prohibited, and its invariable effect on the human frame when used as a beverage — I trust learned biblical expositors will examine the question and give results.—ED.

A
SHORT SERMON
FROM THE
NEW TESTAMENT.

TEXT:

FIRST THESSALONIANS, CHAP. V: 5, 6, 7 AND 8 VERSES.

"Ye are all the children of light, and the children of the day: we are not of the night, nor of darkness. Therefore let us not sleep, as *do* others; but let us watch and be sober. For they that sleep, sleep in the night, and they that be drunken, are drunken in the night. But let us, who are of the day, be sober, putting on the breast plate of faith and love; and for an helmet, the hope of salvation."

Also EPHESIANS V, 18 VERSE.

"And be not drunk with wine, wherein is excess; but be filled with the Spirit;"

Remarks.—Learned scholars, who have examined the text from Thessalonians, declare "be sober," in the original means *to be abstinent*, and that the English translation of the 18 verse, V chap. Ephesians, gives a wrong idea to the general reader.

No. 17.

TEMPERANCE

A SOURCE OF NATIONAL WEALTH.

By Hon. MARK DOOLITTLE, of Belchertown, Mass.

A PRIZE ESSAY

[From *Am. Tem. Quart. Mag.* Vol. II *Feb.*, 1834.]

The subject of temperance, as connected with *political economy*, is well worthy the attention of every patriot and every philanthropist. It has a direct and important bearing on all the vital interests of nations, being inseparably connected with them, not only in its political effects, but also in its moral influences, involving all that is dear and desirable in the condition and character of a people. Few subjects have engaged the attention of the politician, or the moralist, more than *political economy;* and few have been more loosely and obscurely treated.

Political economy, is defined to be the science which treats of the wealth of nations; in what the wealth of a nation consists; what produces it; what increases it; what perpetuates it; what diminishes it. Writers have different views on all those points. It is not my design to go into the consideration of the comparative excellence of the different systems that have been embraced by different writers, on this subject. Devenant and Stewart, contend that commerce is the great source of the wealth of a nation; and that those who engage to the greatest extent, in this branch of industry and enter prise, deserve the appellation of political economists. M. Quesnai contends that agriculture is the principal source of national wealth. Dr. Adam Smith derives the wealth of a nation from agriculture, commerce and manufactures, and has illustrated his principles, with much good sense and sound reasoning, appended to which, is some theory and speculation of doubtful practicability. Sir William Petty says, the wealth of a nation consists in the totality of the private property of its individuals; others say it consists in the abundance of its commodities; others, in the *exchangeable* value of its nett produce, and some make it consist in what is superfluous. M. Connard calls wealth the accumulation of surplus labor; and Lauderdale says it consists in all that a man desires that is useful or delightful to him.

Without objecting to the views of others, I shall define political economy, the science directing to the best mode of providing for the wants, guarding the rights, securing the interests and means of prosperity and happiness of a nation. In this view is embraced not only the science treating of the wealth of a nation, and the means of acquiring and perpetuating it, but also the application of wealth, as a means of national prosperity.

A rule for the application of wealth as the means of advancing the common interest, is the great desideratum in political economy : and this is equally true, whether applied to nations, to small communities, or to an individual. A nation may have great wealth, while the subjects of that nation, in countless multitudes, are suffering the extremes of poverty and wretchedness; or a nation may have great wealth, and the means of making it still greater, while it is placed at such immense hazard, either in the acquiring or sustaining it, that they could not be justly entitled to the distinction of political economists. Again, a nation may acquire great wealth by conquests, or by treaty, while they multiply the draw-backs and expenditures, resting on their resources to a much greater amount; in such a policy, there could be no economy. Economy is *frugality, discretion in expenditure or investment, a distribution of everything in its proper place*, whether practiced by a nation, or by an individual, it matters not, the one or the many who disregard the principle, cannot claim the character dependent on the principle ; it is a principle of universal application, it cannot be changed by time, place or circumstances.

By the unalterable constitution of things in this world, our wants both of body and mind, urge themselves upon us with perpetual demands. These wants must be supplied, or man could never attain to the station for which he is designed; he could not exist as a rational and intelligent being in the world; our own efforts are necessary to develop the means and furnish these supplies; in this we see the wisdom of Providence, in connecting our own enjoyment with our own efforts in attaining it. *Labor, diligence in useful employment*, is the source of wealth to both individuals and nations, it is the source of national strength and prosperity; not only is it the source of wealth, but it is the capital of the nation, and the government whose system of policy induces the greatest number of its subjects to be usefully employed, may take the palm for practicing the best system of political economy. Imagine for a moment, a community exhibiting such a spectacle, where all are engaged in mitigating the ills of life, in supplying the wants, in improving the mind, in purifying the morals and elevating the character of those within the sphere of their influence, and we should have presented to the mind an emblem of heaven. Any acts of the government tending to induce idleness, dissipation of mind or morals, declare war with every principle of political economy, and send disease to the very vitals of the body politic. They open the store-houses of misery in the land. Legislators should be the guardians of the public morals. Their business should be to act for the public good.

Laws imposing restraints upon the evil passions and propensities of men, have always been found necessary. As vice increases, these laws must be multiplied. Livy tells us that when Rome was *pure*, she had no law against embezzling the public money, but when this crime began to appear, laws against it became necessary, and expense and danger to the public followed in their train. *Idleness produces vice.* By the laws of *Solon*, idleness was made a *crime*. By these laws each citizen was required to give an account of the manner of his obtaining a livelihood; the wisdom of this law-giver raised Athens to its highest glory. Vice creates an amazing tax upon industry and honesty; it fastens all the fruits of their exertions in a mortgage from which there is no redemption.

I have said that *labor* is the source of wealth, the capital of the nation. Land is also called a source of wealth; but without labor it would be of comparatively no value; even the few spontaneous productions of the earth useful to men, require *labor* in fitting them for such use.

I shall attempt to prove that *labor* applied to the production of what is *useful and beneficial* to society is *always accumulative* in its nature; all the fruits of our industry, so far as they are applied to meet the necessary wants of the community, are *investments for future use.* I use the term *investment* for what is sometimes called *expenditure.* In this connection, for illustration, the man who rears a dwelling, necessary for himself and family, makes an *investment* against future want, as directly, as he does who places his money in stocks for future use; he who labors to furnish himself and family with food and clothing suited to their wants, invests the fruits of his labor for future need, as directly as he does who stores his silver and his gold for a like purpose. Without these supplies the physical and moral energies of man could never be matured or sustained; all would be lost, and earth emptied of its inhabitants. Whatever is applied to the maturing, sustaining and perfecting the physical, intellectual and moral powers of men, and tending to promote that which is useful and beneficial to the community, is a capital applied to advance national wealth and prosperity; to secure the production and the application of such a capital is the duty of every government, and to this end should the science of political economy forever be directed.

An objection may arise to the view here taken, from the fact that labor to some extent in every country is applied to the production of what are denominated the superfluities of life; that these may be beneficial and yet are not among the supplies to meet the *wants* of the community. Be it so. It is not at variance with my position. The question how far a government can by its acts and its laws, patronize the production of the superfluities and luxuries of life in accordance with sound principles of political economy, is not a new one; the advocates for such patronage say it is a stimulus to increase industry; that it tends to develop mind and means for greater usefulness, which but for such a patronage would lie dormant and useless. So far as it has the effect, it is capital invested for future use. For example: the man who can purchase for himself a suit of clothes for fifty dollars, equally comfortable and equally durable, as a suit that would cost a hundred dollars, but for reasons which seem to him substantial, purchases the most expensive suit, and is induced by it to double his diligence and the fruits of his industry, loses nothing; by an increase of diligence and of skill, he invests in himself a new and increased capital for future profit; but suppose he has not increased his labor or his skill, to meet the extra amount of cost, then it is loss to him. Still, so far as his wants were supplied, it was a good investment for future profit.

The government which authorizes the manufacture and traffic in ardent spirits, lends its authority to legalize corruption, and violates the first principles of political economy. In the first place, I say the capital, the labor and the fruits of it directed in this channel are useless; it has often been proved that even to the druggist, ardent spirit is not necessary. Many medical and scientific men have testified to this assertion from their own experience. It is also evident from the fact, that drugs and compounds were as scientifically prepared and as successfully applied in staying the progress of disease, before the discovery of ardent spirit, as they have been since, and as a drink the article is highly pernicious, continually warring against the welfare of men.

If this position be true, government has no right to authorize the traffic; this I infer from several considerations. Every government is bound to protect its citizens in the enjoyment of their natural rights of life, and the use of the elements which surround them. It is as unjustifiable for a government to violate these rights, as it is for one individual to violate them. The government that should assume to make a grant to one or more, giving authority to corrupt the air, or the water which is for his neighbor's use, or to sell as healthful aliment, such kinds of food as injure his health, as manifestly acts without right, as the government would that should attempt to repeal the commands of the decalogue, or any other statute of heaven. It is violating the first great principles on which society is founded, and the rights which are granted by the unalterable laws of God. The legislature that assumes such a power, incurs a fearful responsibility. Many, while shielded by such authority, will carry on a traffic without remorse, at which the whole soul would be in agony but for the trappings of such an armor. In this way legislators become the patrons of iniquity; so it has been, and so it continues to be; every vile passion, and every evil propensity becomes clamorous for indulgence under legislative sanctions; they have often gained an influence fatal to the prosperity of a people, carrying degradation and misery in their train. Such influence has been witnessed from the licensing of lotteries, of theatres, and gambling houses, and has been fearfully illustrated in licensing the traffic in ardent spirit.

In what aspect would that government be viewed by a Christian community, or by a civilized world, which should directly authorize the commission of the same crimes, which are the legitimate fruits of the *traffic* which they do authorize? Strip the license law of its false attire, and it would read thus: "Be it enacted by the authority of government, that any person who will pay into the public treasury for the use of the government, one dollar, shall be permitted to become idle, dissolute, profane and abandoned in his character, to abuse his own family and commit violence on the property and persons of others, whenever he is thus disposed, or induce others to do it if he thinks proper." Such a law would be harmless, when compared with the law authorizing the traffic in ardent spirit. The license law throws off the restraints against the commission of crime, while it multiplies to an hundred fold the propensities for the commission of crime. Legislators cannot say they are ignorant of the effects of this traffic. Even if they could, they must know that voluntary ignorance can never excuse them. The legislator probably knows the effect of the *license* law, as well as he does the effect of any other law. Does he know the effect of the law made for the execution of the murderer, and for chaining down in perpetual solitude, the burglar and the robber? and does he know that on one page of his statute are written the penalties which await the perpetrators of crime, and on the next, a license for administering the very aliment which brings the sufferer to feel them? This is cruelty! *legalized cruelty!!* And is it right? I ask again, is it right? If it is not, it is wrong; there is no middle latitude on this compass. Again, I would ask the legislator, who sanctions the traffic in ardent spirit, what he would say of a traffic, furnishing an article to the very swine he feeds, if it should have the same effect on them that ardent spirit has on the human species, producing no nourishment to the animal, but bringing disease and premature death, even against the counteracting effects of all the nutritious aliment that could be administered? would not the swine be entitled to legislative protection against the common enemy of their species, and would not the trade be denounced as a great public calamity?

The *traffic in ardent spirit violates the first principles of political economy.* It diminishes the productive labor of the nation. It is computed that about one in ten of the adult male population of our country is disabled by the use of ardent spirit from performing the usual labor of a man. His mere disability, if it cost nothing to support him, would require one-tenth more labor to be performed by the residue, and when we add the expense of support to the disabled one, we shall increase the burden upon industrious sobriety nearly as much more; for he that does not contribute his share to the common supply is a pensioner upon the bounty of his fellow men.

The capital, materials and labor converted into ardent spirit, becomes a TOTAL LOSS *to the world*, and the community is taxed to make up the loss. Though the producer obtains his exchange, the manufacturer his reward, and the retailer his profit, the *consumer loses the whole.* Is it not so? do the avails of his purchase feed, or clothe, or instruct, or improve, or in any way benefit him or his? Place the mind on this point with all the intenseness of minute discovery, and point me to the benefit which the *consumer* has derived from his purchase; if some benefit is not derived and cannot be derived, then it must be a *total loss*, involving all the capital, labor and profit which the purchase cost. It is loss to the world, and doubly so to the *consumer*, for with this loss his physical and mental powers are impaired, the very capital which he had invested for future use. Had the devouring element consumed the purchase and spared the purchaser, his loss would have been comparatively small. When labor and the resources of the country are applied in advancing the great objects for which man was created and civil and political communities formed, to mature and elevate and purify the mind of man and perfect all his powers, they become *beneficial investments* for the *public good;* the more deeply this principle becomes fixed in the minds of men, the greater will be the demand upon these investments for carrying on the great purposes of improving the world, till man arrives to the highest elevation of which he is susceptible, in his present state of existence.

The argument for the manufacture and sale of ardent spirit derived from the fact that these employments afford occupation for multitudes, when viewed in its bearings on *political economy*, will be seen to be unsound. What one gains another loses. Even if the government derive a revenue from the manufacture or the sale, it changes not the case, the *consumer loses the whole.* The government can never be benefitted by a traffic, the result of which is a *total loss* to every one of the entire amount of the article which is the object of the traffic. For illustration, suppose the government should import infection for spreading the *cholera* or the *plague* through the country, and a revenue should be derived from a traffic in the article, and an army of druggists and of the medical faculty and attendants should find full employment, the business become extended, the revenue increased till one half of the population of the country was required for administering relief to the wants of the other half; would the government be profited? would this be a wise system of political economy? Just so far as the moral or physical energies of a people are diseased or palsied by the acts of the government, just so far the government is weakening, impoverishing and ruining itself. In this respect what is true of a single family is true of a nation; as well might the father of a family imagine that he was accumulating wealth from a traffic which should bring idleness, profligacy, disease and death within his own doors, as a government could imagine itself deriving a *beneficial revenue* from a traffic producing similar consequences upon its own citizens. Take another view of the same *general principle*, of revenue from human suffering merely as a question of *political economy.* Suppose the government barters the lives, the health, the means of usefulness of its subjects for gain. A revenue is derived from the traffic, *human scalps or amputated limbs*, by supposition, are in great demand in a foreign market; the government *possessing the power* "*to enforce the wrong, dooms and devotes its subjects as their lawful prey,*" furnishes that market till the avails should fill the government treasury to overflowing, would it be a *saving policy* for the nation? Their energies crippled and all their powers palsied, the remainder helpless, miserable, wretched remnants of humanity, a charge on public charity, and objects of pity at which even savage mercy would weep tears of blood. Apply the illustration to the effects which ardent spirit is producing in the land, and these effects are but faintly represented. It is ascertained that *thirty thousand* die annually in the United States by intemperance, probably many more. A portion of these are for a time cast on the public for support. The loss to the community of the labor of each, for a single year, is at least fifty dollars, which he might have earned more than the supply of his own wants. By this traffic he is made a pensioner on the public to a like amount. Thirty thousand such cases would cause a loss of three millions of dollars annually. If the government has gained in revenue, it has granted no equivalent to the victims of the traffic.

Another argument in favor of this traffic is, that *producers* might be multiplied to an injurious extent, were it not for a class of *consumers*. It is said that what was not likely to be consumed would not be produced: the argument is an old one and is simply this, the producer will not apply his labor to supply his own wants and to increase his own comforts, unless he can apply a portion of his produce to support the idle and the profligate; a fact is assumed in this case which has nothing to support it. Examination will prove the reverse of the proposition, the assumed fact is mere delusion.

Six years ago, there were in the county of Hampshire, Massachusetts, about forty distilleries; the county contains about thirty thousand inhabitants. At many of these distilleries, there were consumed annually for each one, several thousand bushels of grain. These have ceased to operate, and our grain bears a higher price uniformly than when they were in operation. What is true in that county, is true elsewhere; we may discover a reason why it is so. The *mere consumer* does nothing to benefit the producer. Like the horse leach, he cries give, give; like the devouring element, he makes no return. If he returns an equivalent for what he receives, it is the fruit of others' labors, and might as well have passed to the hands of the producer, without his interference, as with it; all he possesses is as pensioner on the bounty of others, reaping where he has not sown, and gathering where he has not strawed.

Again, no government has ever acted on the principle that a class of *mere consumers* is necessary or useful, and such a class has never existed but as objects of compassion or of dread. If such a class be necessary, the true policy of the government would be to designate them with reference to their moral character, and that their number be such as would produce the greatest amount of labor to the nation. The principle, as bearing on the economy of the nation, may be seen under the inquiry, *who remunerates* the *producer* for what is furnished to the *mere consumer?* It is very evident that the *mere* consumer cannot, for he has nothing to pay with; the answer may be the *government*. And who is the government in this connection, and what the means and source of its wealth? this is *labor*, the industry of the *producer*. This mode of market-making brings us to this anomaly in political economy, that for the purpose of creating a market for our surplus produce, we must have a class of *mere consumers*, and that the *producers* must pay themselves for what is thus consumed, and do we not come to the same result as before, that it is a *total loss?* The price of labor cannot increase but by an increase of the funds from which it is to be remunerated. Every effective laborer taken from the producing class, diminishes the general fund. To increase the effective labor of a nation, must increase its wealth and all its resources, and this in its turn again increases the rewards to active industry. Hence every member of the community is interested in increasing the means for remunerating the laborer, that they become as abundant as possible. The prosperity and *increasing* wealth of a nation furnish the richest rewards to the laborer, and are an inducement to activity and diligence in the active pursuits of life. The mere consumer hangs as a continual discouragement upon the active industry of the country. The truth of this principle may be illustrated by adverting to such judgments upon the fruits of the field as produce a scarcity: here is a *consumer*, but is it beneficial to the public. Have patriots or Christians ever desired the visits of blast or mildew on the fruits of the field, for the purpose of creating a *consumption*, or making a market for the surplus produce of the laborer? The locusts and caterpillars of Egypt, were *con-*

sumers, but no blessing to the nation. By the unalterable laws of God, labor is the source whence our wants are to be supplied, and without it the world would be depopulated. In savage life, labor is *limited* and supplies *scanty;* labor does not go beyond the production of mere necessaries; yet something in the form of labor does exist, and no nation can exist without it. The grave would hardly be more barren of supplies for the wants of life, than the earth without the aids of active industry. To discontinue the traffic in ardent spirit would increase the wealth of the nation almost beyond calculation. In a few years the value of our lands would be doubled, purchasers would be multiplied, active labor greatly increased, and wealth accumulating for the useful purposes of life. New investments and applications of capital would give elasticity to mind and enterprise in action; these in their turn would become accumulative and seek new investments for purposes beneficial to the public. Railroads and canals, would bring into commercial nearness the most distant parts of the land; means of instruction in the useful arts of life, would be furnished and directed to the improvement of the intellectual and moral powers of man. It is not within the scope of my design to carry out in statistical detail, the effects of suppressing the traffic in ardent spirit, neither could it come within the limits prescribed for this essay; all that can be done here is to present *general principles*, leaving the details and the application of them for others.

Probably more than *one hundred millions* of dollars have been lost annually to these United States, for a succession of years in this traffic; it is a *total loss*, and whether it be more or less than the computation here made, is of little moment to the patriot or the Christian. We cannot here follow out the demoralizing effects of the traffic upon the community; three-fourths of the crime of the land, three-fourths of the expense of our criminal code, three-fourths of the occurrences which jeopardize life and property by night and by day, by sea and by land, and three-fourths of all the misery which the righteous retribution of infinite justice visits on our land is the offspring of this traffic. These effects merely on the financial concerns of the country, must arrest the attention of every patriot; he must act, and he will act till these streams of desolation are dried at their fountain. *Temperance* is the means to produce the change, the redeeming power which alone can accomplish the work. By this, thousands of drunkards will be reclaimed, and tens of thousands of free drinkers saved from a drunkard's end. By this, vast numbers of the idle, the profligate, and the abandoned, will be turned to honest and useful employment. By this our alms-houses, our penitentiaries, our jails and our state prisons, will be converted into apartments for free, useful and profitable industry. By this, many families will be taken from the sinks of degradation, and misery, and restored to comfort, and to competence, and instructed in the useful arts of life. Legislators should begin this work and place this traffic on the contraband list, as filled with contagion to the community. Such an act of prohibition on the traffic would soon change the whole aspect of things; prosperity would be written on all the employments of men, and give stability and perpetuity to the government: forty thousand public prosecutions for crimes would be saved for a single year, at an expense of two millions of dollars; an army of pensioners on public charity, and officers for executing the penalties of law upon transgressors, would be disbanded, and seek useful and productive employment. It was said of one of the former kings of England, that during his reign, "none needed the public charity, because none were idle." The emphatic language of the celebrated Burke, should forever be kept in mind, that, "*Patience, labor, frugality, sobriety, and religion,* are the support of *political economy, true benevolence, and real charity,* and all the rest is *down right fraud.*"

Remarks.—The above article is re-published in this volume for preservation, and to show the present and the rising generation the kind of argument which was used over thirty years since by great and good men, now for the most part no more, to arouse the American people to the serious consideration of an evil which was rapidly sapping the very foundation of our nation's greatness. Let the above be read by all men who love the human race and seek for its advancement in all that is good and great. Never was there a period in *our nation's history* when the wisdom contained in the above essay, should sink deeper into every patriotic heart. God grant that it may so be, and produce fruits a thousand fold.—Ed.

South Ballston, *Nov.* 8, 1864.

No. 18.

REDUCTION

IN RATE OF

INSURANCE ON TEMPERANCE SHIPS.

[Extract from Article II (2) in the *American Quarterly Magazine, Oct 1st*, 1834, on the Reduction in the Rate of Insurance on Temperance Ships, and before the great principle of total abstinence from all that can intoxicate had become universal, as the basis of all organized temperance labors.]

The temperance reformation is gradually, but steadily, and we trust irresistably extending its influence into every class of society, and every pursuit and relation in life. And well it may, for no practice or custom can be mentioned which had ever gained such universal prevalence in a civilized community, producing so much evil without any countervailing good, as the use of intoxicating drinks. Our fervent prayer is that the friends of this cause may never cease their efforts until the only remedy and the only preventive, *total abstinence from all that can intoxicate*, shall be a universal motto.

This great reformation differs from all others that have ever been undertaken by human instrumentality alone, in several particulars. It addresses man as a moral and intellectual, as well as a social and physical being. It has a bearing both on his temporal and eternal interests. All other great attempts at reformation have had some one specific object in view, and have been based upon such principles or have united such elements as have entirely forbidden their universal adoption. But this addresses itself equally to the king on his throne and the beggar on the dunghill; to all denominations in religion, and to men of no religion; to all parties in politics; to the patriot, to the political economist, to men in every profession, to the poor and to the rich; to the farmer, the merchant, the mechanic and the laborer; to parents and children; to husbands and wives; and in short to man in all conditions, circumstances and relations. It moreover offers no compromise. It proposes the entire abandonment of a habit almost universal, and the substitution of one directly opposite, under a full and unequivocal assurance that nothing but good shall result from the change.

But it is not our intention, in our further progress, to dwell upon the common views of this subject. Our readers will have perceived, at the head of this article, that we have a new text. The unmixed, uncompensated evils resulting from the use of alcohol have been spread before the public, supported by such an accumulation of evidence as would appear to be irresistable; it would seem that the world must be aroused, and that every man who loves his own or his neighbor's body or soul, must enlist in a war of extermination against so deadly a foe to his race. This effect, however, has not been produced; and although victory after victory has been achieved, still the enemy is strong, and numbers amongst his hosts many of the rich, the honorable, the talented, the respectable and the *pious* of the land: indeed these alone sustain him; these form his van guard; these are his shield and his only efficient protectors. The drunkards! They are powerless. Their minds and bodies are enfeebled; their property is mostly wasted; they are captives to alcohol, not his defenders; many of them struggle to escape from his chains, but alas! they are unable, for whichever way they turn they are headed and hemmed in by officers and soldiers in the army of alcohol, under the guise of respectable temperate drinkers and respectable dealers, who by their *example, solicitations* and *temptations*, drive the helpless victim back to heavier chains and deeper degradation.

But we would say to the friends of temperance, take courage! A new ally has appeared; a fresh victory is won; a wide and promising field for future operations is opened; you have only to persevere, and by the help of God your success will be complete. And whilst we encourage our friends we would also present to those who are indifferent or neutral and to those who still oppose, the fruits of our recent acquisitions, affording as they do the strongest possible evidence of the goodness of our cause and the truth of our principles; and we would earnestly, but kindly, ask them to unite with us, and thus save themselves and the perishing around them.

The recent proceedings of the marine insurance companies of the city of New York, in relation to temperance, are of so interesting and important a character, and afford such delightful encouragement to the friends of temperance, and to the best friends of the human race, that we have felt sure that we could not better serve the cause than by laying their proceedings before our readers, with our general views of the subject, and our estimates of some of the results that may reasonably be expected to follow the proposed measures.

Copy of a Letter from Edward C. Delavan to the Committee appointed by the Board of Underwriters of the city of New York.

To the Committee appointed by the Board of Underwriters, to take into consideration the expediency of allowing a discount on the premium of insurance on all vessels sailing without ardent spirit:

GENTLEMEN:

I have submitted to your consideration a document embracing the experience of very many of the most intelligent masters and ship owners in the Union, which clearly demonstrates, that a very large proportion of all the losses of life and property on the ocean, are occasioned directly or indirectly by the use of ardent spirit, and as an inducement to all interested in navigation to give the subject serious attention, I would most respectfully suggest, that you recommend the adoption of a rule by all Insurance Offices in the city of New York, to return five per cent on the premium of insurance, on all vessels on return to port, or at the termination of the risk, on satisfactory evidence being given, by the officers of vessels insured, that no ardent spirit has been used as a drink, by officers or men, during the voyage or voyages.

I am, Gentlemen, with great respect,

Your obedient servant,

(Signed,) EDWARD C. DELAVAN.

The undersigned, to whom was referred the above communication from Mr. E. C. Delavan, believing that its adoption would subserve the cause of humanity, raise still higher the character of American vessels, and increase the security of our navigation, do hereby recommend, in accordance thereto, that the Board of Underwriters should resolve to hereafter allow a deduction of five per cent upon the nett premium *earned* by any of the Insurance Companies of this city, on any vessel or vessels insured by them, upon the presentation of a deposition from the commander and mate, that no spirituous liquors had been drank by officers or men, on board their vessel during the passage, voyage, or term for which she has been insured.

(Signed,) ABR. OGDEN, J. R. HURD, ADAM TREDWELL, *Committee.*

New York, Oct. 1, 1834.

At a special meeting of the Board of Underwriters, held at the office of the American Insurance Company, in the city of New York, on the 2d October, 1834, present,

Mr. WM. NEILSON, President, and

Mr. ABM. OGDEN, Vice-President of the Board, and the following members:

Messrs. J. R. Hurd,	Messrs. F. Diblee,
J. P. Tappan,	A. Tredwell,
H. Cotheal,	N. G. Rutgers,
J. C. Delprat,	J. K. Hamilton,
C. McEvers, senr.,	J. R. Skiddy,
B. McEvers, jun.,	C. C. Walden, and
J. L. Hale,	W. R. Jones.
B. Balch,	

Mr. OGDEN, chairman of the committee, to whom was referred a communication from E. C. Delavan, Esq., on the subject of temperance ships, made a report recommending that the Insurance Companies of this city make a deduction of five per cent on the premiums arising on ships navigated by crews not using ardent spirits.

Whereupon the following resolution was unanimously adopted.

Resolved, That the different Marine Insurance Companies in the city of New York, will allow a deduction of five per cent, on the nett premiums which may be taken after this date, on all vessels, and on vessels together with their outfits if on whaling and sealing voyages, terminating without loss, provided the master and mate make affidavit, after the termination of the risk, that no ardent spirits had been drank on board the vessel, by the officers and crew, during the voyage or term for which the vessel or outfits were insured. WM. NEILSON, President.

WALTER R. JONES, Secretary of the Board.

List of Insurance Offices, with Officers and Capital.

Name	*President.*	*Secretary.*	*Capital.*
New York	C. McEvers	T. B. Satterthwaite	500,000
Ocean	A. Ogden	I. S. Schermerhorn	350,000
American	Wm. Neilson	P. Hoyt	500,000
Union	J. P. Tappan	W. J. Van Wagenen	500,000
Atlantic	J. L. Hale	J. R. Pentz	350,000
Neptune,	J. R. Hurd	A. B. Neilson	250,000
National	J. K. Hamilton	W. T. Jones	250,000
Jackson	F. Diblee	L. Gregory	400,000
New York State,	J. Bolton	C. C. Walden	300,000
Commercial	B. Balch	E. Hale	300,000
	Total capital		$3,700,000

NOTE.—At a subsequent meeting of the Board of Underwriters, $1500 was voted out of the funds of the Board), to print for the use of the American sailor, 100,000 Temperance Tracts, adapted to their need, which order was duly executed.

The directors and officers of these companies are as respectable a body of men as can be collected in any community. They are selected to manage the concerns of these important institutions on account of their intelligence and their good standing in the commercial world. These qualifications are indispensable in order to insure the good management of the affairs committed to them, and in order to command the public confidence. They are no enthusiasts. They know nothing, in their collective capacity, of parties in politics or sects in religion. They have probably never been called upon to express themselves on any question purely religious, moral or political, nor would they, as directors of these companies, have listened, for a moment, to any suggestion whatever of such a character. These gentlemen, and the stockholders whom they represent, each for himself, acts in these particulars according to the dictates of his own conscience. Their only aim, as a body, is, to manage the affairs of their institutions with skill and integrity; and their success, and the high standing they enjoy, both at home and abroad, afford the best possible evidence of their ability and uprightness. In the consideration of the matter in question they inquired only for facts in their bearing upon this question alone. Nothing but the most irresistible evidence in favor of temperance, nothing short of a full assurance that total abstinence from ardent spirits would promote the safety of property on the ocean, could have induced them to embark thus publicly in promoting the great temperance reformation.

Let us look for a moment at the facts presented to them. It has been ascertained beyond a dispute that by far the greater part of the shipwrecks and accidents at sea, are occasioned, directly or indirectly, by ardent spirits; that vast amounts of property lost, thousands of lives sacrificed, a great share of the insubordination and mutinies may be traced to this cause alone. It was moreover shown satisfactorily, on the testimony of numerous respectable ship owners and masters, that ships can be navigated in all parts of the world, and on the longest voyages, without ardent spirit; that the seamen enjoy better health, that they are better able to endure hardships, and that in every respect their comfort and safety are promoted by entire and total abstinence from the article. It was shown that several hundred ships have already made voyages, of every description, from this country, upon this principle, with the most satisfactory results; and that the superior safety and good order of our temperance ships was exciting attention in Europe. The action had by the Insurance Companies fully confirms these statements; their knowledge of every thing that relates to commerce being such as would enable them at once to refute any erroneous representations.

It may be set down as certain, therefore, that ardent spirits, in all circumstances and in all climates, on the ocean, are not only unnecessary, but that they are hurtful and dangerous. The insurers of ships in New York publicly offer an inducement to all ship owners and seamen to abandon their use.

A GOOD CREATURE OF GOD.

The Rev. Dr. Guthrie, of Scotland says:

"I have heard a man with a bottle of whisky before him have the impudence and assurance to say: 'Every creature of God is good, and nothing to be refused, if it be received with thanksgiving;' and he would persuade me that what was made in the still-pot was a creature of God. In one sense it is so; but in the same sense so is arsenic, so is oil of vitriol, so is prussic acid. Think of a fellow tossing off a glass of vitriol, and excusing himself by saying that it is a creature of God. He would not use many such creatures, that's all I'll say. Whisky is good in its own place. There is nothing like whisky in this world for preserving a man when he is dead. But it is one of the worst things in the world for preserving a man when he is living. If you want to keep a dead man, put him in whisky; if you want to kill a living man, put the whisky into him. It was a capital thing for preserving the dead admiral, when they put him in a rum puncheon; but it was a bad thing for the sailors when they tapped the cask, and drank the liquor till they left the admiral as he never left his ship—high and dry."—*N. Y. Observer.*

BREAD is the staff of life, and liquor the stilts—the former sustaining man, and the latter elevating him for a *fall.*—*N. Y. Observer.*

No. 19.

LONDON STAR AND LONDON TIMES

ON

TEMPERANCE, ETC., ETC.

[From the *London Star*.]

"The motives and objects of the Prohibitory Bill promoters must of necessity command the high respect and cordial sympathy of all who have at heart the welfare of humanity, for the cancer which they are striving to extirpate is one of the most virulent that ever ate into the vitals of a nation. No words can be too vivid to paint the hideousness of the myriad evils of which intemperance is the prolific parent. Excess* in the use of strong drink peoples the hospital, the lunatic asylum, the work house, and the gaol. It poisons the bodies, emasculates the minds, empties the pockets, and corrupts the morals of its victims, whose self-wrought destruction of body and soul adds enormously to the burthens of sober and decently-conducted taxpayers. The homes which it has desolated may be counted by thousands, and imagination shudders at the contemplation of the huge army of immortal beings hurried by it to perdition. There exists no difference of opinion among rational men with regard to the vast power and intense malignity of this foe to human happiness and human progress—the only question

*All use as a beverage is "excess."

is as to the most efficient means of checking its advances and securing its definitive defeat."

[From the *London Times*.]

"It may happen that our curious foreigner may in other parts of the world have seen the contortions of Arabs under the influence of *hasheesh;* he may have seen a Malay furious from bang, a Turk trembling from the effects of *opium*, or a Chinaman emaciated from inordinate indulgence in the same vice; but for a scene of sterling vice, and lust, and filth, and frenzy, all drawn into one pit, and fermenting *under the patronage of the law*, he might search the world all over and never find a rival to that object of ambition to respectable vintners, and that creation of Middlesex magistrates—a thriving public house in a low gin-drinking neighborhood."

James Haughton, Esq., J. P., of Dublin, alluding to the above quotation from the *London Times*, remarks:

"A more severe, a more terrible, a more just anathema, has, perhaps, never been uttered against the cruel liquor traffic of these countries. It will not do to say that men should drink liquors in moderation. No nation that uses them has ever done so; and the 600,000 drunkards which it has been computed are ever floating in these United Kingdoms are sufficient evidence that so-called moderation in their use is a recommendation which will not and cannot be followed; so that if we would get rid of the fearful drunkenness which is our shame and our disgrace, some better means must be resorted to.

That Christian British Poet, Cowper, born 26th April, 1731, and died 25th April, 1794, well understood the nature of the license system and its effects: a brief extract is given from the Task, Book IV:

"Pass where we may, through city or through town,
Village or hamlet of this merry land,
Though lean and beggar'd, every twentieth pace
Conducts the unguarded nose to such a whiff
Of stale debauch forth issuing from the sties
That LAW HAS LICENSED, as makes temperance reel.

There sit involved and lost in curling clouds
Of Indian fume, and guzzling deep, the boor,
The lackey, and the groom. The craftsman there
Takes Lethean leave of all his toil;
Smith, cobbler, joiner, he that plies the shears,
And he that kneads the dough, all loud alike,
All learned and all drunk. The fiddle screams
Plaintive and piteous, as it wept and wailed
Its wasted tones and harmony unheard.
Dire is the frequent curse, and its twin sound
The cheek-distending oath. *'Tis here they learn*
The road that leads from competence and peace,
To indigence and rapine; till at last
Society, grown weary of the load,
Shakes her incumbered lap, and casts them out.
But censure profits little; vain the attempt
To advertise in verse a public pest,
That like the filth with which the peasant feeds
His hungry acres, stinks, and is of use.
Th' excise is fattened with the rich result
Of all this riot: The ten thousand casks,
Forever dribbling out their base contents,
Touched by the Midas finger of the state
Bleed gold for Parliament to vote away.
Drink and be mad, then; 'tis your country bids;
Gloriously drunk—obey the important call;
Her cause demands the assistance of your throats;
Ye all can swallow, and she asks no more."

Remarks.—Mr. Houghton is right. When Mr. Gladstone was urging the wine bill through Parliament as a Temperance measure (I was present at the discussion), the *London Times* was with him. During the agitation of the question, however, that influential paper made the admission that "*wine is less poisonous than gin,*" thereby coming up in a degree to the standard of the learned chemists of the world. Still the Times is in error: intoxicating wine is not "less poisonous than gin." If a glass of gin contains 100 drops of alcohol and a certain number of glasses of wine or any other fermented drinks, contain the same number of drops, the account is balanced, the evil is the same to those drinking the same amount of alcohol in wine or in gin.

The Duke of Orleans in 1838, who was at the time the Commander in Chief of the armies of France, stated that the allowance of one bottle of the light wine of the country as a day's ration to the soldier, was the direct cause of most of the intemperance in the army. That this ONE bottle, as weak as it was, had the stimulating effect on the appetite to create the desire for another bottle, and still another, and to satisfy this desire caused by the first bottle *given* by the government as a ration, the small pay of the soldier was exhausted to purchase additional bottles to satisfy the cravings induced by the alcohol contained in the first; then followed disobedience of orders, crime, court martials and punishment. The first bottle *here*, like the first glass *everywhere*, is the origin of all the drunkenness of the world, and until it is given up by all classes, drunkenness with all its train of horrors will continue to curse this world. Intoxicating drink, what is it? why is it so called? If it takes six glasses of this poison to make a man drunk, what share in producing this madness should attach to the first of the six glasses? This is a vital question, settled in the minds of some, but not yet settled as it should be, in the minds of all. A learned professor has stated: "The line which divides temperate (so called) from intemperate drinking HAS NOT YET BEEN DRAWN."

There can be no temperate use of alcohol in any drink, no matter how genteel or aristocratic in *name*. Any use of such liquor as a beverage, is abuse—is "excess." Let the terms "moderate use" and "excess," be abandoned as *implying temperance* (there is no truth in them), by those who wish to place the reformation on a solid and lasting foundation.

With due respect, I would ask of those who ridicule the "fallacies" and "follies" of temperance advocates, if they would take upon themselves the responsibility of recommending the moderate use of hasheesh or opium, and licensing men to vend *them* for common use. Opium and hasheesh are acknowledged to be poison, and when used as a medicine should, like other poisons, be prescribed with the greatest caution. Alcohol is a poison in the same sense as opium and hasheesh, a slow poison to the more cautious, but a swift one to the incautious. Understanding the question as I now do, and after a study and *experimented practice* of near forty years, for *me* to use intoxicating drinks as a beverage *is sin.* I have no right to judge others, but I would advise every one to examine the question seriously (aside from preconceived opinions or habits, which are sometimes very blinding), with the light of the Bible and science before them, and if after such examination, they find that God has declared alcohol (and without any qualification) "a mocker," and science has also settled the question that it is *a poison*, it is hoped they will join our ranks, and with their influence and labors and means as far as convenient, assist in rolling back the mighty flood of intemperance which now threatens to overwhelm us, and ruin those we hold most dear. With a concerted action—a simultaneous movement in the right direction by the wise and the good, and the republic again united, the nation's debt would soon be wiped out by the increased wealth resulting from true temperance habits.

It is thought by many who have studied the question, that a vast body of good men, the excellent of the earth, have in some degree at least, overlooked the *one* great cause of a large proportion of the destitution, misery and crime in our great cities. It is an evil which if not arrested, will exert such a controlling influence as will in time over-ride good influences and culminate in rendering our great cities pandemoniums of vice and corruption. The licensed grog shops before the war, caused about three-fourths of our local taxes, *placing a first mortgage on the real and personal property of the state.* The good and benevolent of our cities should at once turn their attention to this great question. By devoting one-tenth of the tax now created by the license system and contributions to alleviate the sufferings of families, made wretched by its agency, in enlightening the masses and the public mind generally as to the necessity of breaking up that system, they would soon see a change that would astonish them.

An experienced physician, when called to a patient, first applies himself to study the disease, its nature and its cause. He does not recommend the continuance of habits which created the disease, but at once says, "stop those habits or you must die." So with our license system; it causes through its effects the destitution of vast numbers, breaks down their characters, and renders them unworthy of the ballot. It has been stated that every grog-shop controls on the average at least twelve votes.

Look at the vote on the 8th Nov., 1864, in New York. I am no partisan in politics—parties change, and each is glad to receive the rum vote. But let virtuous politicians of all parties (and there are plenty of such), look well into this matter, and do all in their power to purify the ballot—else the rum vote will control the nation, and then its days as a republic are numbered.

In closing, we give another extract from the *London Times*, taken from the *N. Y. Observer*, of the 15th December, 1864:

The *London Times* is preaching temperance. The world does move. Hear what the "leading" newspaper of England says of the use of intoxicating liquors:

"It is a peculiarity of spirit drinking that money spent upon it is, at the best, thrown away, and in general far worse than thrown away. It neither supplies the natural wants of man, nor offers an adequate substitute for them. Indeed, it is far too favorable a view of the subject to treat the money spent on it as if it were cast into the sea. A great portion of the harvest of Sweden, and of many other countries, is applied to a purpose compared with which it would have been better that the corn had never grown, or that it had been mildewed in the ear. No way so rapid to increase the wealth of nations and the morality of society could be desired, as the utter annihilation of the manufacture of ardent spirits, constituting as they do an infinite waste and an unmixed evil."

Good doctrine that, for all countries and times.

THE

INFLUENCE OF WINE DRINKING,

Hundreds of Centuries before the Art of Distilling was known.

Tantoquo opere, tanto labore et impendio constat, quod hominis mentem mutet ac furorem gignat, millibus scelerum huic deditis.

TRANSLATION.

(So vast are our efforts, so vast our labors, and so regardless of cost, which we lavish on a liquid—[wine], which deprives man of his reason, and drives him to frenzy and the commission of a thousand crimes.)—PLINY.—*London Tem. Spectator.*

In the early movement in favor of Temperance Reform in this country, distinguished and learned writers denied that wine contained alcohol, therefore could not produce drunkenness. They were entirely right, if they referred to the *un*-intoxicating wine, wine a blessing; but wrong if they referred to *in*toxicating wine, wine a curse, when used as a beverage, and the kind of wine which Pliny refers to.—[ED.

FABRICATORS

OF

FALSIFIED LIQUORS, IN LONDON, GETTING THEIR DUES.

De Witt and Wright, the two men concerned in the extensive wine frauds in London, were tried at the Central Criminal Court on Wednesday. The jury returned a verdict of guilty; and previous convictions having been proved against both prisoners, they were each sentenced to *fifteen years* penal servitude.

No. 20.

SCHEDULE OF BIBLE TEXTS

RELATIVE TO WINE, Etc.,

FROM THE LONDON EDITION OF

DR. NOTT'S TEMPERANCE LECTURES,

CORRECTED BY DR. F. R. LEES.

I.—*Texts in which the* Fruit of the Vine, *or some one of its preparations, is spoken of with* approbation, *in its natural, or at least, unintoxicating state, i. e. the state in which it exists in the cluster where it grows, or the press and the vat in which it is put; the state being evident from the text, or deducible from the products classed with it, or from the sequel of its use, or from its absence being regarded as a loss.*

(1.)—Hebrew, TIROSH (Vintage Fruit)—Approved.

Texts.		Authorized Version.	Septuagint.	Vulgate.	Context.
Genesis	27: 28	wine	οἶνος	vinum	Dew and rain, as causing the growth of corn and other blessings.
"	27: 37	"	"	"	
Deuteronomy ..	11: 14	"	"	"	
"	33: 28	"	"	"	
"	28: 51	"	"	"	Corn failing through drouth, or otherwise by way of judgment.
Isaiah	24: 7	new-wine	"	vindemia	
Hosea	2: 9	wine	"	vinum	
"	9: 2	new-wine	"	"	
Joel	1: 10	"	"	"	
Haggai ,......	1: 11	"	"	"	
Nehemiah	5: 11	"	"	"	The restoration or increase, of natural things.
Psalms........	4: 7 (8)	"	"	"	
Hosea	2: 22	"	"	"	

Explanation.—The figures within ( ) refer to the Hebrew text. Bis (*i. e.* twice). The general terms *oinos* and *vinum* are put in the Nominative Case; but for the exceptional renderings, the Case as in the original text has been preserved.

Book	Ch.	Verse	English	Greek	Latin	Remarks
Joel	2:	19	wine	οἶνος	vinum	Corn, plenty, and rejoicing, as blessings.
2 Kings	18:	32	"	"	"	
2 Chronicles	32:	28	"	"	"	
Isaiah	36:	17	"	"	"	
"	62:	8	"	"	"	
Jeremiah	31:	12	"	"	"	
Deuteronomy	7:	13	"	"	vindemiæ	Vines, grapes, and vats.
Zechariah	9:	17	new-wine	"	vinum	
Judges	9:	13	wine	"	"	
Proverbs*	3:	10	new-wine	"	"	
Isaiah	65:	8	"	ῥὼξ	granum	
Joel*	2:	24	wine	οἶνος	vinum	
Micah	6:	15	sweet-wine	"	mustum	
Numbers	18:	12	wine	"	vinum	First fruits, tithes, and offerings.
Deuteronomy	12:	17	"	"	"	
"	14:	23	"	"	"	
"	18:	4	"	"	"	
2 Chronicles	31:	5	"	"	"	
Nehemiah	10:	37	"	"	vindemiæ	
"	10:	39 (40)	new-wine	"	vinum	
"	13:	5, 12	"	"	"	
Hosea	2:	8 (10)	wine	"	"	Named as a mere luxury.
"	4:	11	"	"	"	

* The Hebrew words in these texts translated 'burst out' and 'overflow' signify *abundance*.

(2) Hebrew, YAYIN—used with approbation.

Texts.		English.	Septuagint.	Vulgate.	Context.
1 Chronicles ...	27: 27	wine	οἶνος	vinariis	
Nehemiah	5: 18	"	"	vinum	
"	13: 15	"	"	"	
Job	32: 19	"	γλεῦκος	mustum	
Psalms	104: 15	"	οἶνος	vinum	
Canticles	5: 1	"	"	"	
"	7: 9 (10)	"	"	"	For the most part, wheat, grapes, vine-yards, ingatherings, wine presses, etc.
"	8: 2	"	"	"	
Isaiah	16: 10	"	"	"	
Deuteronomy ..	28: 39	"	"	"	
Jeremiah	40: 10	"	"	vindemiam	
"	" 12	"	"	vinum	
"	48: 33	"	"	"	
Lamentations .	2: 12	"	"	"	
Hosea	14: 7 (8)	"	"	"	
Amos	5: 11	"	"	"	
"	9: 14	"	"	"	
Joel	1: 5	"	"	"	
Genesis	14: 18	"	"	"	
Deuteronomy ..	29: 6 (5)	"	"	"	

Zephaniah ...	1: 15	wine	οἶνος	vinum	
Judges	19: 19	"	"	"	
1 Samuel......	25: 18	"	"	"	
2 Samuel......	16: 1, 2	"	"	"	
1 Chronicles ..	12: 40	"	"	"	
2 Chronicles ..	2: 10(9) 15(14)	"	"	"	Corn, oil, raisins, fruit, and other natural productions.
"	11: 11	"	"	"	
Nehemiah	5: 15	"	"	"	
Ezekiel	27: 18	"	"	"	
Ecclesiastes ...	9: 7	"	"	"	
Exodus	29: 40	"	"	"	
Leviticus......	23: 13	"	"	"	
Numbers	15: 5, 7, 10	"	"	"	
"	28: 14	"	"	"	
1 Samuel......	1: 24	"	"	"	Oil, offerings, etc.
"	10: 3	"	"	"	
"	16: 20	"	"	"	
1 Chronicles ...	9: 29	"	"	"	
Hosea	9: 4	"	"	"	
Deuteronomy ..	14: 26	"	"	"	A feast.
Proverbs	9: 2	"	"	"	As mixed by wisdom (with water).
Zechariah	9: 15	"	"	"	
"	10: 7	"	"	"	
Canticles	1: 2, 4	"	"	"	Comparison with different things.
"	4: 10	"	"	"	
Genesis	49: 11	"	"	"	
Psalms........	78: 65	"	"	"	
Isaiah	29: 9	"	"	"	
"	51: 21	"	"	"	

II. *Specific Terms, used variously.*

Ausis	Canticles	8: 2	juice	νάματος	mustum	With other natural productions.
	Joel	1: 5	new-wine	οἶνος	dulcedine	
	"	3: 18	"	γλυκασμόν	dulcedinem	
	Amos ..	9: 13	sweet-wine	"	"	
Æshishah .	2 Samuel	6: 19	flagon of wine	λάγανον απο τήγανου	similam frixam oleo	With food as needful for men, women and children.
	1 Chron.	16: 3	"	αμορίτην αρτον	"	
	Canticles	2: 5	flagons	αμύροις (a cake)	floribus	
	Hosea ..	3: 1	flagons of wine	πέμματα	vinacia (husks)	
Sobhe	" ..	4: 18	drink		convivium	Tendency to turn sour.
	Isaiah ..	1: 22	wine	οἶνος	vinum	Adulteration by water spoiling it.
	Nahum .	1: 10 (bis)	drunken as drunkards		convivium pariter potantium	Consuming stubble or thorns.
	Deuteron	21: 20	drunkard	οἰνοφλυγέι	convivium	
	Proverbs	23: 20, 21	"	μέθυσος	conviviis potatorum vacantes potibus	Drunkenness.
	Isaiah ..	56: 12 (13)	fill		impleamur	
Mesech ...	Proverbs	23: 30	mixed-wine	πότοι	calcibus	Inebriety.
	Psalms .	75: 8 (9)	mixture	κεράσματος	misto	Anger of God.
	Isaiah ..	65: 11	drink-offering	κέρασμα	libatis	Forsaking God.
	" ..	5: 22	mingle	κεράννυντες	miscendam	Inebriety.
	Psalms .	102: 9	mingled	εκίρνων	miscebam	Ashes.
Shemarim .	" ..	75: 8 (9)	dregs	τρύγιας	faex	Dregs.
Ihamra, etc.	Daniel ..	5: 1, 2, 4, 23	wine	οἶνος	vinum	Royal festivity.
Hhamar ...	Psalms .	75: 8 (9)	red	ἀκράτου	meri	Dregs.
Hhamer ...	Deuteron	32: 14	pure	οἶνος	meracissimum	Butter, milk, etc.

III.—*Texts in which* YAYIN *is spoken of with* DISAPPROBATION; *usually, if not always, in its artificial state, the* state (*as good or bad*) *being deducible from the context.*

TEXT.		A. VERSION.	SEPTUAGINT.	VULGATE.	CONTEXT.
Genesis	9: 21, 24	wine	οἶνος	vinum	Drunkenness—of Noah — Nabal — Ephraim —prophets —priests—drunken men—nations—Hannah supposed drunk, but denied.
1 Samuel......	25: 37	"	"	"	
Proverbs......	23: 31	"	"	"	
Isaiah	28: 1, 7, 7,	"	"	"	
Jeremiah......	13: 12 (bis)	"	"	"	
"	23: 9	"	"	"	
"	51: 7	"	"	"	
1 Samuel......	1: 14, 15	"	"	"	
Genesis	19:32,33,34,35	"	"	"	Incest—Lot.
2 Samuel......	13: 28	"	"	"	Murder of Amnon.
Deuteronomy ..	32: 33	"	"	"	Poison of dragons — the mocker—astonishment—violence—drunkenness—whoredom.
Proverbs......	20: 1	"	"	"	
"	23: 30	"	"	"	
Psalms........	60: 3 (5)	"	"	"	
"	75: 8 (9)	"	"	"	
Proverbs......	4: 17	"	"	"	
Jeremiah	23: 9	"	"	"	
Hosea	4: 11	"	"	"	
Genesis	27: 25	"	"	"	Falsehood and deception.
Joshua........	9: 4	"	"	vinarios	
"	" 13	"	"	vinum	
Micah	2: 11	"	"	"	
Amos	2: 8	"	"	"	The condemned.

Deuteronomy ..	32: 38	wine	οἶνος	vinum	Idolatry — transgression. In Hab. 2:15 called 'poison' (*hhemah*).
Habakkuk.....	2: 5	"	"	"	
Proverbs	21: 17	"	"	"	
Ecclesiastes ...	2: 3	"	"	"	
"	9: 7	"	"	"	
Isaiah	5: 11,12,22	"	"	"	
"	22: 13	"	"	"	
"	56: 12 (13)	"	"	"	
Hosea	7: 5	"	"	"	Festivity— licentiousness and feasting. Again called 'poison' in Hos. 7:5.
Amos	6: 6	"	"	"	
Joel	3(4): 3	"	"	"	
Esther	1: 7	"	"	"	
"	1: 10	"	"	mero	
"	5: 6	"	πότω	vinum	
"	7: 2	"	"	"	
"	7: 7, 8	"	συμποσίον	convivium	
Leviticus......	10: 9	"	οἶνος	vinum	Prohibition for priests, Nazarites, and the mother of the strong man.
Ezekiel	44: 21	"	"	"	
Numbers	6: 3	"	"	"	
Judges	13: 4, 7, 14	"	"	"	
Proverbs	31: 4, 6	"	"	"	
Amos	2: 12	"	"	"	
Jeremiah	35: 2, 5	"	"	"	Temptation to priests, Nazarites and Daniel.
Daniel	1: 5, 8	"	"	"	
Jeremiah	35: 6, 8, 14	"	"	"	
Daniel	1: 16	"	"	"	Refusal by Rechabites, and by Daniel.
"	10: 3	"	"	"	

IV. SHECHAR—(THE ROOT OF SUGAR—SWEET-DRINK.)

TEXT.		ENGLISH.	GEEEK.	LATIN.	CONTEXT.
Leviticus ...	10: 9	strong drink	σίκερα	omne quod inebriare potest	Prohibition to priests and Nazarites.
Deuteronomy	14: 26	"	"	"	A feast.
Numbers ...	6: 3 (bis)	"	"		
Judges	13: 4	"	μέθυσμα	siceram	Prohibition to the mother of Sampson.
"	" 7	"	"	"	
"	" 14	"	"	"	
1 Samuel....	1: 15	"	μέθυσμα	omne quod inebriare potest	Drunkenness erroneously alleged.
Psalms	69: 12 (17)	drunkards	οἱ πίνοντες τὸν οἶνον	qui bibebant vinum	Drunkards.
Proverbs....	20: 1	strong drink	μέθη	ebrietas	
"	31: 4, 6	"	"	"	
Isaiah	5: 11, 22	"	σίκερα	ebrietatem	
Micah	2: 11	"	μέθυσμα	"	
Isaiah	28; 7 (thrice)	"	σίκερα, μέθη	ebrietate	Drunkenness and woe.
"	29: 9	"	"	"	
"	56: 12	"	"	"	
"	24: 9	"	"	potio	Bitter in contrast with *sweet*, its original state.
Deuteronomy	29: 6 (5)	"	"	"	
Numbers ...	28: 7	strong-wine	"	siceram vini	Sacrifice.

No. 21.

SUMMARY

OF THE

TEMPERANCE SCRIPTURE ARGUMENT;

CONDENSED FROM THE

WORKS OF DR. F. R. LEES,

MEANWOOD LODGE, LEEDS, ENG.

SUMMARY.

The Divine Works and Word, correctly interpreted, *must* harmonize; not less on the Temperance question than any other; and since this is a practical topic, connected with morals and religion at many points, the Bible may fairly be expected to have recorded special instructions upon it. When we come to examine it, impartially, in the light of Facts, and correct principles of Interpretation, it is even found to have *anticipated* the ordinary wisdom of men and the developments of modern Science. The great physicians of Europe — Levy, Lallemand, Lehmann, Chambers, Smith, etc., express the last verdict of Science when they affirm the old Temperance doctrine that Alcohol is simply a narcotic *Poison*, and not *Food*, in any true or ordinary sense of that word. The property of such a poison, is to seduce, mock, deceive; to generate an ever-increasing appetite for itself amongst men; and to make the soul subject to the craving tyranny of the sensual nature. The express language of Scripture is but the echo of this conclusion. "Wine is a *mocker*." "Be not *deceived* thereby." The cry of the drunkard is, "They have stricken me, but I *felt it not*. I will seek it yet again." The voice of a warning Wisdom is, "Look not upon the Wine, when it is red; when it giveth its eye in the cup," (marks of fermentation); for at last it *stingeth like a serpent*." Nay, more, in three plain texts, the only word in Hebrew for 'Poison' (HHEMAH) — the word six times so translated — is applied to this very species of drink which "stingeth *like* a serpent." The evil wine was "like the *poison* of dragons" (Deut. 32:33.) The princes made the King "sick with *poison* of wine." (Hos. 7:5). And a woe is hurled against him who giveth *such* drink to his neighbour — who "putteth thy *poison* to him"— (Hab. 2:15) — the consequence being that God's poisoned cup of wrath (HHEMAH) shall be turned to him. Is it not pure insanity to suppose that *such* an element is identical with the contents of "the cup of blessing?"

The facts of the Bible are not less clear and decisive as regards the evils of Drinking.—1st. God uses *intoxicating* wine as the constant symbol of wickedness and punishment. *Hhemah* is the poison of the cup of wrath — the *maddening* element — which is to the soul what physical poison is to the body. From Moses to John this expressive symbolism prevails. 2d. God shows us in the biography of his People, how prophets, patriarchs, and Priests fell into sin "through wine" and were "swallowed up" of strong drink. 3d. God teaches us that the great cause of perversion in his People, as Church and Nation, after centuries of varied education and discipline, of unexampled laws and privileges, social, sanitary, and political,—was "the love of drink." "What *more* could I do for you?" saith the Lord. "Why, then, when I looked for grapes, do I find poisonous (or wild) grapes?" The answer of the prophets is still the same. Amos sums up the whole in *four* transgressions; and the four resolve themselves into one cause. (1). The Judges passed unjust verdicts, to get fines *for drink* to be consumed in the holy places. (2). They commanded the prophets to cease, unless they would prophecy of wine and strong drink. (3). They tempted the Nazarites to break their pledge, because their sobriety was a standing rebuke to themselves. (4). They cared not for the "affliction of Joseph," but drank wine in bowls. (Compare Amos 2:6;

Micah 2:11: and Isaiah 5:). For these sins, it is said, "Therefore shall they go into captivity;" and it is remarkable that they learned sobriety at last in the Court of Cyrus, the Magian teetotaler, where royal fashion and the Persian philosophy co-operated to that end. In this sublime history we see *evil* constantly associated with intoxicating drink; and exhibited as the *hindrance* to God's own teaching. How vain, then, to expect that our laws and crotchets will triumph over this sin where His failed. THE CHURCH CAN ONLY CURE INTEMPERANCE BY BANISHING ITS CAUSE.

With equal clearness are the blessings and benefits of Abstinence exhibited. 1. Paradise was *not* wrongly constructed; yet, amidst the perfect adaptations of food and drink to the wants of our perfect originals, alcohol found no place. To you, "*it* shall be for meat," applied to grain and fruit—not to that artificial and fiery product which results from their fermentative destruction. 2. God appoints or approves in other ways, the practice of Abstinence, both by Individuals and Societies. "In the beginning," as the Lord argued, concerning marriage, the *modern* system was not. The first of men and the fairest of women, were constituted teetotalers. Samson, the strong man, Samuel the Holy founder of the School of the Prophets, and John, more than a prophet, were striking examples of God's favor upon the system. It could not be for no reason in the nature of things, that Teetotalism was made the antecedent to physical power, to mental intelligence, and to spiritual purity. 3. The Nazarites were a Society of Religious Abstainers, whose pledge was drawn out by God, to do honor to Him; and were ranked on the same level with his Prophets. 4. The Rechabites were probably voluntary imitators of them; outside Kenites or Arabians; and were highly commended by the Almighty for their fidelity to the pledge. 4. The Bible implies that Teetotalism is a physiological law or truth. The case of Adam and Eve involves this, as part of the best possible condition. The Nazarites, Daniel, etc., prove it by their experience, for they were "ruddier, and fairer, and fatter in flesh" than the drinking Jews, who were black and 'withered.' But Samson's case is still more emphatic, since an angel was twice sent with instructions as to abstinence, before the birth of the strong-one. Dr. Smith's Experimental Researches say: "Alcohol greatly lessens muscular tone." Tom Sayers and Heenan, the well-mated champions of the Prize Ring, are obliged to *train* on Teetotalism. These, then, are but reverberations from a truth well known in Heaven nearly 3,000 years ago. The Rechabites, again, have their faithfulness made the ground of their *perpetuity as a race*—a promise founded in nature, and vindicated by their multiplication and continuance to the present day. 5. *God's Remedy* for Intemperance, when that vice interfered with the services of the sanctuary, was of total and everlasting abstinence. And what was neither needless, nor unwise, nor extreme in God, cannot be so with man. 6. Abstinence was taught as a necessary physical preparation for moral purity and spiritual efficiency: (*a.*) In the cases of Samuel and John the Baptist. (*b.*) In the case of the Priests (Lev. 10), that they might *distinguish* holy from profane. (*c.*) In the case of the Nazarites, that they might illustrate at once, and voluntarily, the virtues of self-denial and purity. The law of prohibition to the Priests means this: "as men, do your own work your own way, but while bearing my *insignia*, and acting as *my servants*, the work shall be done in your natural state, free from strong-drink." That to the Nazarites implies that "as I accept sacrifices only that have no spot and taint, so I accept your living sacrifice only on condition that you are *unpolluted* with the poison and the mocker." (*d.*) To this we may add the significant advice "It is not for Kings to drink wine."

In the common Version of the Bible, even, there is but ONE TEXT *that gives God's* APPARENT *sanction to intoxicating wine,* namely, Deut. 14 : 26, where 'strong drink' is named as a permissible element in a sacred feast. The answer is conclusive — that no word for 'strong' exists in the original Hebrew. The term there is SHEKAR — the original of *saccar*, sugar, and other terms. It denoted *Palm-wine,* which exists in various states, unfermented, sweet, and syrupy, as well as intoxicating and 'bitter.' Hence, as Bishop Lowth observes, the antithesis of Isaiah — "Thy *shechar* (sweet-wine) shall become '*bitter*'— i. e., deteriorated. About 60 texts of the authorized version refer to wine (or what is supposed to be wine) with approbation, where the context shows or implies it to be a natural or unfermented product. Not more than 52 texts exist which can be *proved,* by the context, to refer to *intoxicating* wine — and not one of these is connected with the Divine blessing. On the contrary, one half of them describe it as an evil, as a mocker and stupefier, or *prohibit* it either in general, or in special cases.

These special implications of the evil *quality* of a particular kind of wine, cannot be got rid of by saying that the Bible warns against *excess,* and thus implicitly sanctions a lesser use. In reality, it does both warn against the *use*, and the excess. But the principle of the objection is false. It is the same as to say, that if you are prohibited from killing a man, as in the Decalogue, you are *allowed* to maltreat him short of killing! But not only does the Old Testament commend abstinence and condemn drink, the New Testament frequently and distinctly exhorts to it; and Church history furnishes illustrious examples of it in the first ages. It was, as Prof. Jewett admits, ranked "among the counsels of perfection." The Bishop of Ephesus — Timotheus — was an extreme Abstainer, and seemed to need an apostolic prescription to induce him to use "a little wine" even as a medicine.

What sort of wine it was, we do not know; but we do know that Athenæus says of the Sweet-Lesbian, called *protropos*, it was "very good for the stomach." (ii. § 24).

The fact that teetotalism prevailed throughout the East for thousands of years — that it was a part of the discipline of the Oriental priesthoods from Egypt to India, that it pervaded Judea in the time of our Lord, and was manifested in the sympathetic sects of the Essenes and Therapeutæ,— are circumstances which *compel* the impartial critic to give a plain and literal sense to the language of the Scriptures, when it at once *corresponds* with historical practices and scientific verities. The presumption is strong against the supposition that our Lord would transform innocent water into *intoxicating* wine — an element that the Essenes called "Fool's physic," which after Christians designated as the "invention of the evil one"— though, as Augustin witnesses, they readily drank the *juice of grapes;* which the Saint somewhat illogically condemns as inconsistent! All that our blessed Lord did, was to discountenance the Dualistic mistakes of the Persian philosophy, with a foresight of the Manichœan revival of it, that there was *essential* evil in matter, and therefore in Marriage and in Wine. But as his countenance of a pure marriage gives no sanction to a corrupt one, neither does his conversion of pure water into pure wine, involve the slightest approval of that essentially impure and corrupt element which *is* "a mocker," and "*wherein* is excess." Here, again, we find the true modern conception anticipated by Divine Wisdom: in that miracle which, though the first in order of time, was recorded only in the last of the Gospels, when the error it meets was creeping into the church.

All the critical mistakes of those who have vainly striven to enlist the Bible on the side of sensuality, arise from the acceptance of *false principles* of Interpretation, and from ignorance of *Facts*, no text referring to intoxicating wine can have any validity unless it be associated with *Divine sanction.* No such text exists — but many exist associated with varied evil. Such wine, no doubt, was permitted to be used, by both good and bad men, but so were divorce, polygamy, concubinage, slavery, permitted. This was "for the hardness of their hearts," not because the practice was good. The sole critical argument of the Tipler is this: that the word 'wine' is the same in connexion with the drunkenness of Noah, and the blessing of God upon wine in the Psalms, etc. Quite so: but that does not argue sameness of *nature* or quality. 'Man,' 'spirit' 'angel,' 'wife,' etc., are, like 'wine,' general words — but for that very reason cannot denote the *specific* differences amongst the class of things to which they are applied: as good or bad, pure or corrupt. Ignorance of facts is displayed in the common assertion that wine signifies "the *fermented* juice of the grape." The ancients did not, and could not, know anything of such a conception, inasmuch as they were ignorant of the process of fermentation itself. Hence the old Hebrew books—as the *Gemara* and the Chaldee paraphrase—speak of "the *wine* (yayin) which Messiah shall drink," as being "reserved in its grapes from the beginning;" a striking comment upon the language of our Lord at His Last Supper. Hence also, in the thirteenth century, the great logician and theologian, Thomas Aquinas, decides that grape juice is of *the specific nature of wine* (vinum), and may be used in the celebration of the Eucharist. The definition attempted to be palmed upon us, therefore, is false in history, and confounds the *genus* with the *species:* the 'Man' with 'Negro."

The original Scriptures in Hebrew and Greek, are not less clearly in favor of Abstinence than the common version. The Hebrew has many distinct words, which are all confused into the English phrases — 'wine' — 'new-wine' — 'sweet-wine' — 'flagons of wine' — and 'wine on the lees.' The real distinctions are as follows: 1. TIROSH — a collective term for 'the fruit of the vine' in its natural state, from the early "*tirosh* in the cluster" to the richer "blessing within it"— of the full, ripe grapes, ready for consumption or use. Hence Micah's phrase, "Thou shalt *tread* tirosh, but shall not *drink* yayin" (its juice), for the fruit should be withered. (6:15.) It is thus associated as a thing of growth and of the fields, with *corn* and orchard-fruit (*yitzhar* — not oil): dependent upon the dew, rain, etc. In the Latin, French, German, Italian, and Spanish versions, it is generally, but wrongly translated *mustum, mosto*, etc. It is no where implied to be either intoxicating, or liquid. "Whoredom, wine, and new-wine"— does not make sense; but Idolatry, Inebriety, and Luxury" does — represented by "Whoredom, Wine, and Grapes," which "take away the heart." The words in Prov. 3:10, and Joel 2:24, translated 'bursting and 'overflowing,' respectively, in the original signify no more than abundance.

2. ÆSHISHAH, 'sweet cake,' is the word translated 'flagons-of-wine — but erroneously, as all scholars now concede.

3. SHEMARIM, in Isaiah from *Shamar* 'to preserve,' means 'preserves,' well refined — not 'dregs' or 'wine.' It only occurs *once* in the supposed sense of wine. The older translators regarded it as "sweet and dainty things."

4. MESECH signifies 'mixture' simply, which might be good or bad. The mingled-wine of *Wisdom* (boiled grape juice mixed with water), or the wine of Sensuality. "Who hath *woe?* They that are mighty to *mingle* sweet drink" with inebriating drugs.

5. YAYIN is the generic term for wine, including the '*pure* blood of the grape,' preserved-juice, and the fermented and drugged juice. It is applied in all these varied ways. "They washed their *garments* in wine." "They *gathered* wine." "Wine is a *mocker*:" it stingeth like a serpent.'

" *Their* wine is the *poison* of dragons." No where do we find divine sanction associated with *yayin,* where the context shows it to be intoxicating.

This word being general, necessitated in the latter ages of Jewish literature, the use of two or three *specific* terms tc indicate particular kinds of wine. As for example —

6. HHAMER: fresh 'foaming'-wine in its first sense. But since the wine when it ferments, becomes *red,* the idea of redness got associated with the Chaldee use of the word: and perhaps 'thickness' also. It is the word related to the *foam* of the sea, and the *bitumen* of pits.

7. AUSIS, from *asas,* 'to tread,' signifies the same as the classic *protropos* — 'first trodden' or 'running'-wine. "The mountains shall drop-down *ausis.*"

8. SOBHE is 'boiled-wine.' It is the *sapa* of the Romans, the *sabe* of the French and Italians. It was the luxurious-drink of the rich: but of course not intoxicating.

9. OINOS is the generic Greek word corresponding with the Hebrew *yayin,* and is applicable to *all* sorts of wine. The context alone can determine the specific nature of the wine.

10. GLEUKOS only occurs once in the New Testament, and is not associated with any Divine approval. It is, classically the name of *rich-grape-juice,* or unfermented wine; perhaps in some cases, for initially fermented wine.

The New Testament distinctions and instructions are not less in harmony with Teetotalism than those of the Hebrew Bible.

1. ENGKRATIA — self-control — is the word four times translated 'Temperance' — and in its other forms, twice *temperate* and once *continent.* In 1 Cor. 7 : 9; 9 : 25, it has evidently a negative application equal to *abstaining.*

2. EPI-EIKEES: Forbearing — translated only once *moderation;* thrice *gentle;* once *patient.*

3. SOPHRONEO — sedate, discreet — translated *sober* — *so-*

ber-minded — and *in* a *right-mind.* This is mental 'sobriety — or the state when we can obey reason, and resist appetite. This can have nothing to do with drinking, which at best is but the gratification of a sensuous appetite.

Mental temperance being thus expressed by the preceding terms, we shall want a word for *Abstinence* in regard to the body. This is found in a compound formed from the negative particle *nee* (not), and *pio* (to drink) = *neephō.* Neepho occurs in the Apostolic exhortations seven times; in its adjective form (*neephalios*), thrice; in such peculiar connections, that it seems absurd to put upon it any secondary or metaphorical meaning. The primary sense of the word, beyond all cavil, is that of *Abstinence;* its secondary sense of 'wakeful,' being derived from the condition in which people *are* who abstain from narcotics. "Without doubt," says Dean Alford, "the word signifies Abstinence, but Dr. Lees is bound to prove that it means *total* abstinence!" Now we are bound to prove, no more than this — that it means *not-drinking;* and that the Apostles use it in that, its primary sense. Josephus, one of their contemporaries, says of the Priests — "They *abstained* from wine" — (apò âkratou neephontes). So Paul and Peter, who use the word *along with* the proper words for mental temperance and for watchfulness. Thus:—

I Tim. 3:2. Be (neephalion) ABSTINENT (teetotal), sound minded.

I Thes. 5:6. Let us *watch* and DRINK-NOT neephōmen.

I Pet. 4:7. Be sound-*minded,* and ABSTINENT unto prayer.*

I Pet. 5:8. (Neepsate) DRINK NOT, be *vigilant,* because your adversary seeketh whom he may *drink-down* (kata-pië)."

Why Josephus, Philo, Plutarch, and Porphyry should mean *abstinence* from drink by this word, but, as some strangely con-

* So Tertullian (*De Jeju.*) By prayer, sobriety, and *abstinence.*"

tend, the Apostles signify *drinking* a *little*, we will not inquire: for we will not follow perversity and appetite into the Den of Idols.

The objection that the Deacons are not to be "given towards *much* wine," and the Deaconesses (aged-women) "not to be enslaved to *much* wine," falls before the fact that unfermented wine was allowed to women and to men after a certain age.* If it be said, Why warn against excess in that which does not intoxicate? — we answer, why does Solomon inform us that "To eat *much* honey is not good?"— if no one ever did. This is the fallacy of interpreting the language of the ancients by the customs of the moderns. Pliny and many others show us that the abuse of syrupy and sweet-wines was a *special vice* of the day. Lucian has this passage: — "I came, by Jove, as those who drink *gleukos*, require an emetic"—before they drink again.

Josephus says of the Jewish priests, that on account of their office, they "had prescribed to them a double degree of purity." So Paul deemed a *special* and *extreme* form of Abstinence proper to be urged upon a Bishop: just as the 'Law Book of the 'Ante-Nicene Church' commands that a Bishop shall not enter a Tavern except on necessity. To this end, Paul uses a word, which is equivalent to the modern pledge—"*discountenance* the drinking usages"—viz., namely, *mee*, (not) — *par* — (over, or in company)—*oinon* (wine). In 1 Tim. 3: 2–3; and Titus 1: 7–8; in connexion with being *no-drinker*, sound-minded, and no-striker, it is commanded that a Bishop shall be *mee-par-oinos* — "not near wine"—not in its company.

Thus, it will be seen, even from the bare summary of the case, that the varied language of the Old and the New Testa-

* Titus 2: 2, and 1 Tim. 3: 11, command that the *Elders* and their wives shall be *neephalious* (abstinent.)—i. e., no-drinkers of another sort of wine.

23

ment, and the known-facts of antiquity, conspire to establish every portion of our Critical Theory ; thus does each separate fact and phrase find its fitting place in the Temple of Truth ; and thus, too, is it made manifest that Holy Scripture concurs with moral and physical Science in teaching abstinence from narcotic poisons — a doctrine which needs to be reiterated afresh from the pulpits of Christendom, until the torpid conscience is aroused, and the great obstacle to the progress and triumph of the Gospel is removed out of the way. " Where fore, take unto you the whole armour of God, that ye may be able to withstand in the evil-day ; and having done all — to stand."

MR. R. COBDEN, M. P

Mr. Cobden's sympathy for the abstinence cause is well known. At Bradford he once made a speech, of which the following is a portion:—

You are all aware, or, at least, some of you, that out of the 658 members of the House of Commons, Col. Thompson was able to endure the fatigue and annoyance of those long, dreary, and dull speeches better than any other man. He was more constantly upon the benches than any other member of that House; and, I believe, the member who came second to him was Mr. Brotherton. (Cheers.) Now, it appears very oddly (and I tell it as a secret to those teetotalers who are present, that they may tell it to those who are absent), that both Col. Thompson and Mr. Brotherton are teetotalers. (Loud cheering.) And from what I have seen in the House, I must say that I have the belief, that the men who are the most temperate are the men who bear the fatigue of the House the best. I remember, on one occasion, that Col. Thompson, Mr. Bright, and myself, went on an agitation tour—during the heat of the League's agitation—into Scotland. We separated, and went through Scotland, lecturing every night and holding public meetings, and sometimes two meetings in a day. We rendezvoused together on coming back. On comparing notes we found that during all our tour in Scotland, not one of us had paid a farthing for fermented or intoxicating drinks of any kind. (Cheers.) I remember at one house, where we met, we were visited by a number of the bailies—bailies, in Scotland, are what our aldermen are in England—who called for glasses of whiskey-toddy. The way in which they twisted and turned it out from a large glass into a small one! I remember Colonel Thompson and all of us tried to imitate that twist, but could not. (Laughter.) These bailies stayed with us until two o'clock in the morning. They had glass after glass of toddy, and still they went on in the process of twisting it out of a tumbler into the wineglass. (Laughter.) Just as they were going off, we told them the circumstances under which we could not join them. In consequence of the hard work, we were obliged to confine ourselves exclusively to the pump—(laughter)—and I remember one of those bailies looked up with a rather maudlin expression—for it was late, and he spoke at the bottom of three or four glasses of stiff toddy—and said, "Hey mon! but you water-drinkers will upset the world." (Cheers and laughter.) I do think that water-drinkers *will* upset the moral world—(cheers)—and will turn it round with a much better face to us when they have done with it. (Renewed cheering.)—*Alliance News*.

No. 22.

DR. JOHN HIGGENBOTTOM, F. R. S.,

NOTTINGHAM, ENGLAND,

ON

CONSTITUTIONAL DIFFICULTIES.

I have been a guardian of the health of the public for nearly sixty years, and have labored as much as possible to prevent as well as to cure disease. Pecuniary emolument has been a secondary object, having been influenced more by a sense of duty than of interest. I have constantly and carefully studied the constitutions of my patients: *constitutional difficulties*—a phrase I never heard before teetotalism commenced. I recollect the first time I heard it, about a quarter of a century ago. I was attending a clergyman's wife during her confinement. On my second visit a maid-servant came into the bedroom with a basket containing several bottles of wine—a present from a lady in the neighborhood. I told my patient wine was improper for her. "Oh, no," she said, "my London doctor told me my constitution required such stimulants, and I have always been in the habit of taking them." I directly saw it was the indomitable force of habit which was her constitutional difficulty.

Dr. Samuel Johnson says: "The diminutive chain of habit is scarcely heavy enough to be felt until it is too strong to be broken." The lady's habit had become too strong to be broken; it would have been in vain to have told her that no constitution ever required an alcoholic stimulant. No; her

London doctor's opinion just agreed with her constitution—or to speak truly, with her habit, and depraved and unnatural appetite. The doctor had signed her death warrant; her destination and destruction were fixed; my patient was not satisfied with wine, but took brandy, and died of disease of the liver in the prime of life, adding another victim to the many I have witnessed.

The lady who sent my patient the wine died an inveterate drunkard; and she shortened the days of a poor asthmatic patient who lived near her, and who I attended gratuitously. In this poor woman I was surprised to find disease of the liver, which led me to inquire if she was in the habit of taking spirits; her daughter informed me that the lady had supplied her with rum regularly. The three patients lived only in one small circle compared with the many large circles of my patients.

I could a tale unfold!

I am grieved with my professional brethren making use of such a pretext—or in plainer terms, such a falsehood; indeed, I consider it impious in a medical man saying that any constitution requires alcoholic stimulants; it is a reflection on his Maker. Our bodies were not made so as to require the incendiary alcohol, or liquid fire, to permeate or to pass through every organ, to sear, burn, and destroy the delicate and beautiful structures of our body. Why do medical men allow it? Sixty years ago the celebrated Dr. Trotter, in his essay on drunkenness, said: "Society must be undergoing the last state of vitiation when the faculty of medicine receives gold and returns poison." I must confess it is a dangerous experiment at the present time for a medical man to become an ultra-teetotaller, never to prescribe or allow brandy, wine, porter, or bitter beer, &c., in his practice; half of his living would be taken away. Alcoholic liquids are in common use, and doing their deadly work from the cradle to the grave. A finger cannot be pointed to any part of that most invaluable and instructive picture of Cruickshank's "Worship of Bacchus" without showing a group of individuals who are making plenty of work for the doctors; beginning where the doctor, who is giving malt liquor to his lying-in patient, and ending where the doctor is introducing the publican to his patient—as the honest Yorkshireman said, "*to finish the job!*" and in truth to prepare him for the next scene, the funeral. Medical men, unfortunately, are the greatest foes to teetotalism or true temperance. Many of them become intemperate, and fall victims. A medical writer in 1859, says of the drunkenness of medical men (we blush to write it), "That no class of persons who have received a liberal education are so addicted to it."

I am sorry some of our distinguished medical men who have written on temperance have not been thorough teetotalers. I have reason to think that good Dr. Miller, of Edinburgh, would have become so had he lived. He informed me "that he was led to make out as good a case as he could for alcohol as a medicine, in order that he might reconcile people to part with it as food." He added, "Perhaps I have been led to rate alcohol as a medicine too highly in consequence." If Dr. Miller had become an ultra-teetotaller, never to prescribe or allow alcoholic fluids in his practice, he would most certainly have lost his reputation as a medical man; he being the surgeon to the Queen, and to Prince Albert the Good, would not have much availed him. It has long been my opinion that if an angel came down from heaven, and could cure all diseases, if brandy, wine, porter, or bitter beer were not allowed in the treatment, the attendance of the angel would be dispensed with; not desired by the patient, who would seek for a fallen one, who would be selected instead.

None of my medical opponents have tried both ways, with and without alcoholic fluids in their practice, not even for a single year; therefore they have no practical ground to rest upon, so as to enter into any satisfactory controversy upon the subject.

I have amply tried both ways. I gave alcohol in my practice for twenty years, and have now practised without it for the last thirty years or more. My experience is that acute disease is more readily cured without it, and chronic disease much more manageable. I have not found a single patient injured by the disuse of alcohol, or a constitution requiring it; indeed, to find either, although I am in my seventy-seventh year, I would walk fifty miles to see such an unnatural phenomenon.

If I ordered or allowed alcohol in any form, either as food or as medicine, to a patient, I should certainly do it with a felonious intent.

REMARKS.—It is my solemn conviction, that until the medical profession adopt Dr. Higgenbottom's standard, and professing christians *return* to the use of the fruit of the vine, free from alcohol, at the Sacrament, the progress of true temperance will be slow; and more especially so, should these two vital questions be ignored by leading temperance advocates. ED.

[From the *London Spectator*.]

SACRAMENTAL WINE.—One of the chief hindrances to the Temperance Movement has hitherto been the use of intoxicating wine at the Lord's Supper. It is difficult to make men understand how that can be a bad thing on their own table which is deemed a good thing on the Lord's table. The exception in the pledge, made in favor of alcoholic wine at the Sacrament, is always felt to be a kind of indirect testimony against the principle of entire abstinence. *It is a source of weakness.* Nor is this all. There is real danger in the case. The late REV. B. PARSONS, in his "*Anti-Bacchus*," says—"Not long ago, a reformed drunkard, and apparently a converted man, approached the Lord's Table of a church which I could name; he ate the bread and drank the wine, but mark the result—the taste of the drunkard for alcohol is like that of the *blood-hound for blood*, a single sip makes him thirst for more; so here, the wine tasted at the sacred communion, revived the old passion and he who seemed a saint, was corrupted by the sacramental wine, went home, got drunk, and died a drunkard." DR. CARPENTER, in his admirable lecture "*On the Use of Intoxicating Wine at the Lord's Supper*," referring to the above, says—"One of my friends has assured me that no fewer than TWELVE similar cases had come to his own knowledge." In view of this awful danger some ministers have trembled lest certain reformed drunkards in their congregations should seek admission to the Lord's Table.

No. 23.

THE PATHOLOGY OF DRUNKENNESS,

OR THE

PHYSICAL EFFECTS OF ALCOHOLIC DRINKS,

WITH

DRAWINGS OF THE DRUNKARD'S STOMACH.

A LETTER ADDRESSED TO EDWARD C. DELAVAN, ESQ.,

BY THOMAS SEWELL, M. D.,

*Professor of Pathology and the Practice of Medicine in the Columbian College, District of Columbia**

PLATE I.—*Fig.* I. Represents the internal or mucous coat of the stomach in a healthy state, which, in color, is slightly reddish, tinged with yellow. It was drawn from an individual who had lived an entirely temperate life, and who died under circumstances which could not have changed the appearance of the organ after death.

Fig. 2. Of the same plate, represents a portion of the internal coat of the stomach of the Temperate Drinker—the man who takes his grog daily, but moderately, or who sips his wine with his meals. The blood vessels of the inner surface are so far enlarged, as to be visible, and are distended with blood.

PLATE II.—*Fig.* 1. Represents the stomach of the habitual drunkard, or hard drinker, and shews the mucous or internal coat, to be in a state of irritation, with its blood vessels, which are invisible while in a healthy state, to be enlarged and distended with blood. It was drawn from the stomach of one who had been an habitual drunkard for many years. It bears a strong resemblance in its vascular structure, to what

* From the first volume of the "Enquirer," published 1841, now republished in 4th edition of this work, by the written request of Judge Black, of Lancaster, Pa., being called for as explanatory of Dr. Sewell's stomach diagrams, page 22.

are denominated the rum blossoms, sometimes seen upon the face of the hard drinker.

Fig. 2. Of the same plate, represents the inner coat of the stomach, corroded with small ulcers, which are covered with white crusts, with the margin of the ulcers elevated and ragged.

PLATE III.—*Fig.* 1. Represents the mucous, or internal surface of the stomach of the drunkard, after a debauch of several days. It shows a high degree of inflammation, extending over the surface, changing its color to deep red, and in some points exhibiting a livid appearance.

Fig 2. Of the same plate, represents the appearance of the cancerous stomach; and was taken from the case of a sea captain, who had been an habitual drinker of ardent spirits, and often in an undiluted state. The stomach is thickened, and scirrous, with a corroding cancer of the size represented in the plate.

PLATE IV. Represents the state of the internal coat of the stomach of a drunkard, who had died in a state of Delirium Tremens. It is covered by a dark brown, flaky substance, which on being removed, shews the stomach to have been in a state of high inflammation before death. In some points it is quite dark, as if in an incipient state of mortification.

TO EDWARD C. DELAVAN, Esq.:

Sir—From a consideration of the deep interest which you have taken in the Temperance Reformation, and the eminent services you have rendered to this and other countries, by a series of philanthropic efforts to eradicate one of the greatest evils of the age, I am induced to comply with your request, by furnishing the accompanying drawings of the Drunkard's stomach, with a few remarks upon the pathology of intemperance; delineating certain morbid changes produced by alcoholic drinks, as they have fallen under my observation.

The following remarks will explain the circumstances under which these cases occurred, and the phenomena attending them:

For upwards of thirty years, I have been more or less

engaged in pathological researches ; during which I have enjoyed many opportunities of inspecting the stomach of the drunkard after death, in the various stages and degrees of inebriation; and these drawings will be found to present a pretty accurate delineation of the principal morbid changes produced upon that organ by intemperance ; changes which are eminently worthy of being brought to the view of the unsuspecting sufferer, and which I should hope, might have some effect in deterring the temperate from the use of alcoholic poison.

If the morbid effects of intemperance are in some degree various in different individuals : if they are not developed with the same degree of power and rapidity in one case as in another, it is nevertheless true that alcohol is a poison forever at war with man's nature, and in all its forms and degrees of strength, produces irritation of the stomach, which is liable to result in inflammation, ulceration and mortification, a thickening and induration of its coats, and finally scirrous, cancer and other organic affections ; and it may be asserted with confidence, that no one who indulges habitually in the use of alcoholic drinks, whether in the form of wine or the more ardent spirits, possesses a healthy stomach.

In addition to the morbid specimens which I furnish, I present you with one drawing of the healthy stomach, which will enable you to institute a comparison, and the more fully to appreciate the morbid changes produced by alcohol.

To enable the unprofessional reader the better to understand the morbid effects of alcoholic drinks upon the stomach, as represented in the drawings, I beg leave to call your attention to a few remarks upon the anatomy and physiology of the digestive canal.

Digestion is one of the most important of all the functions of the animal economy; indeed it is indispensable to the due performance of all the other functions ; consequently whenever this becomes impaired, the whole system languishes, and all the other functions become sooner or later affected also. The object of digestion is to convert the food into nutriment fitted to sustain and renovate the system, and to supply the waste that continually takes place in every part.

As food is seldom found in a state fit for nutrition, it has necessarily to undergo various changes in the digestive organs; changes which require that these organs should be extensive and complicated in their structure, and healthy in their action.

The digestive canal is divided, according to its physiological arrangement, into, 1st, the mouth; 2d, the pharynx and œsophagus; 3d, the stomach; 4th, the small intestines, and 5th, the large intestines.

The mouth is the part concerned in masticating or grinding the food; by the pharynx and œsophagus, it is swallowed and conveyed to the stomach, where it undergoes a most important change, commonly called digestion, by which it is converted into a substance denominated chyme.

The stomach is situated in the cavity of the abdomen, occupying the epigastric, and a portion of the left hypochondriac region. It is a hollow organ, somewhat conoidal in its figure, and has been compared in its form to a bag-pipe. It is capable of containing in the adult, when moderately distended, about one quart. The left half of the organ is much larger than the right. It has two curvatures, the greater and the less. It has two openings; the first is called the cardiac, and the second the pyloric orifice. The cardiac orifice is situated in the lesser curvature, near the left extremity of the organ, communicates with the œsophagus, and is the passage by which the food is received into the stomach. The lower or pyloric orifice is situated at the right extremity, communicates with the intestines, and forms the passage by which the food, after the process of digestion is completed, is conveyed out of the stomach. This latter opening is garnished by a circular band of muscular fibres, by which it is capable of becoming completely closed during the process of digestion. The stomach is composed of three coats. The first is the peritoneal or serous coat; which is extremely thin, and forms the outer covering. The second is the muscular coat, and is composed of muscular fibres running in different directions, and is that coat upon which the contraction of the organ depends when it is empty. The third is the mucous or internal coat, and is about a line in thickness. It presents, when the stomach is contracted to its smallest dimensions, a corrugated or wrinkled appearance, which disappears as soon as the organ is distended. This coat exhibits to the eye somewhat of a mottled appearance; of a reddish complexion, slightly tinged with yellow. Its surface resembles velvet, from which the term villous coat has been applied to it. In its texture it is soft, loose and easily lacerated. It has, opening upon its surface, a multitude of minute orifices, which lead to small glands designed to secrete mucous. These three coats are connected to each other by the intervention of cellular substance, but are separable by maceration and dissection. The stomach is very largely supplied with blood-vessels, nerves, and absorbents. Indeed the nervous texture of the organ is so largely supplied and fully expanded between the mucous and muscular coats as to form, apparently, a fourth covering, sometimes denominated the nervous coat.

The digestion of the food in the stomach is performed by the action of the gastric juice, a fluid secreted by the mucous or internal coat; or by some small glands seated in this coat, and which possesses the extraordinary power of dissolving animal and vegetable substances, which are first deprived of the principle of life; but upon living bodies it has no action, as shewn by the experiments of Spallanzani and others. For example, if the legs and feet of a living frog be thrust down into the stomach of a lizard, and be confined in that situation, the gastric juice has no action upon them, so long as the frog lives; but if the frog be killed and be replaced in this situation, they are digested to a pulp in a few hours. The gastric fluid has even the power of dissolving the stomach itself when the organ is deprived of life; and consequently in some persons who die suddenly and in a state of full health, the stomach is found a few hours after death, softened, broken or dissolved.

There are some substances, however, though destitute of vitality upon which the gastric juice has no action, or if any, it has not the power of converting them into nutriment; and alcohol is one of this number.

The small intestines, while they form numerous convolutions, constitute one continuous tube, extending from the pyloric orifice, or right extremity of the stomach, and terminating abruptly in the large intestines. This portion of the digestive tube gradually diminishes in size as it descends.

The food having been digested by the stomach and converted into chyme, passes out at the pyloric orifice into the small intestines, when the nutritious is separated from the innutritious portion, as it mingles with the bile and pancreatic juice; two fluids which are poured into the intestines near their upper extremity. The nutritious portion is absorbed by a set of vessels denominated lacteals, which open their numerous mouths upon the inner surface of the canal. By these it is transported under the name of chyle, to the blood-vessels, and there unites with the blood in a state prepared to renovate this fluid, and render it fit to sustain and nourish the system, and supply the waste continually going on; while the innutritious part of the food passes on to the large intestines.

The large intestines form the lower portion of the digestive canal, and though much greater in diameter than the small intestines, are far shorter. They form a mere reservoir for the innutritious portion of the chyme. The small and large intestines together, constitute one continuous tube, which is nearly six times the length of the body. Except in two small sections, they have three coats, corresponding with those of the stomach, and like that also are supplied with blood-vessels nerves and absorbents.

Having thus briefly described the anatomical and physiological arrangement of the digestive canal, I will now proceed to notice some of the morbid effects of alcoholic drinks upon it, as they have been presented to my notice.

In PLATE I. *Fig.* 1*st*, we have a representation of the internal surface of the stomach in a healthy state, taken from an individual who was entirely temperate, which is copied from a sketch furnished by Professor Horner, of Philadelphia, one of the ablest anatomists of the country or age. The subject from which it was originally drawn, came under Professor Horner's own observation, and the dissection was made by his own hand; and he says that the individual was not only healthy, but remarkably temperate and regular in all his habits; he therefore considers the case invaluable, as furnishing a standard of observation. It is of a color slightly reddish, tinged with yellow, and exhibits something of a mottled appearance; although supplied with a multitude of blood-vessels, none of them are so large as to be visible to the naked eye. This healthy and natural appearance of the stomach would doubtless continue from the period of childhood to that of old age, if it were acted upon only by appropriate food and drink.

In *Fig.* 2*d* of the same plate, we have exhibited the internal surface of the stomach of the temperate drinker, the man who takes his glass of mint sling in the morning, and his toddy on going to bed; or of him who takes his two or three glasses of Madeira at his dinner. And here the work of destruction begins. That beautiful network of blood-vessels which was invisible in the healthy stomach, being excited by the stimulus of alcohol, becomes dilated and distended with blood, visible and distinct. This effect is produced upon the well known law of the animal economy, that an irritant applied to a sensitive texture of the body, induces an increased flow of blood to the part. The mucous or inner coat of the stomach is a sensitive membrane, and is subject to this law. A practical illustration of this principle is shown by reference to the human eye. If a few drops of alcohol or any other irritating substance, be brought in contact with the delicate coats of the eye, a network of fine vessels which were before invisible, become distended with blood and easily seen. If this operation be repeated daily, as the temperate drinker takes his alcohol, the vessels become habitually increased in size and distended with blood.

It is by this temperate drinking that the appetite of the inebriate is first acquired; for by nature man has no taste or desire for alcohol; it is as unnatural and averse to his constitution as to that of the horse or the ox; nor is there any apology for its use by man, that does not equally apply to the brute.

Plate II. *Fig.* 1*st*, of this series, represents the stomach of the confirmed drunkard; the man who has become habitually accustomed to the use of alcoholic drinks. And here we find the blood-vessels of the inner coat, which in the temperate drinker were only slightly enlarged, so fully developed as to render the most minute branches visible to the eye, like the rum blossoms on the drunkard's face; and this enlargement does not depend upon the perpetual presence of alcohol, as in the temperate drinker, but it has become so permanent and fixed, that they maintain their unnatural size even after death; unless indeed the inebriate has for some time previous to this event abandoned the use of alcohol. and given nature time to restore them to their natural size. In this state, the inebriate is never easy or satisfied, unless his stomach is excited by the presence of this or some other narcotic poison. Whenever these are withheld, he is afflicted with loss of appetite, nausea, gnawing pain and a sinking sensation at the stomach, lassitude, debility and temporary disturbance of all the functions of the body.

It is under these circumstances, and in this condition of the stomach, that the drunkard finds it so difficult to resist the cravings of his appetite, and to reform his habits. Difficult but not impossible. Thousands thus far sunk to ruin have reformed, and thousands are now undergoing the experiment. But it is only by total abstinence, that reformation can be accomplished. No one may hope to reform by degrees, or to be cured by substituting one form of alcohol for that of another. So long as he indulges in the smallest degree, so long will his propensity to drink be perpetuated, and his stomach exhibit traces of disease.

What takes place in the stomach of the reformed drunkard, the individual who abandons the use of all intoxicating drinks? The stomach by that extraordinary power of self-restoration with which it is endowed, gradually resumes its natural appearance. Its engorged blood-vessels, become reduced to their original size, and its natural color and healthy sensibility return. A few weeks or months, according to the observations I have made, will accomplish this renovation; after which the individual has no longer any suffering or desire for alcohol. This process, however, is greatly facilitated, and rendered more easy to the sufferer, by cupping, blistering and other counter irritation over the region of the stomach; by the use of cooling medicines and vegetable diet. It is nevertheless true, and should ever be borne in mind, that such is the susceptibility of the stomach of the reformed drunkard, that a repetition of the use of alcohol in the *slightest degree*, and in any form, revives the appetite; the blood-vessels again become dilated and the morbid sensibility of the organ is re-produced. Abstinence, therefore, total abstinence, at once and forever, must be the pledge of him who means to stand.

PLATE II. *Fig. 2d*, presents a view of the ulcerated or

apthous condition of the drunkard's stomach; a state which frequently exists, but is not readily apprehended on account of the obscurity of the attendant symptoms. It consists in numerous small ulcerations extending over the internal coat, and which are usually covered with a white crust, producing the apthous appearance. Upon wiping off the crust, the mucous surface was found broken and covered with small corroding sores, of greater or less size and depth, with ragged and inflamed edges; and sometimes the inflammation extends over the intervening spaces. These ulcerations are produced by the irritating effects of alcoholic drinks. I cannot better give you an account of this affection, than by a reference to the observations of Dr. Beaumont, a gentleman who has produced one of the most rare and interesting works ever published upon the powers of the gastric juice and the functions of the stomach. You will recollect that while these experiments and observavations bear with peculiar force upon the subject of alcoholic drinks, they were instituted prior to the commencement of the temperance enterprise, and were made without the slightest reference to this subject. Dr. Beaumont cannot, therefore, be suspected of having his mind prejudiced, or of a desire to adapt the results of his researches to the opinions of the present time, or to promote the cause for which they are here introduced. The following account will explain the occasion of his researches, and show the authority upon which his observations are based.

In the year 1822, Alexis St. Martin, a Canadian boy, of French descent, aged 18, of robust and healthy constitution, received a shot from a musket in the left side, by which the integuments, muscles and a part of one rib was carried away, and the stomach perforated. In this state he fell into the hands of Dr. Beaumont, then a distinguished army surgeon of the United States, stationed upon our northern frontier. The boy was cured, but the edges of the wound in the stomach became adherent to the wound in the side of the chest, and the opening from without into the stomach remained unclosed; being two and a half inches in circumference ; so that the food and drink could only be retained by the use of a tent, and subsequently by the protrusion of a fold of the inner coat of the stomach. This state of the aperture afforded Dr. Beaumont an opportunity of making important observations and experiments upon the digestion of food, and of ascertaining by occular inspection, the condition of the interior of the stomach, the state of its mucous coat, and the influence of various agents upon it, particularly the effect of different kinds of food and drink. At length St. Martin was brought to the city of Washington, where I had many opportunities of witnessing the Doctor's experiments, and can testify to the accuracy with which they were made and are detailed. Commencing with the 237th page of his work, I find the following record:

" July 28, 9 o'clock A. M. Weather clear. Wind N. W., brisk. Thermometer 66°. Stomach empty, not healthy, some erythema (inflammation) and apthous patches on the mucous surface. St. Martin has been drinking *ardent spirits* pretty freely for eight or ten days past ; complains of no pain, nor shows symptoms of any general indisposition ; says he feels well and has a good appetite.

"August 1, 8 o'clock A. M. Examined stomach before eating anything ; inner membrane morbid ; considerable erythema and some apthous patches on the exposed surface; secretions vitiated; extracted about half an ounce of gastric juice ; not clear and pure as in health ; quite viscid.

"August 2, 8 o'clock A. M. Circumstances and appearances very similar to those of yesterday morning. Extracted one ounce of gastric fluids, consisting of unusual proportions of vitiated mucus, saliva and some bile, tinged slightly with blood, appearing to exude from the surface of the erythema and apthous patches, which were tenderer and more irritable than usual. St. Martin complains of no sense of pain, symptoms of indisposition, or even of impaired appetite. Temperature of stomach 101°.

'August 3, 7 o'clock A. M. Inner membrane of stomach unusually morbid; the erythematous appearance more extensive, and spots more livid than usual; from the surface of some of which exuded small drops of grumous blood; the apthous patches larger and more numerous; the mucous covering thicker than common, and the gastric secretions much more vitiated. The gastric fluids extracted this morning were mixed with a large proportion of thick ropy mucus, and considerable muco-purulent matter, slightly tinged with blood, resembling the discharge from the bowels in some cases of chronic dysentery. Notwithstanding this diseased appearance of the stomach, no very essential aberration of its function was manifested. St. Martin complains of no symptoms indicating any general derangement of the system, except an uneasy sensation, and a tenderness at the pit of the stomach, and some vertigo with dimness and yellowness of vision, on stooping down and rising again; has a thin yellowish brown coat on his tongue, and his countenance is rather sallow; pulse uniform and regular; appetite good; rests quietly and sleeps as well as usual.

"August 4, 8 o'clock A. M. Stomach empty; less of those apthous patches than yesterday; erythematous appearance more extensively diffused over the inner coats, and the surface inclined to bleed; secretions vitiated. Extracted about an ounce of gastric fluids consisting of ropy mucus, some bile and less of the muco-purulent matter than yesterday; flavor peculiarly fœtid and disagreeable; alkalescent and insipid; no perceptible acid; appetite good; rests well and no indications of general disease or indisposition.

"August 5, 8 o'clock A. M. Stomach empty; coats less morbid than yesterday; apthous patches mostly disappeared; mucous surface more uniform, soft, and nearly of the natural, healthy color ; secretions less vitiated. Extracted two ounces of gastric juice, more clear and pure than that taken for four or five days last past, and slightly acid, but containing a larger proportion of mucus, and more opaque than usual in a healthy condition.

"August 6, 8 o'clock A. M. Stomach empty; coats clean and healthy as usual; secretions less vitiated. Extracted two ounces gastric juice, of more natural and healthy appearance, with the usual gastric acid flavor; complains of no uneasy sensations, or the slightest symptom of indisposition; says he feels perfectly well, and has a voracious appetite, but not permitted to indulge it to satiety. He has been restricted from full and confined to low diet, and simple, diluent drinks for the last few days, and has not been allowed to taste of any stimulating liquors, or to indulge in excesses of any kind.

"Diseased appearances, similar to those mentioned above, have frequently presented themselves in the course of my experiments and examinations, as the reader will have perceived. They have generally, but not always succeeded to some appreciable cause. Improper indulgence in eating and drinking has been the most common precursor of these diseased conditions of the coats of the stomach. The free use of *ardent spirits, wine, beer, or any intoxicating liquor*, when continued for some days, has invariably produced these morbid changes. Eating voraciously or to excess; swallowing food coarsely masticated or too fast; the introduction of solid pieces of meat, suspended by cords into the stomach, or of muslin bags of aliment secured in the same way, almost invariably produce similar effects if repeated a number of times in close succession.

"These morbid changes and conditions are, however, seldom indicated by any ordinary symptoms or particular sensations described or complained of unless when in considerable excess, or when there have been corresponding symptoms of a general affection of the system. They could not, in fact, in most cases, have been anticipated from any external symptoms, and their existence was only ascertained by actual occular demonstration.

"It is interesting to observe to what extent the stomach, perhaps the most important organ of the *animal* system, may become diseased without manifesting any external symptoms of such disease, or any evident signs of functional aberration. Vitiated secretions may also take place, and continue for some time without affecting the health in any *sensible* degree.

"Extensive active or chronic disease may exist in the membranous tissues of the stomach and bowels, more frequently than has been generally believed; and it is possible that there are good grounds for the opinion advanced by a celebrated teacher of medicine, that most febrile complaints are the effects of gastric and enteric inflammations. In the case of the subject of these experiments, inflammation certainly does exist to a considerable extent, even in an *apparent* state of health—greater than could have been believed to comport with the due operations of the gastric functions."

We cannot place too high a value upon the observations and experiments of Dr. Beaumont, as they are the result of occular demonstration, an actual looking into the interior of the stomach from hour to hour, and from day to day, for a number of successive years; accurately noting the different states of the organ in health and disease, and the effect of the various kinds of food, drinks and other agents upon it.

I beg you to mark his words. "The free use of *ardent spirits, wine, beer or any of the intoxicating* liquors," says he, "when continued for some days has *invariably* produced these morbid changes."

Here we find that *wine and beer* produce these morbid changes as well as ardent spirits; and well they may, since they contain alcohol as their basis, as well as rum, brandy, whiskey and gin, though in rather smaller proportion.

There is another fact stated by Dr. Beaumont, to which I wish to call your special attention. Having spoken of the effects of intemperance in producing the morbid appearances referred to in the stomach of St. Martin, he says, "These morbid changes and conditions are, however, *seldom indicated* by any *ordinary symptoms* or particular sensations described or complained of unless when *in considerable excess*. They *could not, in fact, have been anticipated* by any *external symptoms, and their existence was only ascertained by actual occular demonstration.*"

Here is a most important pathological fact brought to view and established by occular demonstration, and one which should be ever present to the mind of him who uses alcohol. It is this: that the stomach may become extensively deceased from the influence of alcoholic drinks, without there being present any general constitutional derangement, or other obvious manifestations of its morbid state. This fact is particularly applicable to the temperate drinker, for in his case the narcotic poison of alcohol so blunts and deranges the healthy sensibility of the stomach, that it holds out no signal of its sufferings. But though the manifestations of disease may be absent, he should be aware that morbid changes, extensive and fatal may exist; and that while he is sipping his wine, or regaling himself upon his brandy and water, he is laying the foundation of a broken constitution, and premature decay and death. And this is what doubtless takes place with the temperate drinker, and is the true cause of the marked difference between his constitution, when prostrated by disease, and that of the man who leads a life of total abstinence; a difference seen and appreciated by every practitioner of medicine. In the one case disease is easily vanquished, the system reacts, and the patient soon recovers his wonted energy—in the other case, if he does not sink under the disease, he lingers and every attack leaves him in a more broken and enfeebled state; a consequence inevitable since all the other functions of the body are intimately connected with, and dependant upon that of the stomach. Whenever this organ fails to perform its office, all the other functions become deranged, and the whole system languishes.

From a careful observation of this subject during many years of practice, I am persuaded that tens of thousands of temperate drinkers, die annually of diseases, through which the abstemious would pass in safety.

PLATE III. *Fig.* 1*st* represents the state of the drunkard's stomach after a debauch. It was drawn from the case of one who had been for several days in a state of inebriation, but who came to his death suddenly from another cause. It shows the internal coat of the organ to have been in a state of high inflammation, and presents several livid spots, with dark grumous blood oozing from the surface.

I have had several opportunities of inspecting the stomach under similar circumstances, and I believe this plate presents about the ordinary appearance of the organ when excited to a state of inflammation by excessive indulgence in the use of alcoholic drinks. It has been remarked, that the symptoms attendant upon the ulcerated state of the stomach, and especially if unaccompanied by much inflammation, are often obscure, and such as not to denote much constitutional derangement. But in this condition of the organ the whole system suffers. There is loss of appetite, nausea, vomiting, ardent thirst, pain in the head, red eyes, bloated face, coated or red tongue, frequent pulse and symptomatic fever. These symptoms are more or less intense, according to the duration of the debauch, the quantity of liquor drank, being modified in some degree, by the constitution and habits of the individual. They are, in some respects, such as attend the ordinary inflammation of the stomach, produced by other causes, and the appropriate treatment in both is found to be nearly the same. It consists in total abstinence from all stimulating drinks, general bleeding, cupping, leeching and blistering over the stomach, cooling and mucilaginous drinks, and general perspiration with entire rest.

The following case so fully confirms the principles here laid down, and at the same time furnishes so valuable an admonition, that I must beg leave to present you with the outlines of its history.

A gentleman equally distinguished for the powers of his mind, and the great influence which he wielded in the counsels of the nation, unfortunately acquired in early life, the habit of intemperance; but it was not that intemperance which is perpetual, it only came over him at distant periods, not oftener than once or twice in a year. In the intervals he practiced entire abstinence, while at these periods he wholly abandoned himself to his propensity, and would continue drinking until his stomach was wrought up to a high state of inflammation. I was called to attend him in at least twelve of these paroxysms, during as many years, and conducted him safely through the storm. It was done upon the principle of withholding at once all stimulus and allowing the free use of iced water, with other cooling drinks, with cupping and blistering over the stomach.

In ten or twelve days he was usually well and able to attend to his business. Unfortunately, in his last paroxysm, he came under the care of those who advised that he should not abandon his cup at once, but wind off his debauch by degrees. The advice was followed, and he fell a victim to the experiment. He died suddenly, in the vigor of his days, and the height of his usefulness; lamented and wept by all who knew him.

No one may hope to be weaned from the love of alcoholic drinks, or to be cured of a fit of intoxication by diminishing the quantity alone, or by substituting one form of the poison for another. As well might the culprit who receives his fifty lashes to-day, expect a palliation of his sufferings by the infliction of forty lashes to-morrow, and thirty the day after, or by substituting the cow-hide for the cat-of-nine-tails. The practice is opposed to all experience, and to every principle of man's constitution.

The stomach is inflamed, and must be cured like inflammation produced by other causes, by withholding stimulants, and instituting a cooling antiphlogistic treatment.

Fig. 2d of the same plate presents a specimen of the cancerous stomach. It was drawn from the stomach of a gentleman who had for many years followed a seafaring life. He was not regarded as intemperate, but used his grog daily, and was much in the habit of taking a glass of brandy in the morning, undiluted, to excite an appetite for breakfast. At length dyspepsia came on, with pain and a burning sensation in the region of the stomach, vomiting of his food an hour or two after his meals, followed by extreme emaciation and death. Upon examination of the body, the whole of the stomach, except a small portion at the left extremity, was found in a scirrous state, its coats thickened to the extent of about two inches, and the cavity of the organ so far obliterated as scarcely to admit the passage of a probe from the left to the right extremity; so that for a considerable time before death, none of the nutriment derived from food and drink could have passed into the intestines. Near the right extremity of the stomach was a cancerous ulcer of the size and appearance represented in the drawing.

Since the foregoing case occurred, two others of the same character, and produced by the same case, have fallen under my observation. In both these, the one a male and the other a female, the stomach was thickened, scirrous and cancerous, and so extensively disorganized as not to admit of the passage of the chyme out at the pyloric orifice. The prominent symptoms in these two cases also, were excruciating pain, a vomiting of the food in a half digested state, followed by extreme emaciation. These subjects had indulged freely in the use of alcoholic drinks for years, and continued the habit till the stomach would no longer receive it.

PLATE IV. represents the appearance of the stomach of the drunkard who dies in a state of mania a potu, or delirium tremens.

The history of the case from which this drawing was made, and which occurred in my practice some years since, will illustrate the character of the disease, and the morbid condition of the stomach.

The subject was a man, amiable in disposition, courteous in manners, high in public life. By degrees he became intemperate, and although he drank daily, his excessive indulgence was confined to paroxysms of greater or less duration. Several times during the continuance of these paroxysms, he was thrown into a state of delirium tremens, but from which he soon recovered. At length one of his paroxysms of drinking came upon him, which was of longer continuance than usual, and of greater severity. For more than a week his mind was entirely deranged, and it required two persons to confine him to his room. He imagined that his nearest friends were his greatest enemies and persecutors, and were constantly laying plans for his destruction. He fancied that he saw spectres and devils, and files of armed soldiers entering his apartment, deadly serpents crawling over his bed, and wild beasts ready to devour him. There was one individual in particular, a certain man who had often won his money at the billiard table, whom he imagined he saw grinning and skulking round the chamber, waiting an opportunity to rob him of his money. His bodily functions became more and more disturbed, accompanied with great debility; a cold, profuse, clammy sweat, and small and sinking pulse. These symptoms were followed by general spasms, which soon closed the scene.

After death the body was examined. Upon laying open the

stomach it presented the appearance exhibited in the plate It contained a considerable quantity of dark fluid resembling coffee grounds; the inner surface was covered with a dark brown flaky substance, upon removing which, it exhibited marks of having been in a high state of inflammation; some portions appearing of a deep red or mahogany color, and others quite black, as if in a state of incipient mortification. It was obvious that the dark flaky matter which lined the inner coat, as well as that lying loosely in the cavity of the organ, was blood which had exuded from the vessels of the inflamed surface, and had been acted upon by the gastric juice, converting it into the black vomit.

I have had several opportunities of inspecting the body after death of those who have fallen by intemperance in a state of delirium tremens; and have found not only the symptoms attending the affection, but the morbid appearance upon dissection to be extremely uniform, and my observations fully confirm the opinion entertained by most modern pathologists, that the disease has its seat originally in the stomach, and that the affection of the brain is purely sympathetic and secondary; an opinion sustained also by the course found most successful in the treatment of the disease.

I have thus briefly spoken of intemperance as affecting the condition of the stomach only; but it should be borne in mind that while alcoholic drinks make their first and stongest impression here, their morbid effects are not limited to this organ; the whole of the intestinal canal participates more or less in their influence. The internal coat becomes irritated, inflamed and ulcerated, and occasionally affected with those other organic changes delineated in the drawings of the stomach. Nor are the consequences of intemperance confined to the digestive canal alone. The distant parts of the body become in time affected also. The liver, the brain, the heart, the lungs and the kidneys become the seat of alcoholic influence, an influence which is transmitted to them in two ways. The first is upon the principle of sympathy; the second is through the medium of the circulation, and the immediate action of the alcoholic principle upon the organs as it passes through them, mingled with the blood. Both may be illustrated by familiar examples. The individual who has become exhausted by labor and fasting, finds his muscular power diminished and his whole system enfeebled. Upon partaking of his food his strength is immediately restored—restored long before his food is digested, or any nourishment can have been derived from it. This effect is produced by the stimulus of the food upon the stomach, which impression is transmitted to all the other organs of the body through the medium of the nervous system, upon the principle of sympathy. The second, through the medium of the circulation, may be shown by two facts. The odor of the drunkard's breath, furnishes us with one of the earliest indications of intemperance. This is occasioned by the exhalation of the alcoholic principle from the bronchial vessels and air cells of the lungs; not of pure alcohol, as taken into the stomach, but as it has been absorbed and become mingled with the blood and subjected to the action of the different organs of the body, and not containing any principle which contributes to the nourishment or renovation of the system, is cast out with other excretions as poisonous and hurtful. Magendie long since ascertained by experiment, that diluted alcohol when subjected to the absorbing power of the veins, is taken up by them, is mingled with the blood, and afterwards passes off by the pulmonary exhalents. The case of a drunkard is mentioned who used to amuse his comrades by passing his breath through a narrow tube and setting it on fire as it issued from it. The perspirable matter which passes off from the skin, becomes charged with the odor of alcohol in the drunkard, and in some cases furnishes evidence of the kind of spirit drank. Two cases are related by Dr. McNish, the one in a claret and the other in a port drinker, in which the moisture exhaled from their bodies had a ruddy complexion, similar to the wine upon which they had committed their debauch. These facts show us that alcoholic drinks are absorbed, mingle and circulate with the blood, and therefore act immediately upon the different organs of the body.

It is upon these two principles that alcoholic drinks produce their morbid effects upon the different organs.

The liver. Alcohol in every form and proportion produces a strong and speedy effect upon this organ when used internally. Its first effect usually is to increase the action of the liver, and sometimes to such a degree as to result in inflammation. Its secretion often becomes changed from a bright yellow to a green or black, and from a thin fluid to a substance resembling tar in its consistence; and this change not unfrequently leads to the formation of billiary calculi, or gall stones. There often follows an enlargement of the organ, and a change in its structure. Aware of this fact, the poultry dealers of England are in the habit of mixing a quantity of spirit with the food of their fowls, in order to increase the size of the liver; that they may be enabled to supply the epicure with a greater abundance of that part of the animal which he regards as the most delicious. I have met with cases in which the liver has become so enlarged from intemperance as to weigh from eight to twelve pounds, instead of four or five, its usual weight. The inflammation of the organ not unfrequently terminates in suppuration and the formation of extensive abscesses. The liver sometimes, however, even when it manifests upon dissection great organic change in its structure, is found rather diminished in volume. This was the case in the person of the celebrated tragedian, George Frederick Cook, who died several years since in the city of New York. This extraordinary man was long distinguished for the profligacy of his life, as well as the native vigor of his mind and body. At the time of his death, his body was opened by Dr. Hosack, who found that the liver, while it was rather diminished in size, was in a state of induration, and surprisingly hard, so as to make considerable resistance to the knife; and it was of a lighter color than natural. The whole substance of the organ was studded with tubercles, and the blood vessels, which are numerous and large in the healthy state, were nearly obliterated; shewing that the circulation had nearly ceased long before death. I have met with several cases in the course of my dissections in which the liver had become shriveled and indurated; its blood vessels diminished and the organ greatly changed in its structure; the evident consequence of long continued habits of intemperance.

The brain. This organ also suffers from intemperance. Inflammation, and engorgement are frequent consequences of the use of alcoholic drinks, and may take place at the time of a debauch, or arise sometime afterwards, during the stage of debility from a loss of the healthy balance of action in the system. Inflammation of the organ, when it is acute, is usually attended by furious delirium and other indications of high cerebral excitement. It may arise from sympathy with an inflamed or irritated stomach, or it may take place from the immediate action of alcohol upon it as it is transfused into the system. In the following case the affection of the brain seems to have arisen from the latter cause. A man was taken up dead in the streets of London, soon after having drank a quart of gin upon a wager. He was carried to the Westminster Hospital and dissected. In the ventricles of the brain there was found a considerable quantity of limpid fluid, distinctly impregnated with gin, sensible to the taste, the smell, and to the test of inflammability. The liquid was supposed to be about one third gin.

Dr. Armstrong, an eminent physician of England, who possessed ample opportunities for investigating this subject, says that he has found the free use of intoxicating liquors, a frequent cause of chronic inflammation and engorgement of the brain and its membranes.

It is a fact familiar to anatomists, that alcohol has the effect of hardening the brain and other organs which contain albumen, when subjected to its action; and it is a common practice to immerse the brain in ardent spirit for a few days, in order to render it firmer for dissection; and upon examining the brain after death, of such as have long been accustomed to the use of ardent spirit, it is said that the organ is generally found harder and less elastic and yielding, than in temperate persons.

The heart. It has generally been supposed that the heart is less frequently affected by intemperance than most of the other vital organs; but from several cases which have fallen under my observation, and from the fact that it sympathises strongly with the stomach, and is thrown into a state of unnatural excitement by the use of alcoholic drinks, the very effect produced by the violent agitation of the passions, the influence of which upon this organ is found so injurious, I am inclined to think that it seldom escapes uninjured in the habitual drunkard.

The following case came under my notice several winters since. A large, athletic man, long accustomed to the use of ardent spirit, on drinking a glass of raw whiskey dropped instantly dead. On carefully dissecting the body, no adequate cause of the sudden cessation of life could be found in any part except the heart. This organ was free from blood, hard and firmly contracted, as if affected by spasm.

A few years since I saw an individual while engaged in public debate, drop instantly dead from an affection of the heart, being at the time highly stimulated by alcohol, and under a strong excitement of his passions. I am convinced that many of those cases of sudden death which take place with intemperate persons, are the result of spasmodic action of the heart from sympathy with the stomach, or some other part of the system.

The use of ardent spirit no doubt tends to produce an enlargement of the organ, promotes the ossification of its valves, as well as the development of other organic affections.

The lungs. Respiration in the inebriate is generally oppressed and laborious, especially after eating or violent exercise; and he is teased with a cough attended by copious expectoration in the morning, and especially after his recovery from a fit of intoxication; and these symptoms go on increasing, and, unless arrested in their progress, often terminate in fatal bronchitis and consumption.

This affection of the lungs is produced in two ways: first, by the immediate action of the alcoholic principle upon the highly sensitive membrane which lines the trachea, bronchial vessels and air cells of the lungs, as it is poured out by the exhalents; and second, by the sympathy which is called into action between the lungs and other organs, already in a state of disease, and more especially that of the stomach and liver.

I have met with meny cases in the course of my practice, of cough and difficult breathing, which could be relieved only by regulating the functions of the stomach, and which soon yielded on the patient's ceasing to irritate this organ with ardent spirit. I have found the liver still more frequently the source of this affection, and on restoring the organ to its healthy condition by laying aside the use of alcoholic drinks, all the pulmonary symptoms have subsided.

On examining the lungs of the drunkard after death, they are frequently found adhering to the walls of the chest hepatized, or affected with tubercles.

The kidneys. These organs and others immediately associated with them, are seldom found in a healthy state after death in the inebriate; and the use of alcoholic drinks, even in a temperate degree, lead to some of the most harassing and fatal affections to be found in the whole catalogue of diseases. But though an important subject, and upon which much might be said in reference to intemperance, I pass on to notice an affection, which, though common, seems scarcely to have attracted the attention of those who have written upon the effects of alcoholic drinks. It is, *Paralysis of the lower extremities;* but not that paralysis which takes place suddenly from an affection of the brain, or spinal marrow, but a gradual diminution of the power of sensation and of motion. Several of these cases have occurred to me within the last twenty years, three of which I will state.

Tho first was in an active business man of forty-five, who gradually acquired the habit of tippling, though he never drank to intoxication. His practice was to take small quantities of brandy, gin, wine, &c. at short intervals. He at length began to complain of debility, a sense of numbness in his lower limbs, and an inability to walk with his accustomed activity. These symptoms gradually increased, and were soon followed by other mortifying indications of imbecility. The complaint increased till he could neither walk nor stand, and for months before his death, he was lifted from his bed to his chair. Several times during the progress of the case he partially recovered, but it was only in proportion as he suspended the use of alcoholic drinks.

Upon examination after death, the mucous coat of his stomach was found in a state of irritation, such as is usually met with in the case of the confirmed drunkard, and as represented in the second plate, figure first. The small intestines through the greater part of their extent, seemed to have participated in the irritation of the stomach.

The second case was that of a highly respectable man, who made shipwreck of fair prospects and a good character, by contracting the habits of intemperance upon entering public life. I was frequently called to attend him, on account of indisposition produced by paroxysms of inebriation, and yet so assiduously did he conceal his intemperance, that it was long before any one but myself suspected the cause. He seldom drank any ardent spirit, but kept his demijohn of old Madeira, which he used profusely. He first complained of weakness and want of sensibility in the lower extremities, and an inability to walk, especially to ascend long flights of steps. Upon a full representation of his situation, and the consequences that must ensue, he was induced to abandon his wine, and almost immediately recovered all his powers; but upon returning to it sometime afterwards, he relapsed into all his former weakness, and if now living is lost to his family and country.

The third case is that of a Mr. ———, a man of thirty, of fine, robust constitution. He gradually acquired the habit of tippling, but it was not upon ardent spirit. He was never drunk, and no one suspected him of intemperance but his family. He had not exactly the drunkard's breath, nor much of his demeanor or aspect. He consulted me several times on account of a numbness and loss of power in his lower limbs. It was not for a considerable time that I came at the real cause of the difficulty, so carefully did he conceal his habits. At length I discovered that he kept in his grocery a pipe of wine for his own use, of which he drank frequently through the day, and would often visit his store at an early hour in the morning and late at night to renew his potations. I informed him that wine was the cause of all his complaints, upon which he abandoned the traffic and his habit of drinking together. His limbs almost immediately regained their accustomed energy. He is now, after six years, in good health and a sober man.

But time would fail me, were I to attempt an account of half the pathology of drunkenness. *Dyspepsia, jaundice, emaciation, corpulence, dropsy, ulcers, rheumatism, gout, tremors, palpitation, hysteria, epilepsy, palsy, lethargy, apoplexy, melancholy, madness, delirium tremens and premature old age,* compose but a small part of the catalogue of diseases produced by alcoholic drinks. Indeed, there is scarcely a morbid affection to which the human body is liable, that has not, in one way or another, been produced by them; there is not a disease but they have aggravated, nor a predisposition to disease which they have not called into action; and although their effects are in some degree modified by age and temperament, by habit and occupation, by climate and season of the year, and even by the intoxicating agent itself; yet the general and ultimate consequences are the same.

But I pass on to notice one state of the system produced by alcoholic drinks, too important and interesting to leave unexamined. It is that *predisposition to disease and death* which so strongly characterizes the drunkard in every situation of life.

It is unquestionably true, that many of the surrounding objects in nature are constantly tending to man's destruction. The excess of heat and cold, humidity and dryness, noxious exhalations from the earth, the floating atoms in the atmosphere, the poisonous vapors from decomposed animal and vegetable matter, with many other invisible agents, are exerting their deadly influence; and were it not that every part of his system is endowed with a self-preserving power, a principle of excitability, or in other words, a vital principle, the operations of the economy would cease, and a dissolution of his organic structure take place. But this principle being implanted in the system, reaction takes place, and thereby a vigorous contest is maintained with the warring elements without, as well as with the principle of decay within.

It is thus that man is enabled to endure from year to year, the toils and fatigues of life, the variations of heat and cold, and the vicissitudes of the seasons—that he is enabled to traverse every region of the globe, and to live with almost equal ease under the equator, and in the frozen regions of the north. It is by this power that all his functions are performed from the commencement to the close of life.

The principle of excitability exists in the highest degree in the infant, and diminishes at every succeeding period of life; and if man is not cut down by disease or violence, he struggles on, and finally dies a natural death; a death occasioned by the exhaustion of the principle of excitability. In order to prevent the too rapid exhaustion of this principle, nature has especially provided for its restoration by establishing a period of sleep. After being awake for sixteen or eighteen hours, a sensation of fatigue ensues, and all the functions are performed with diminished precision and energy. Locomotion becomes feeble and tottering, the voice harsh, the intellect obtuse and powerless, and all the senses blunted. In this state the individual anxiously retires from the light, and from the noise and bustle of business, seeks that position which requires the least effort to sustain it, and abandons himself to rest. The will ceases to act, and he loses in succession all the senses; the muscles unbend themselves and permit the limbs to fall into the most easy and natural position; digestion, respiration, circulation, secretion, and the other functions, go on with diminished power and activity; and consequently the wasted excitability is gradually restored. After a repose of six or eight hours, this principle becomes accumulated to its full measure, and the individual awakes aud finds his system invigorated and refreshed. His muscular power is augmented, his senses are acute and discriminating, his intellect active and eager for labor, and all his functions move on with renewed energy. But if the stomach be oppressed by food, or the system excited by stimulating drinks, the sleep, though it may be profound, is never tranquil and refreshing.

The system being raised to a state of feverish excitement, and its healthy balance disturbed, its exhausted excitability is not restored. The individual awakes, but finds himself fatigued rather than invigorated. His muscles are relaxed, his senses obtuse, his intellect impaired, and his whole system disordered; and it is not till he is again under the influence of food and stimulus that he is fit for the occupations of life. And thus he loses the benefits of this wise provision of repose designed for his own preservation.

Nothing, probably, tends more powerfully to produce premature old age than disturbed and unrefreshing sleep.

It is also true, that artificial stimulus, in whatever way applied, tends constantly to exhaust the principle of excitability of the system, and this in proportion to its intensity, and the freedom with which it is applied.

But there is still another principle on which the use of alcohol predisposes the drunkard to disease and death. It acts on the blood, impairs its vitality, deprives it of its red color, and thereby renders it unfit to stimulate the heart and other organs through which it circulates; unfit, also, to supply the materials for the different secretions, and to renovate the different tissues of the body, as well as to sustain the energy of the brain; offices which it can perform only while it retains the vermillion color and other arterial properties. The blood of the drunkard is several shades darker in its color than that of temperate persons, and also coagulates less readily and firmly, and is loaded with serum; appearances which indicate that it has exchanged its arterial properties for those of venous blood. This is the cause of the livid complexion of the inebriate, which so strongly marks him in the advanced stage of intemperance. Hence, too, all the functions of his body are sluggish, irregular, and the whole system loses its tone and its energy. If alcohol, when taken into the system, exhausts the vital principle of the solids, it destroys the vital principle of the blood also, and if taken in large quantities produces sudden death; in which case the blood, as in death produced by lightning, by opium, or by violent and long continued exertion, does not coagulate.

The principles laid down are plain, and of easy application to the case before us.

The inebriate having, by the habitual use of alcoholic drinks exhausted to greater or less extent the principle of excitability in the solids, the power of reaction, and the blood having become incapable of performing its offices also, he is alike predisposed to every disease, and rendered liable to the inroads of every invading foe. So far, therefore, from protecting the system against disease, intemperance ever constitutes one of its strongest predisposing causes.

Superadded to this, whenever disease does lay its grasp upon the drunkard, the powers of life being already enfeebled by the stimulus of alcohol, he unexpectedly sinks in the contest, but too frequently to the mortification of his physician, and the surprise and grief of his friends. Indeed, inebriation so enfeebles the powers of life, so modifies the character of disease, and so changes the operation of medical agents, that unless the young physician has studied thoroughly the constitution of the drunkard, he has but partially learned his profession, and is not fit for a practitioner of the present age.

These are the reasons why the drunkard dies so easily, and from such slight causes.

A sudden cold, a pleurisy, a fever, a fractured limb, or a slight wound of the skin, is often more than his shattered powers can endure. Even a little excess of exertion, an exposure to heat or cold, a hearty repast or slight emotion of the mind, not unfrequently extinguishes the small remains of the vital principle.

That fearful epidemic, the Asiatic Cholera, which so lately spread consternation and dismay over more than half the civilized world, wherever it appeared, singled out the intemperate for its victims, in a marked and most extraordinary manner If in some instances the sober and temperate were borne off in the common ruin, it was seldom, except when some powerful predisposing or exciting cause, overwhelmed the system.

I have thus endeavored, according to your request, to furnish a few remarks upon the pathology of drunkenness. The sketch I have given is brief and imperfect, and forms a mere outline of this important subject, but so far as it extends, it is based upon facts, which I have no fear, will bear the test of future observation. You will perceive that a few passages are extracted from my address, already before the public, but they are here introduced as applicable to the occasion.

Allow me in conclusion, to congratulate you and your co-laborers, upon the good already achieved by your efforts. Multitudes have been emancipated from a state of the most degrading servitude; disease has been arrested in its ravages; enterprise brought back in a thousand instances, fresh and vigorous to the great purposes of the age; banished happiness restored to the social circle; and new worshippers called around the altar of God. For the universal consummation of such blessings, every philanthropist will pray, and every patriot extend the helping hand.

The following notice of the first volume of the Enquirer, appeared in the Albany Argus about twenty-five years since, over the signature of I. That noble Christian gentleman and patriot, whose memorable words "IF ANY ONE ATTEMPTS TO HAUL DOWN THE AMERICAN FLAG, SHOOT HIM ON THE SPOT," and which words sent a thrill of patriotism through the honest American heart, at the opening hour of the great rebellion, is the writer of the following—ED.

REVIEW OF ENQUIRER—No. 1, Vol. I, by I.

The publication which bears the above title, is in quarto form containing forty-eight pages, and consists of a series of letters to professing Christians, by Edward C. Delavan, on the kind of wine proper to be used at the Lord's Supper, and a copious appendix. It was published in this city on the 1st inst. and, appears by a notice on the first page, is to be issued quarterly. The object of this article is not to take part in the important question, which it discusses, but to refer to some of the principal communications which it contains, and the positions taken by the writers.

The first fourteen pages are occupied by Mr. Delavan's letters, the object of which is to show that the wines in ordinary use in this country are highly drugged and adulterated, and are not suitable for the communion service; that they are not, in fact, the Fruit of the Vine, which the Divine institutor of the sacrament ordained, and that a large portion of those wines are manufactured from whiskey, and contain not a single drop of the juice of the grape. The distinction made by Mr. Delavan, and those who sustain his positions, is that the wine used by the Saviour was unfermented and without the alcoholic properties generated by the process of fermentation; and he asserts that this distinction is indispensable to reconcile passages of scripture, condemning wine on the one hand and commending it on the other, and which can only be rendered harmonious by the supposition that two kinds of wine, the fermented and the unfermented, were in use in the time of our Saviour. On the testimony adduced in support of this position it is not the design of this article to comment. It must speak for itself. It is presented with great candor, and, indeed, all the letters of Mr. Delavan are written in a spirit which is entirely unobjectionable, and which is calculated to disarm all hostility, even on the part of those who dissent from his positions.

Among the articles contained in the appendix, will be found a lecture by Dr. Nott, the President of Union College, written in his clear and forcible style, and which it appears is one of a series delivered at Schenectady three years ago. Dr. Nott takes decided ground in favor of the use of unfermented wine, upon the general reasonings referred to by Mr. D., and throws a flood of light upon the whole subject. Chancellor Walworth, in a letter which is given in the appendix, concurs in the general view of the subject taken by those who are in favor of substituting the unfermented wine in the communion service for the fermented. There are also letters to the same purport from a number of distinguished clergymen in the United States. The Enquirer professes to aim at a free discussion of the subject, and the sincerity of the profession is manifest in the fact that it contains letters on the other side of the question, by gentlemen who dissent, to a greater or less extent, from Mr. Delavan's opinions.

One of the most interesting portions of the paper is an Essay on the Pathology of Drunkenness, by Dr. Thomas Sewall, professor of pathology and the practice of medicine in the Columbian College, District of Columbia. This essay is illustrated by several drawings of the stomach of the drunkard, exhibiting it in a healthy state and in the various stages of disease produced by the use of alcoholic stimulants. It is certainly a very interesting as well as remarkable paper, and it is put forth with the guaranty of the author's name and professional character in favor of the truth of its statements.

A few facts appear by the testimony produced, which in justice to those concerned, ought to be stated in this article.

1. The discussion was originally forced upon them by the opponents of the total abstinence principle, who asserted that as the Saviour miraculously made and drunk intoxicating wine, it was a reproach to him to recommend entire abstinence from it. This led to the inquiry whether there was not two kinds of wine in use, one intoxicating and the other not so; and whether the kind consecrated by him to religious uses, was not unfermented and free from the intoxicating principle.

2. That the course of Mr. Delavan and his associates has been uniform; that they have never advocated the exclusion of wine from the communion, but merely the use of the unfermented juice of the grape.

3. That the pure juice of the grape, without fermentation, can be obtained in sufficient quantity for the purpose; and

4. That the question at issue is between the pure juice of the grape, and intoxicating or adulterated wines, a large portion of which are the product of distillation.

Finally, the Enquirer asks a candid examination of the subject and a fair comparison of opinions formed with deliberation and in a spirit of honest inquiry; believing that on all subjects, and on questions of morals especially, TRUTH has nothing to fear from calm and enlightened discussion, and that it is only error which shrinks from investigation as a test, which it cannot endure.—[*Alb. Argus.* I.

THE EXPEDIENCY DOCTRINE EXPLAINED AND VINDICATED.

The doctrine of expediency, when rightly applied, has its origin from above; when wrongfully applied, its origin is from below. It is always expedient to do right—never expedient to do wrong. St. Paul would not eat meat, for reasons stated by himself. The meat he was willing to abandon for the good of others, was good health-preserving meat, not putrid, rotten, life-destroying meat. The law of Christian expediency could not apply to this kind of meat to be given up for the good of others, could it? The great Apostle was willing to give up wine, good wine, the wine direct from the cluster and the press, breaking out from the vat, and so preserved, as a healthful drink and a medicine, as grapes are for persons in health and in sickness; and the existence of this kind of wine was as well known when St. Paul wrote, as the wine termed by God, and without any qualification as to quantity—"a mocker," biting like a serpent and stinging like an adder, and not to be looked upon even; and why so? because ALCOHOL, a deadly poison, through the *after* process of fermentation, had been produced. Could St. Paul, in his willingness to abandon wine, have had any reference to the kind of wine containing alcohol, a poison which has occasioned all the drunkenness in the world.? I think not. Space will not permit me to enlarge, but in closing this last page of this little Temperance scrap-book, I would make an earnest appeal to the clergy of all denominations, as well as the benevolent physician—the former for the sake of the soul, the latter for the body's sake, to take this subject into earnest and speedy consideration —ED.

REMARKS ON DR. SEWALL'S LETTER.

It appears to us quite impossible for an unprejudiced mind to rise from the perusal of the foregoing admirable letter of Dr. Sewall without a deep conviction that one of the greatest delusions that has ever held possession of the human mind, causing an amount of wretchedness and loss of wealth which the most fertile imagination finds it impossible to estimate, is about to be dissipated, and we trust forever. Providence, in the case of Alexis St. Martin, provided a subject to establish beyond all contradiction the great principle on which the Temperance cause is now based, which is, *that intoxicating drinks are never beneficial, but always injurious to persons in health.* All can now understand why wine, intoxicating wine, is declared by God to be "*a mocker*;" it will be seen it at once disturbs the healthful action of the stomach, and consequently the mind feels the injurious influence We recollect when engaged in business, and while drinking two or three glasses of intoxicating wine at dinner, the bargains made in the afternoon were frequently disapproved the following morning ; at the time we were much mortified at this unaccountable vacillation of mind within a few hours ; the reason never occurred to us until we abandoned the use of wine altogether. We then found that we had been "mocked," and that our judgment had been impaired in proportion to the alcohol we had indulged in. We found, too, that after drinking a glass or two of wine at dinner on the Sabbath, we listened to the afternoon service with very different feelings than to the morning service, and often accused the preacher of stupidity, when it was our own stupidity occasioned by that wine which "is a mocker." Until we abandoned the use of this "mocker," we could never account for this difference of feeling between the morning and afternoon services of the sanctuary ; we then made the discovery that we were under the influence of the "mocker" in the house of God. For all the sin we have committed, in times long passed, through ignorance of the true nature of all intoxicating liquors, we have asked, and we trust we have obtained, pardon.

A friend recently informed us that he had frequently watched the influence of a single glass of wine at dinner-parties on the eye, and that he had invariably noticed a change not only in the expression, but in the pupil.

Doctor Sewall has our warmest thanks for furnishing his important letter, as also for the drawings of the human stomach. We believe all coming generations will hail him as a great public benefactor. We are informed that it is the first time the human stomach has been thus exhibited, through all its changes, from the use of alcohol. May God in his mercy bless the effort made, we well know, under pressing professional duties and ill health; may it serve to arrest the temperate drinker in his dangerous course; may it bring to a full stand the poor diseased drunkard, and induce him to flee at once to Total Abstinence from all that can intoxicate—and in his case, as well at the communion table as a medicine. We trust the press, now scattering its hundreds of millions of sheets yearly, will sound the alarm, and will not be backward in proclaiming the truth now so clearly established by science, founded on the Word of God; and may the Church rejoice at these developments; they are opening a bright day for her, and may she speedily cast out from her sanctuary those fabricated and intoxicating substances, and substitute in their place the Fruit of the Vine—pure and *un*intoxicating; and may the time soon come when not one of her members shall be found making, vending, drinking, or giving others to drink, that "mocker," the use of which has so long filled the world with pauperism and crime, and kept from entering within her walls millions of perishing beings.

May all classes, from the monarch to the beggar, be admonished; let them remember that God has said, and that, too, without any qualification, that "*wine* [intoxicating] *is a mocker*," AND THAT SCIENCE CONFIRMS IT. Let all know that alcohol, whether in the purest wine or in the most disgusting beer or whisky, is a poison—an enemy to health and happiness; that to use it in health is a species of suicide—an outrage on one's self, on the community, and when its character is understood, as we understand it, its use is a sin against the God of heaven.—E. C. D., *Enquirer, Dec.*, 1841.

No. 24.

DOCTORS AND DRINK.

The London *Weekly Record,* in its review of the progress of Temperance last year, makes the following highly important statement on the use of alcoholic stimulants in the medical treatment of typhus fever, etc. :

"In this connection we may refer to the progress attained during the past year on the physiological question. The National Temperance League has had no specific conference during the year with the medical profession. But it has had communication and free scope for many of its most fundamental principles with the physicians and surgeons of Great Britain through the medium of the medical journals. Our movement comprises not a few members of that learned profession, who can take their stand with the most distinguished of their compeers, and some of whom (for example, Dr. Munroe, of Hull) have rendered during the past year invaluable service to the good cause by their addresses, lectures, and contributions to the medical journals. In this and other ways the subject has got into these influential exponents of medical principles and practice, and cheering results have been reached both in regard to the properties of alcohol, and the wisdom of its prescription in numerous cases in which it has hitherto been freely administered.

"As regards the properties of alcohol and its effects on the human body, the more intelligent of our readers are aware of the light thrown on this subject by Dr. Perry twenty-five years ago. His experiments clearly proved that alcohol is no sooner received into the system than it is absorbed into the circulation and carried to the brain and other organs with which it has affinity, where it is discovered unchanged; but its further history was left undetermined. This gave scope for Liebig's theory, that it was burned in the blood; and thus, though not a flesh-former—which, from its want of nitrogen, it could not be—it was still a heat-former, or supplier of fuel to the vital furnace, and as such entitled to the name of food. Twenty years passed, and the theory, plausible in itself, and shielded by a great name, enjoyed its day. But the experiments, five or six years ago, of Lallemand and his Parisian *confrères,* by means of the bichromate-of-potash test, exploded it to atoms, proving as they did that the system expels alcohol unchanged, and does so when taken in minute as well as in large doses. Many attempts have since been made to bolster up the fallen fortunes of the blue fiend, but to no purpose. The results gained by those Parisian investigators, and so ably expounded by Professor Carpenter in the *Westminster Review* for January, 1861, remain where the latter writer then put them, as warranting the conclusion that 'alcohol has no claim whatever to rank among articles of food.' Dr. Edward Smith's experiments shortly after confirmed the same conclusion, with the remarkable addition that the chromic test detected the eliminated alcohol in the perspiration as well as in the breath. Discussion and controversy very naturally and most desirably followed; and this year has been more prolific of discussional articles in the medical journals, on the physiology of Temperance, than many previous years. The *Lancet*, with much of a mixed complexion, has made many important concessions, which nothing could have extorted but the force of truth. The *British Medical Journal*, whose habitual spirit is most fair and candid, contained in September an important leader, entitled, 'Is Alcohol Food?' in which it openly declares that, 'on the face of it, the teetotalers have, from a scientific point of view, the best of the argument.' It then goes on to say that 'our greatest and most esteemed authorities' have come to the conclusion 'that alcohol is not food,' but that it is simply 'eliminated as alcohol from the body.' 'The body,' adds the writer, 'regards alcohol as a very dangerous enemy; for as soon as ever spirits of wine has found its way into man, his eliminating organs, every one of them, are called into operation for the very purpose of unlodging the unwelcome stranger.' This is the natural and inevitable conclusion. Dr. Anstie, as a last resort, urges the very immaterial circumstance, that the whole of the alcohol imbibed has not in any case been yet recovered, as the result of elimination. But to this Dr. Smith very decisively replies: 'Is there any instance in which a substance taken into the body is uniformly in part transferred and in part eliminated? I believe not. Then, in the absence of this analogy, when we show that a portion of alcohol passes off as alcohol, are we not entitled to affirm that the whole does so, and the more so that it passes off by every outlet of the body, and for many hours, and under all circumstances, and always as alcohol?'

"As regards the practical aspects of the medical question, this too, in the papers referred to, has been ably and amply discussed. The result has been to demolish completely Dr. Todd's plausible doctrine, on which so many medical men have long been confidingly acting. In the stand made by Dr. Anstie and others for this theory, the ground taken was of the most minute and infinitesimal compass. Small doses only were contended for, and even these only in certain contingencies, under conditions so subtile and computations so intricate as to come practically to nothing, or worse—for prescription on no better basis than this would be very dangerous practice. Thus Dr. Todd's theory became a dissolving view, and by this time, we fear, is nowhere. But one of the most important results of recent experience in regard to the prescription of alcohol is that which appeared in the *Lancet* of March 12th, 1864, and which may here be simply alluded to as capping the climax of practical disproof of the claims of alcohol to be freely administered, and that, too, in the case of all others in which its prescription has been deemed most unquestionable—the case of typhus fever. Dr. Gardner, physician to the Royal Infirmary of Glasgow and Professor of the Practice of Physic in the University of that city, brought the matter to the test of extended and comparative experiment. The cases treated by him with this view amounted to nearly six hundred —a very ample basis from which to deduce conclusions. Of these the mortality among the patients who were treated with alcoholic stimulants amounted for all ages to 17½ per cent., this being nearly the same as in the English hospitals; whereas among those who were treated with milk and other milder substitutes, the mortality fell short of 12 per cent., and in the case of young people was less than 1 per cent. He accordingly concludes that to the young in particular, 'in typhus, and very probably in most other fevers, stimulants are not less than actively poisonous and destructive, unless administered with the most extreme caution and in the most special and critical circumstances.' On these and other grounds we have abundant reasons for self-gratulation on the distinct and legible mark in our favor which the past year has left on the physiology of Temperance, and which coming years are sure to bring out in ever bolder relief."

Aunt Dinah's Pledge. 12mo, 318 pages. By Miss MARY DWINELL CHELLIS, author of "Temperance Doctor," "Out of the Fire," etc., ... **$1 25**

Aunt Dinah was an eminent Christian woman. Her pledge included swearing and smoking, as well as drinking. It saved her boys, who lived useful lives, and died happy; and by quiet, yet loving and persistent work, names of many others were added who seemed almost beyond hope of salvation.

The Temperance Doctor. 12mo, 370 pages. By Miss MARY DWINELL CHELLIS, ... **$1 25**

This is a true story, replete with interest, and adapted to Sunday-school and family reading In it we have graphically depicted the sad ravages that are caused by the use of intoxicating beverages; also, the blessings of Temperance, and what may be accomplished by one earnest soul for that reform. It ought to find readers in every household.

Out of the Fire. 12mo, 420 pages. By Miss MARY DWINELL CHELLIS, author of "Deacon Sim's Prayers," etc., ... **$1 25**

It is one of the most effective and impressive Temperance books ever published. The evils of the drinking customs of society, and the blessings of sobriety and total abstinence, are strikingly developed in the history of various families in the community.

History of a Threepenny Bit. 18mo, 216 pages, ... **$0 75**

This is a thrilling story, beautifully illustrated with five choice wood engravings. The story of little Peggy, the drunkard's daughter, is told in such a simple yet interesting manner that no one can read it without realizing more than ever before the nature and extent of intemperance, and sympathizing more than ever with the patient, suffering victim. It should be in every Sunday-school library.

Adopted. 18mo, 236 pages. By Mrs. E. J. RICHMOND, author of "The McAllisters," . . . **$0 60**

This book is written in an easy, pleasant yle, seems to be true to nature, true to itself, and withal is full of the Gospel and Temperance.

The Red Bridge. 18mo, 321 pages. By THRACE TALMAN, . . **$0 90**

We have met with few Temperance stories containin so many evidences of decided ability and high literary excellence as this.

The Old Brown Pitcher. 12mo, 222 pages. By the Author of "Susie's Six Birthdays," "The Flower of the Family," etc., **$1 00**

Beautifully illustrated. This admirable volume for boys and girls, containing original stories by some of the most gifted writers for the young, will be eagerly welcomed by the children. It is adapted alike for the family circle and the Sabbath-school library.

Our Parish. 18mo, 252 pages. By Mrs. EMILY PEARSON, . . **$0 75**

The manifold evils resulting from the "still" to the owner's family, as well as to the families of his customers, are truthfully presented. The characters introduced, such as are found in almost every good-sized village, are well portrayed. We can unhesitatingly commend it, and bespeak for it a wide circulation.

The Hard Master. 18mo, 278 pages By Mrs. J. E. McCONAUGHY, author of "One Hundred Gold Dollars," and other popular Sunday-School books, ... **$0 85**

This interesting narrative of the temptations, trials, hardships, and fortunes of poor orphan boy illustrates in a most striking manner the value of "right principles," especially of honesty truthfulness, and TEMPERANCE.

Echo Bank. 18mo, 269 pages. By ERVIE, ... **$0 85**

This is a well-written and deeply interesting narrative, in which is clearly shown the suffering and sorrow that too often follow and the dangers that attend boys and young men at school and at college, who suppose they can easily take a glass or two occasionally, without fear of ever being aught more than a moderate drinker.

Rachel Noble's Experience. 18mo, 325 pages. By BRUCE EDWARDS. **$0 90**

This is a story of thrilling interest, ably and eloquently told, and is an excellent book for Sunday-school libraries. It is just the book for the home circle, and cannot be read without benefiting the reader and advancing the cause of Temperance.

Gertie's Sacrifice; or Glimpses at Two Lives. 18mo, 189 pages. By Mrs. F. D. GAGE, ... **$0 50**

A story of great interest and power, giving a "glimpse at two lives," and showing how Gertie sacrificed herself as a victim of fashion, custom, and law.

Time will Tell. 12mo, 307 pages. By Mrs. WILSON, ... **$1 00**

A Temperance tale of thrilling interest and unexceptionable moral and religious tone. It is full of incidents and characters of everyday life, while its lessons are plainly and forcibly set before the reader. The pernicious results of the drinking usages in the family and social circle are plainly set forth.

Philip Eckert's Struggles and Triumphs. 18mo, 216 pages. By the author of "Margaret Clair," **$0 60**

This interesting narrative of a noble, manly boy in an intemperate home, fighting with the wrong and battling for the right, should be read by every child in the land.

Jug-Or-Not. 12mo, 346 pages. By Mrs. J. McNAIR WRIGHT, author of "John and the Demijohn," "Almost a Nun," "Priest and Nun," etc., ... **$1 25**

It is one of her best books, and treats of the physical and hereditary effects of drinking in a clear, plain, and familiar style, adapted to popular reading, and which should be read by all classes in the community, and find a place in every Sunday-school library.

The Broken Rock. 18mo, 139 pages. By KRUNA, author of "Lift a Little," etc., ... **$0 50**

It beautifully illustrates the silent and holy influence of a meek and lowly spirit upon the heartless rumseller until the rocky heart was broken.

Andrew Douglass. 18mo, 232 pages, **$0 75**

A new Temperance story for Sunday-schools, written in a lively, energetic, and popular style, adapted to the Sabbath-school and the family circle.

Vow at the Bars. 18mo, 108 pages. **$0 40**

It contains four short tales, illustrating four important principles connected with the Temperance movement, and is well adapted for the family circle and Sabbath-school libraries.

Job Tufton's Rest. 12mo, 332 pages, ... **$1 25**

A story of life's struggles, written by the gifted author, CLARA LUCAS BALFOUR, depicting most skilfully and truthfully many a life-struggle with the demon of intemperance occurring all along life's pathway. It is a finely written story, and full of interest from the beginning to the end.

Frank Oldfield; or, Lost and Found. 12mo, 408 pages, ... **$1 50**

This excellent story received the prize of £100 in England, out of eighty-three manuscripts submitted; and by an arrangement with the publishers we publish it in this country with all the original illustrations. It is admirably adapted to Sunday-school libraries.

Tom Blinn's Temperance Society, and other Stories. 12mo, 316 pages, ... **$1 25**

This is the title of a new book written by T. S. ARTHUR, the well-known author of "Ten Nights in a Bar-room," and whose fame as an author should bespeak for it a wide circulation. It is written in Mr. ARTHUR'S best style, composed of a series o tales adapted to every family and library in the land.

The Harker Family. 12mo, 336 pages. By EMILY THOMPSON, **$1 25**

A simple, spirited, and interesting narrative, written in a style especially attractive, depicting the evils that arise from intemperance, and the blessings that followed the earnest efforts of those who sought to win others to the paths of total abstinence. Illustrated with three engravings. The book will please all.

Come Home, Mother. 18mo, 143 pages. By NELSIE BROOK. Illustrated with six choice engravings, ... **$0 50**

A most effective and interesting book, describing the downward course of the mother, and giving an account of the sad scenes, but effectual endeavors, of the little one in bringing her mother back to friends, and leading her to God. It should be read by everybody.

Tim's Troubles. 12mo, 350 pages. By Miss M. A. PAULL, . . **$1 50**

This is the second Prize Book of the United Kingdom Band of Hope Union, reprinted in this country with all the original illustrations. It is the companion of "Frank Oldfield," written in a high tone, and will be found a valuable addition to our Temperance literature.

The Drinking Fountain Stories. 12mo, 192 pages, ... **$1 00**

This book of illustrated stories for children contains articles from some of the best writers for children in America, and is beautifully illustrated with forty choice wood engravings.

The White Rose. By Mary J. Hedges. 16mo, 320 pages, . . **$1 25**

The gift of a simple white rose was the means of leading those who cared for it to the Saviour. How it was done is very pleasantly told, and also the wrongs resulting in the use of strong drink forcibly shown.

Hopedale Tavern, and What it Wrought. 12mo, 252 pages. By J. WILLIAM VAN NAMEE, . **$1 00**

It shows the sad results which followed the introduction of a Tavern and Bar in a beautiful and quiet country town, whose inhabitants had hitherto lived in peace and enjoyment The contrast is too plainly presented to fail to produce an impression on the reader, making all more desirous to abolish the sale of all intoxicants

Roy's Search; or, Lost in the Cars. 12mo, 364 pages. By HELEN C. PEARSON, ... **$1 25**

This new Temperance book is one of the most interesting ever published—written in a fresh, sparkling style, especially adapted to please the boys, and contains so much that will benefit as well as amuse and interest that we wish all the boys in the land might read it.

How Could He Escape? 12mo, 324 pages. By MRS. J. NCNAIR WRIGHT, author of "Jug-Or-Not." Illustrated with ten engravings, designed by the author, ... **$1 25**

This is a true tale, and one of the writer's best productions. It shows the terrible effects of even one glass of intoxicating liquor upon the system of one unable to resist its influences, and the necessity of grace in the heart to resist temptation and overcome the appetite for strong drink.

The Best Fellow in the World. 12mo, 352 pages. By Mrs. J. MCNAIR WRIGHT, autnor of "Jug-Or-Not," "How Could He Escape?" "Priest and Nun," **$1 25**

"The Best Fellow," whose course is here portrayed, is one of a very large class who are led astray and ruined simply because they are such "good fellows." To all such the volume speaks in thrilling tones of warning, shows the inevitable consequences of indulging in strong drink, and the necessity of divine grace in the heart to interpose and save from ruin.

Frank Spencer's Rule of Life. 18mo, 180 pages. By JOHN W KIRTON, author of "Buy Your Own Cherries," "Four Pillars of Temperance," etc., etc., . **$0 50**

This is written in the author's best style, making an interesting and attractive story for children.

Work and Reward. 18mo, 183 pp. By Mrs. M. A. HOLT, . **$0 50**

It shows that not the smallest effort to do good is lost sight of by the all-knowing Father, and that faith and prayer must accompany all temperance efforts.

The Pitcher of Cool Water. 18mo, 180 pages. By T. S. ARTHUR, author of "Tom Blinn's Temperance Society," "Ten Nights in a Bar-room," etc., ... **$0 50**

This little book consists of a series of Temperance stories, handsomely illustrated, written in Mr. ARTHUR'S best style, and is altogether one of the best books which can be placed in the hands of children. Every Sunday-school library should possess it.

Little Girl in Black. 12mo, 212 pages. By MARGARET E. WILMER, ... **$0 90**

Her strong faith in God, who she believes will reclaim an erring father, is a lesson to the reader, old as well as young.

Temperance Anecdotes. 12mo, 288 pages, ... **$1 00**

This new book of Temperance Anecdotes, edited by GEORGE W. BUNGAY, contains nearly four hundred Anecdotes, Witticisms, Jokes, Conundrums, etc, original and selected, and will meet a want long felt and often expressed by a very large number of the numerous friends of the cause in the land. The book is handsomely illustrated with twelve choice wood engravings.

The Temperance Speaker. By J. N. STEARNS, ... **$0 75**

The book contains 288 pages of Declamations and Dialogues suitable for Sunday and Day-Schools, Bands of Hope, and Temperance Organizations. It consists o. choice selections of prose and poetry, both new and old, from the Temperance orators and writers of the country, many of which have been written expressly for this work.

The McAllisters. 18mo, 211 pages. By Mrs. E. J. RICHMOND, . **$0 50**

It shows the ruin brought on a family by the father's intemperate habits, and the strong faith and trust of the wife in that Friend above who alone gives strength to bear our earthly trials.

The Seymours. 12mo, 231 pages. By Miss L. BATES, . . . **$1 00**

A simple story, showing how a refined and cultivated family are brought low through the drinking habits of the father, their joy and sorrow as he reforms only to fall again, and his final happy release in a distant city.

Zoa Rodman. 12mo, 262 pages. By Mrs. E. J. RICHMOND, **$1 00**

Adapted more especially to young girls' reading, showing the influence they wield in society, and their responsibility for much of its drinking usages.

Eva's Engagement Ring. 12mo, 189 pages. By MARGARET E. WILMER, author of "The Little Girl in Black," **$0 90**

In this interesting volume is traced the career of the moderate drinker, who takes a glass in the name of friendship or courtesy.

Packington Parish, and The Diver's Daughter. 12mo, 327 pages. By Miss M. A. PAULL, . . . **$1 25**

In this volume we see the ravages which the liquor traffic caused when introduced in a hitherto quiet village, and how a minister's eyes were at length opened to its evils, though he had always declared wine to be a "good creature of God," meant to be used in moderation.

Old Times. 12mo. By Miss M. D. CHELLIS, author of "The Temperance Doctor," "Out of the Fire," "Aunt Dinah's Pledge," "At Lion's Mouth," etc., . **$1 25**

It discusses the whole subject of moderate drinking in the history of a New England village. The incidents, various and amusing, are all facts, and the characters nearly all drawn from real life. The five deacons which figure so conspicuously actually lived and acted as represented.

John Bentley's Mistake. 18mo, 177 pages. By Mrs. M. A. HOLT, **$0 50**

It takes an important place among our temperance books, taking an earnest, bold stand against the use of cider as a beverage, proving that it is often the first step toward stronger drinks, forming an appetite for the more fiery liquids which cannot easily be quenched.

Nothing to Drink. 12mo, 400 pages. By Mrs. J. McNAIR WRIGHT, author of "The Best Fellow in the World," "Jug-or-Not," "How Could He Escape?" etc., ... **$1 50**

The story is of light-house keeper and thrilling adventures at sea, being nautical, scientific, and partly statistical, written in a charming, thrilling, and convincing manner. It goes out of the ordinary line entirely, most of the characters being portraits, its scenery all from absolute facts, every scientific and natural-history statement a verity, the sea incidents from actual experience from marine disasters for the last ten years.

Nettie Loring. 12mo, 352 pages. By Mrs. GEO. S. DOWNS, **$1 25**

It graphically describes the doings of several young ladies who resolved to use their influence on the side of temperance and banish wine from their entertainments, the scorn they excited, and the good results which followed.

The Fire Fighters. 12mo, 294 pages. By Mrs. J. E. McCONAUGHY, author of "The Hard Master," **$1 25**

An admirable story, showing how a number of young lads banded themselves into a society to fight against Alcohol, and the good they did in the community.

The Jewelled Serpent. 12mo, 271 pages. By Mrs. E. J. RICHMOND, author of "Adopted," "The McAllisters," etc., ... **$1 00**

The story is written earnestly. The characters are well delineated, and taken from the wealthy and fashionable portion of a large city. The evils which flow from fashionable drinking are well portrayed, and also the danger arising from the use of intoxicants when used as medicine, forming an appetite which fastens itself with a deadly hold upon its victim.

The Hole in the Bag, and Other Stories. By Mrs. J. P. BALLARD, author of "The Broken Rock," "Lift a Little," etc. 12mo, **$1 00**

A collection of well-written stories by this most popular author on the subject of temperance, inculcating many valuable lessons in the minds of its readers.

The Glass Cable. 12mo, 288 pages. By MARGARET E. WILMER, author of "The Little Girl in Black," "Eva's Engagement Ring," etc., ... **$1 25**

The style of this book is good, the characters well selected, and its temperance and religious truths most excellent. The moral of the story shows those who sneer at a child's pledge, comparing its strength to a glass cable, that it is in many cases strong enough to brave the storms and temptations of a whole lifetime.

Fred's Hard Fight. 12mo, 334 pages. By Miss MARION HOWARD, ... **$1 25**

While it shows the trials which a young lad endured through the temptations and enticements offered him by those opposed to his firm temperance and religious principles, and warns the reader against the use of every kind of alcoholic stimulant, it points also to Jesus, the only true source of strength, urging all to accept the promises of strength and salvation offered to every one who will seek it.

The Dumb Traitor. 12mo, 336 pp. By MARGARET E. WILMER, **$1 25**

Intensely interesting, showing how the prospects of a well-to-do New England family were blighted through the introduction of a box of wine, given in friendship, used as medicine, but proving a dumb traitor in the end.

Miscellaneous Publications.

Forty Years' Fight with the Drink Demon. 12mo, 400 pages. By CHARLES JEWETT, M.D., . **$1 50**

This volume comprises the history of Dr. Jewett's public and private labors from 1826 to the present time, with sketches of the most popular and distinguished advocates of the cause in its earlier stages. It also records the results of forty years' observation, study, and reflections upon the use of intoxicating drinks and drugs, and suggestions as to the best methods oi advancing the cause, etc. The book is handsomely bound, and contains illustrated portraits of early champions of the cause

Drops of Water. 12mo, 133 pages. By Miss ELLA WHEELER, **$0 75**

A new book of fifty-six Temperance Poems by this young and talented authoress, suitable for reading in Temperance Societies, Lodge Rooms, Divisions, etc. The simplicity of manner, beauty of expression, earnestness of thought, and nobleness of sentiment running through all of them make this book a real gem, worthy a place by the side of any of the poetry in the country.

Bound Volume of Tracts. 500 pages, ... **$1 00**

This volume contains all the four, eight, and twelve page tracts published by the National Temperance Society, including all the prize tracts issued the last two years The book comprises Arguments, Statistics, Sketches, and Essays, which make it an invaluable collection for every friend of the Temperance Reform.

Scripture Testimony Against Intoxicating Wine. By Rev. WM. RITCHIE, of Scotland, . . **$0 60**

An unanswerable refutation of the theory that the Scriptures favor the idea of the use of intoxicating wine as a beverage. It takes the different kinds of wines mentioned in the Scriptures, investigates their specific nature, and shows wherein they differ.

Alcohol: Its Place and Power, by JAMES MILLER; and **The Use and Abuse of Tobacco,** by JOHN LIZARS, ... **$1 00**

Zoological Temperance Convention. By Rev. EDWARD HITCHCOCK, D.D., of Amherst College, **$0 75**

This fable gives an interesting and entertaining account of a Convention of Animals held in Central Africa, and reports the speeches made on the occasion.

Delavan's Consideration of the Temperance Argument and History, **$1 50**

This condensed and comprehensive work contains Essays and Selections from different authors, collected and edited by EDWARD C. DELAVAN, Esq., and is one of the most valuable text-books on the subject of Temperance ever issued.

Bible Rule of Temperance; or, Total Abstinence from all Intoxicating Drinks. By Rev. GEORGE DUFFIELD, D.D., ... **$0 60**

This is the ablest and most reliable work which has been issued on the subject. The immorality of the us , sale, and manufacture of intoxicating liquors as a beverage is considered in the light of the Scriptures, and the will and law of God clearly presented.

Alcohol: Its Nature and Effects. By CHARLES A. STOREY, M.D., **$0 90**

This is a thoroughly scientific work, yet written in a fresh, vigorous, and popular style, in language that the masses can understand. It consists of ten lectures carefully prepared, and is an entirely new work by one amply competent to present the subject.

Four Pillars of Temperance. By JOHN W. KIRTON, . . . **$0 75**

The Four Pillars are, Reason, Science, Scripture, and Experience. The book is argumentative, historical, and statistical, and the facts, appeals, and arguments are presented in a most convincing and masterly manner.

Communion Wine; or, Bible Temperance. By Rev. WILLIAM M. THAYER. Paper, 20 cents; cloth, **$0 50**

An unanswerable argument against the use of intoxicating wine at Communion, and presenting the Bible argument in favor of total abstinence.

Laws of Fermentation and Wines of the Ancients. 12mo, 129 pages. By Rev. WM. PATTON, D.D Paper, 30 cts.; cloth, . . **$0 60**

It presents the whole matter of Bible Temperance and the wines of ancient times in a new, clear, and satis actory manner, developing the laws of fermentation, and giving a large number of references and statistics never before collected, showing conclusively the existence of unfermented wine in the olden time.

The National Temperance Society's Books.

Pamphlets.

John Swig. A Poem. By EDWARD CARSWELL. 12mo, 24 pages. Illustrated with eight characteristic engravings, printed on tinted paper, ... **$0 15**

The Rum Fiend, and Other Poems. By WILLIAM H. BURLEIGH. 12mo. 46 pages. Illustrated with three wood engravings, des gned by EDWARD CARSWELL. . . . **$0 20**

Suppression of the Liquor Traffic. A Prize Essay, by Rev. H. D. KITCHELL, President of Middlebury College. 12mo, 48 pp., **$0 10**

Bound and How; or, Alcohol as a Narcotic. By CHARLES JEWETT, M D. 12mo, 24 pp., . . . **$0 10**

Scriptural Claims of Total Abstinence. By Rev. NEWMAN HALL. 12mo, 62 pp., ... **$0 15**

Buy Your Own Cherries. By JOHN W. KIRTON. 12mo, 32 pp., **$0 20**

National Temperance Almanac and Teetotaler's Year Book for 1874. **$0 10**

Illustrated Temperance Alphabet. **$0 25**

The Youth's Temperance Banner

The National Temperance Society and Publication House publish a beautifully illustrated Monthly Paper, especially adapted to children and youth, Sunday-school and Juvenile Temperance Organizations. Each number contains several choice engravings, a piece of music, and a great variety of articles from the pens of the best writers for children in America. It should be placed in the hands of every child in the land.

TERMS—IN ADVANCE.

Single copies, one year,	$0 25
Eight copies, to one address,	1 00
Ten " " "	1 25
Fifteen " " "	1 88
Twenty " " "	2 50
Thirty copies, to one address,	$3 75
Forty " " "	5 00
Fifty " " "	6 25
One Hundred " "	12 00

The Total Abstainer's Daily Witness and Bible Verdict. 75 Cents.

This is a series of Scripture Texts printed on thirty-one large sheets, arranged so that one can be used for each day in the month. The size of each sheet is 19 by 12 inches, all fastened together with roller and cord, so as to be easily hung up in room, office, workshop, etc.; and turning over a sheet day by day as required.

New Temperance Dialogues.

The First Glass; or, The Power of Woman's Influence.

The Young Teetotaler, or, Saved at Last. 15 cents each. Per dozen, . $1 50

Reclaimed; or, The Danger of Moderate Drinking. 10 cents. Per dozen, ... 1 00

Marry No Man if he Drinks; or, Laura's Plan and How it Succeeded. 10 cents. Per dozen, ... 1 00

Which Will You Choose? 36 pages. By Miss M. D. Chellis. 15 cents. Per dozen, ... $1 50

Aunt Dinah's Pledge. Dramatized, . 0 15

The Temperance Doctor. Dramatized, 0 15

Wine as a Medicine. 10c. Per dozen, . 1 00

The Stumbling-Block. 10c. Per dozen, 1 00

Trial and Condemnation of Judas Woemaker. 15 cents. Per dozen, . . 1 50

Temperance Exercise, ... 0 10

Band of Hope Supplies.

Band of Hope Manual. Per dozen. $0 60

Temperance Catechism. Per dozen, 60

Band of Hope Melodies. Paper, 10

Band of Hope Badge. Enamelled, $1 25 per dozen; 12 cents singly. Plain, $1 per dozen; 10 cents singly. Silver and Enamelled, 50 cents each.

Juvenile Temperance Speaker. - - $0 25

Illuminated Temperance Cards. Set of ten. - - - - 35

Juvenile Temperance Pledges. Per 100, 3 00

Certificates of Membership Per 100, - 3 00

The Temperance Speaker, - - - 75

Catechism on Alcohol. By Miss Julia Colman. Per dozen, - - - 60

Sent by mail, post-paid, on receipt of price. Address

J. N. STEARNS, Publishing Agent,

58 READE STREET, NEW YORK.

www.ingramcontent.com/pod-product-compliance
Lightning Source LLC
LaVergne TN
LVHW020225110826
845151LV00003B/833

* 9 7 8 1 4 2 5 5 3 2 1 7 8 *